GOING FOR A SONG

A Chronicle of the UK Record Shop   Garth Cartwright

Flood Gallery Publishing
3 Greenwich Quay, Clarence Road, London SE8 3EY

www.thefloodgallery.com

First published in 2018 by Flood Gallery Publishing
Copyright © 2018 Garth Cartwright under sole license to Flood Gallery Publishing

Text copyright © 2017 Garth Cartwright

Graphic design by Christine Bone at Aleph Studio
Production coordination by Virginia Naden

Printed in EU

British Library Cataloguing in Publication data.
A catalogue record for this book is available from the British Library
978-1-91137-40-46

Front cover, pages 2/3: Bjork gets busy crate digging in Ray's
Jazz Shop, Shaftesbury Avenue, 1993. Photo by Barry Marsden.

Dedicated with deep affection to the memories of:

Mick Gander
Vicki Fox
Prince Buster
and
Jo Cox

Working in a record shop was pretty much a labour
of love. It's more a vocation than a normal job and
I think that holds true today. I'm not comparing
it to nursing but it has to be up there with teaching.

(David Bowie)

The Britisher must have a song to sing – something
simple and easy to learn. Even the errand boy must
have something to whistle. It is characteristic
of the race ... the masses, highbrow and lowbrow,
representative of all classes, are not interested in the
highly involved patterns of ultramodern dance music
... What they want is a simple, appealing tune.

(A German critic, visiting London in the 1920s, contributes
to *Gramophone* magazine)

The past is never dead. It's not even past.

(William Faulkner)

We are far more united than the things that divide us.

(Jo Cox, 3 June 2015)

Foreword by Stewart Lee

Our understanding of the ancient megalithic culture of these islands is greatly indebted to the gentleman-amateur antiquarians of the seventeenth, eighteenth and nineteenth century. Bewigged and booted, they strode the moorlands to document the disappearing remains of stone circles and burial chambers, even as changing farming practices, ignorance and superstition stripped them away.

Indeed, in 1861, it was the great-grandson of the Cornish antiquarian and priest Dr William Borlase, who intervened when a local farmer was in the very act of converting the Zennor Quoit burial chamber, then still intact after four thousand years of neglect, into a pig sty, preserving the past with a financial sweetener of five shillings. (Lie flat in the liquid cow dung and you can still crawl into the subterranean fogou, a ceremonial chamber, in the farmyard of Borlase's ancestral Pendeen home.)

John Aubrey sketched twenty stones in the Southern Inner Circle of the great Avebury henge in 1649, but by the time of William Stukeley's visit in 1663, fifteen had disappeared, and the subsequent decades he spent studying and sketching the site coincided with its casual destruction, as the sacred stones were uprooted and found their way into the masonry of walls and houses. But the records stand.

In his own way, Garth Cartwright embodies the spirit of these pioneers of preservation. Until recently, for many people, our relationships with record shops were adolescent rites of passage and a touchstone of adult life; clubhouses, information exchanges, temples of a faith in the healing properties of music. But sudden and drastic changes in the way music is consumed and marketed are wreaking havoc upon the models we understood as surely as the farmers and landowners that felled the great henges and the huddled burial chambers and the windswept hilltop circles for dry stone wall rubble.

Many of the record stores Cartwright describes herein will have closed during the writing of the book; others are radically reshaping their business plans. As a travelling comedian, I revisit annually all of Britain's city centres, and watch the disappearance of all that I knew. In Birmingham, where I spent my teenage Saturday job money on formative vinyl, the litany of disappeared stores is a stab in the heart; Plastic Factory, Reddingtons, Tempest, Inferno. The Diskery survives, having never really embraced the passing fad of CDs, now a haven for vinyl collectors; and Swordfish, formerly the punk era outlet Rockers, has relocated to Dalton Street, round the side of a multi-story carpark, its walls decorated with curling black and white photos of '70s and '80s local luminaries, many since lost to rock and roll disease.

And the places I bought records have memories of physical interactions that on-line purchases just don't. In 1994, Nikki Sudden of The Swell Maps, then working behind the counter of a store off Tottenham Court Road, invited me to sniff a 7" Cream acetate; in 1987, the guitarist from The Sea Urchins sold me a single by the singer from The June Brides somewhere on Birmingham High Street; I bought an original copy of John Fahey's The Yellow Princess for £2.99, in 1987, from the improviser and guitarist Rod Poole in Garon Records in Oxford's covered market; in 1989 I watched the legendary sound recordist Michael Gerzon argue with the man behind the counter at Manic Hedgehog, off the Cowley Road, about the relative merits of different Pretty Things recordings.

In the late '80s, I bought Eighties American hardcore from Epic Soundtracks, working at The Notting Hill Record and Tape Exchange; in 1995, in a store in Tucson Arizona, Tammy Allen of 35 Summers took the money for my 35 Summer album, before telling me she was actually in the band; at Edinburgh's Avalanche Records in the late 1980s I bought impossibly exotic imports of New Zealand's Flying Nun records from the man who was single-handedly importing them.

After a decade of visiting Mole Jazz almost weekly, at two different Kings Cross premises, the man behind the counter finally appeared to recognise me; and in 2003, in a Bowery record shop opposite CBGB's, I saw New York jazz musician John Zorn buying New York jazz records. It was the most New York experience I ever had, better than being mugged by a fake taxi driver, or dying on stage, at a two drink minimum comedy club where you perform in front of a fake brick wall.

And for years, the uneasy truce that prevailed on the shared Portobello Road premises of both the Stand Out and Minus Zero record shop counters, each run by a knowledgeable man called Bill, was an unofficial weekend clubhouse for tastemakers, musicians and music fans of all persuasions. Far south, in an antiques market near Hastings, Nick Saloman's Platform One preserves a record retail tradition I recognise, and he sent me home last time lighter to the tune of the cost of the second Storyteller album, which I'd long since given up hope of ever finding.

Record shops gave me all these experiences, and more. Now newspaper think-pieces tell us there's a vinyl revival. But there's a difference between supermarkets and lifestyle shops selling represses of classic records as accessories and a viable culture of information exchange and mutual consumer-artist support. The jury is out. Either way, Garth Cartwright has captured a moment of once unimaginable social transition.

The great Avebury henge may not stand complete as it once did, but at least we have William Stukeley's schematics. The gentleman-amateur antiquaries of old would probably recognise a kindred spirit in Garth Cartwright, documenting a once apparently impregnable culture, even at the moment of the disappearance of its venerated sites.

Stewart Lee, writer/clown

Stock check: Shirley Bassey selects her new releases at Shirley's Record Shop, 1962.

Contents

Foreword by Stewart Lee   6

Introduction: **A Ghost on the High Street ...**   11

Chapter 1   **Shape Shifting 1894–1939**   17

Chapter 2   **Dobell's and All that Jazz:** Soho's Hot Music Temples   30

Chapter 3   **Sounds that Swing:** Record Shops Rock the UK   42

Chapter 4   **Rudie Can't Fail:** Ska Shops Surge   57

Chapter 5   **Hustle and Flow:** Long Firms, Larceny and Loot   71

Chapter 6   **The Beatles, Bowie, Bassey and HMV:** Shops of the Stars   86

Chapter 7   **Maximum R&B:** Mods Get Soul   104

Chapter 8   **Tomorrow Never Knows:** Psych Shops Take Shape   117

Chapter 9   **The Rock Shop Cometh:** Virgin, Andy's and Beggars   130

Chapter 10   **Camden Cowboys:** Rock On's Incendiary 45s   147

Chapter 11   **Steptoe and Shop:** Second-Hand Record Psychosis   159

Chapter 12   **Groove Me:** 1970s Soul, Jazz and Funk   170

Chapter 13   **Word Sound Power:** Reggae's Sonic Shrines   182

Chapter 14   **Rough Trades, Small Wonders:** Inflammable Materials   196

Chapter 15   **Rock in Opposition:** Vanguard Record Shops   208

Chapter 16   **"No Irish, Blacks, Dogs":** Minority Music Marts   220

Chapter 17   **Dance Stance:** The Rap and Rave Massive   234

Chapter 18   **Things Fall Apart:** Apocalypse Now for Record Retail   249

Aftermath: **Remnants of an Underground Empire**   263

Conclusion: **Rave On –** Twenty-First-Century Closure and Renewal   269

Select Bibliography   282

Acknowledgements   286

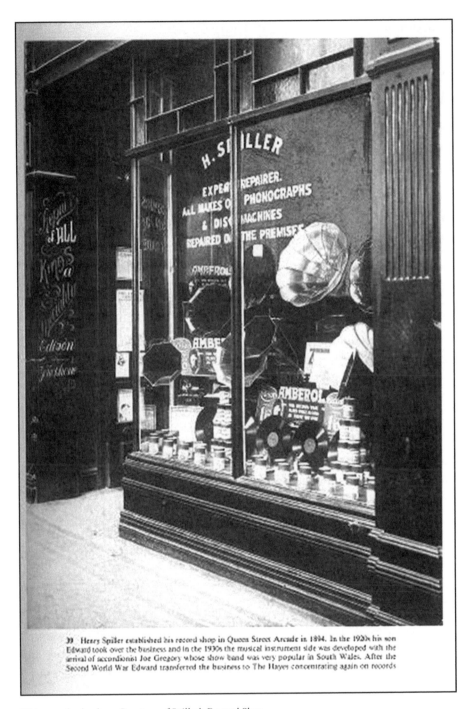

33 Henry Spiller established his record shop in Queen Street Arcade in 1894. In the 1920s his son Edward took over the business and in the 1930s the musical instrument side was developed with the arrival of accordionist Joe Gregory whose show band was very popular in South Wales. After the Second World War Edward transferred the business to The Hayes concentrating again on records

Wales way back when. Courtesy of Spiller's Record Shop.

Introduction: **A Ghost on the High Street ...**

Don't you just know it? Cardiff is the second most musical city in the UK. According to the Performing Rights Society, that is. Perhaps this explains why the Welsh capital is home to the world's oldest record shop. Spillers Records is recognised as such by *The Guinness Book of Records* and its proprietor Ashli Todd is proud to hold this title. However, she notes, being a historic shop does not pay the bills and running Cardiff's only surviving new release record shop is a challenge. "It is kind of a never-ending commitment," Todd says, before adding, "which is fine."

Todd then notes how Spillers, having survived since 1894, has seen off tougher times than the wobbles of today. Depressions, recessions, two world wars, the decline of the docks and mines, stock shifting from wax cylinders to 78s to vinyl to CD to vinyl, the rise and fall of the Virgin and Our Price chains ... Spillers' resilience is not simply commendable but remarkable. Thinking about how, decade after decade, this little Cardiff shop has increased the city's quotient of human happiness by selling recorded music makes me tingle all over.

"Imagine," I say to Todd, "what Cardiff and Spillers were like in the age of the wax cylinder." Todd shakes her head. "No idea," she says, "no idea at all what music they would have sold then." "Although," she adds, "Cardiff was a boom town, with a huge demand for coal, making its port one of the world's busiest." Which is why Spillers thrived: as the wealthy have always embraced novelty and innovation, a talking machine would have represented cutting-edge cool, many a coal baron likely purchasing wax cylinders here. With no documents from a century ago, Todd can't say what cylinders and 78s Spillers once sold but, as Hawaiian steel guitar recordings were popular (Cardiff dockers even formed their own hula combos), I suggest the shop surely sold stacks of Polynesian recordings.

"That's cool," says Todd, "I like the idea of selling hot Hawaiian wax." She then adds that Spillers didn't focus solely on selling records until the 1920s or 1930s. "Right," I reply, "that seems to have often been the case." Recordings were, initially, just another product to be sold alongside gramophones and furniture and washing machines and bicycles. Then an era began when people started to buy lots of recorded music and shops such as Spillers began concentrating on simply selling records.

"Then, at some point," notes Todd, "most people stopped buying music. Which is why there are so few record shops these days." She mentions how a Cardiff dance music shop recently closed "pretty much overnight," leaving behind all kinds of disgruntled creditors. The music industry, I suggest, has never been short of wide boys and chancers. Todd wearily agrees. So why, I ask, does she choose to work in a retail environment that is both capricious and largely associated with older men? She replies: "Firstly, I know lots of women who are just as passionate about music as men so there's no reason I can give as to why record shops tend to be male-oriented environments. See, I grew up in Spillers. My dad started working there in 1974 and, when it came to 2010 and the landlords were saying the shop had to shift out of its premises on the Hayes (where it had been based since the 1940s), he decided to retire. It came down to my sister Grace and I whether we wanted Spillers to continue or not. So, we decided to go for it and it was a huge decision – we had to shift to new premises and set up new accounts with all the record companies as it was a change of ownership – and like any small business you don't switch off from it.

"But, once you get past all that, the excitement of every day literally being like Christmas as you open boxes of new albums and promos coming through makes working in a record shop the best. And you get home and switch on 6 Music and hear something exciting so you grab pen and paper and write it down. Also, it's very rewarding to be talking with people who are as passionate as you are. It's all pleasurable."

Although it is now a pleasure that carries high stress levels: for over a century the record shop was an essential part of a city's fabric, seducing shoppers with beautiful noise and acting as chief muse to latent creative energies. Then, as we started the twenty-first century, the record shop began to appear redundant, a leftover from an analogue age. In a world where you can now have all the music you want on your phone, who needs to enter a bricks and mortar structure to access the sounds you desire? Not, it seems, many people. Across this century, the number of UK record shops operating has fallen from around 1000 in the year 2000 to fewer than half that in 2017.

Even the 2010s vinyl revival, Record Store Day promo and the opening of a number of boutique record shops make little real difference. For the culture has intrinsically changed. The survival of a traditional record shop like Spillers now involves the faithful – a congregation of sorts – who still attend services and receive communion. By championing new independent releases by Welsh artists as well as independent label albums that would find no love (or shelf space) in supermarkets, Spillers survives, a guide and mentor to Cardiff's music lovers.

Across the UK, more than any other nation state, record shops have often operated far beyond their quotidian retail function: musicians have met and formed bands in them and been informed by them; record labels have grown out of them; close friendships and intimate relationships have taken shape across the racks; fanzines, magazines, books and gigs get published/promoted through them; and all kinds of energies (political and personal, intellectual and instinctive) are shared. Most importantly, all manner of music has been engaged with and enjoyed. For, as Kurt Vonnegut noted, "If I should ever die, God forbid, let this be my epitaph: THE ONLY PROOF HE NEEDED FOR THE EXISTENCE OF GOD WAS MUSIC."

God's existence was easy to doubt in 2009 when London's West End resembled something of a record shop ghost town, many long-standing retailers having closed over an 18-month period. To wander past shuttered emporiums now besmirched by fly-posters, their once proud mastheads tatty or shattered, places where I had regularly gone seeking a song, left me feeling ... well, *aghast* says it best. Perhaps I was experiencing something akin to a form of urban mourning, a retail bereavement. That may, I realise, sound silly. I'm certain *The Economist* would not approve of such sentiment. Thing is, I'm not much of a shopper for anything beyond necessities: tins of beans, bottles of ale, loo paper ... but I'm always on the lookout for books and records. *Especially records.* And independent record shops have acted as magnets, instinctively drawing me in, ever since pop first cast its spell on my child self.

As there's previously been no chronicling of the record shop era, this book is very much a work of collective history – or historical memory – as those who worked in and shopped at record shops share recollections. "I liked what I saw. I liked what I heard. I liked how they smelt. I learned more from record shops than I ever did in school," said Jeff Barrett, veteran of many shops – including Bristol's Revolver Records – and now owner of the Heavenly record label. Me too; record shops were where I first gained an inkling of wisdom, of possibilities beyond the extremely circumscribed environment in which I grew up.

"When we opened the first shop in '76 it was really to find a safe haven where we could escape the notion of being part of the everyday working week," explained Geoff Travis of Rough Trade's humble origins. *A safe haven?* Indeed, record shops have provided me with refuge time and again. "I thought of them as secret places where you could go and meet other people who were part of this secret thing," wrote Dave Hickey, the writer who grew up trailing around America with his jazz musician parents. He adds, "thanks to my folks I was privy to this vast, invisible, underground empire that trafficked in nothing but joy." *An underground empire trafficking in joy.* Perfect.

This book then stands as a celebration of those that trafficked in joy. It is not a book of lists; trying to document every song seller that once traded across these fair isles would be even more absurd than what I have attempted to convey here. No, it's more of a homage to an era where record shops acted as sonic temples, oracles of sorts, bringing forth beauty and knowledge, wit and irreverence into the lives of many. I've tried to do this by focusing on a selection of emporiums that, in their uniqueness, made lasting impressions: if tiny shops like Belfast's Atlantic Records and Stamford Hill's R&B Records get more space than voluminous record chains which sold millions and millions of units, this is because the UK record shop epoch exists – if at all – as a secret history.

Certain exalted shops are occasionally noted: I first encountered a reference to R&B Records in an exhibition on Hackney mods, while Van Morrison has always sung the praises of Atlantic Records. Yet most of these music merchants have disappeared leaving few traces. Few independent shopkeepers grew wealthy from their trade but these unsung heroes enriched many lives, adding a mischievous dynamic to high streets and back streets, cities and towns, ensuring many shared the joy.

Oasis sang "Mister Sifter sold me songs when I was just 16" in tribute to a shop in Didsbury, Manchester, which provided Noel Gallagher with inspiration for future tunes. Across the last century many a UK musician, DJ, writer, promoter (among others) gained wisdom of sorts from the record shops they frequented. Spillers served as a sonic womb for the Manic Street Preachers (they still shop here, Todd confirms) and has served Shirley Bassey, Robert Plant, the Super Furry Animals and more. A bright little Cardiff oracle and the perfect place to begin our journey.

Napoleon once dismissed the British as a nation of shopkeepers. Today, in a world awash with corporate chain stores, this strikes me as a characteristic to be celebrated. Time, then, to take the advice funk merchant Jimmy Castor proffered on his memorable 'Troglodyte' 45. "What we gotta do is go back," instructed Jimmy. "Way back ... back into time."

OPENING TOMORROW

Specially designed for record enjoyment with private booths and a coffee lounge —this you MUST see.

SCOTLAND'S MOST UP TO DATE RECORD SHOP

The Disc Jockey Centre

where you can

BUY YOUR RECORDS
MEET YOUR FRIENDS
HAVE A COFFEE

Friday at 7 p.m.
SEE A
ROCK 'N' ROLL
DEMONSTRATION
BY EXPERTS

The Address

102 TORRISDALE STREET
(OFF VICTORIA ROAD AT QUEEN'S PARK STATION)

OPEN TILL 8 P.M. EVERY NIGHT (except Sundays)

The shock of the new: Sheffield's finest sell post cards, phonographs and records, 1902.
Courtesy of Sheffield Archives

Chapter 1

Shape Shifting 1894–1939

Talking machines take off and wax cylinder recordings of Boer War songs prove strong sellers. The 78 fires demand for opera and classical, music hall and crooners. Jazz and the First World War launch the dance band era. Musical instrument and bicycle shops, Woolworths, Marks & Spencer, department stores and market stalls sell records. HMV opens on Oxford Street and Levy's of Whitechapel advertises "100,000 records – all makes and languages." The Depression slows business then the Second World War calls time on much of the trade. Cameos from Sir Edward Elgar, Sidney Bechet, Jack Hylton and Louis Armstrong.

Using 1894 as our oracle's origins, the year Spillers in Cardiff opened, we find the world news cycle dominated by a French anarchist attempting to bomb the Royal Observatory; Tower Bridge opening; Alfred Dreyfuss convicted of treason in France; New Zealand enacting the world's first minimum wage law; and Everton FC and Liverpool FC meeting in the first ever Merseyside derby. Queen Victoria continues to rule over an empire on which the sun, surely, would never set, while horse-drawn carriages not only provide the majority of public transport but a public health problem as equine waste piles up on city streets. The arrival of the wax cylinder player causes furore: *an invention that allowed dead voices to talk!* More exciting, the newspapers thunder, than the telephone! As the British Isles have resonated with music since time out of mind, the initial challenge involves: *what might the public want to hear?*

Wax Cylinder Days

As would be the case for much of the twentieth century, things first got under way in the USA. New Jersey, to be precise, where Thomas Edison patented the tin-foil cylinder phonograph in 1877, believing it useful for office dictation, then did little with it, instead going on to invent the light bulb, carbon microphone and DC power delivery system. Edison's genius did not extend to an appreciation for music so, in 1888, Edward Easton led investors in founding Columbia Records with the express purpose of profiting from Edison's neglected phonograph. Emile Berliner then invented the gramophone to play discs in 1889 and, by 1891, Columbia could offer ten pages of commercial recordings it had made available on wax cylinder. Tech heavyweights Edison and Berliner would slug it out in court over who invented what, while the public were thrilled by the modern world these wizards were busy creating.

During the 1890s, cylinder phonographs began to feature at American fairs and travelling shows, and audiences flocked to hear machines that could talk.

A proto-juke box was invented for bars that amused revellers by, after feeding a coin into a slot, playing a recording of a voice. As demand grew for the cylinders, enterprising showmen strapped the cylinder machines onto a donkey and ventured off to entertain the masses. Everything flows; nothing abides.

Berliner, sensing a fortune to be mined, dispatched William Barry Owen to London in 1897, his mission to establish a gramophone market. Installed at Hotel Cecil in The Strand, Owen formed The Gramophone Company, setting in motion a corporation that, across the next century, would pioneer plenty of technology and – as HMV, EMI, Parlophone and Capitol – record and market vast quantities of music. Berliner had correctly appraised British demand although the American recordings The Gramophone Company (TGC) supplied were not always to UK tastes: a Scottish dealer observed in a letter that what they wanted were "well known airs and songs from modern and popular operas".

Well, Berliner surely said, let's give 'em what they want. The first British recordings were made in London on 9 August 1898, and a range of recordings featuring light opera singers, minstrel bands, Irish and Scottish bagpipes and a flute quartet was soon on sale. A noted early star of the cylinders was Ion Colquhoun, an "iron voiced baritone" who sang patriotic songs made popular during the Anglo-Boer War, 'Soldiers of the Queen' being a favourite with listeners. Such was the cylinder's popularity that, at the dawn of the twentieth century, previously reticent stars of stage began signing recording deals; these included Albert Chevalier and opera icons Enrico Caruso and Nellie Melba. They signed not because the recording quality had improved – it wouldn't until electrical recording took hold in 1925 – but because they were offered lucrative advances and juicy royalties. The hustle and flow of the music industry was under way.

Forever enterprising, Berliner invented the 78rpm (revolutions per minute) record in 1901, discovering that shellac (a South Asian resin) effectively held recorded sound. A year later, Columbia and Victor standardised the formats for records at 7 and 10 inches, while double-sided discs were introduced in 1904. That same year, The Gramophone Company started Zonophone, a discount label focused on selling 78s at 3 shillings and 6 pence (17.5p), subsequently reducing the price to 2 shillings and 6 pence (12.5p). As 78s had retailed for as much as a pound each – equivalent to a week's wages for a manual labourer – Zonophone scooped up a huge market that wanted to own records. Finding it cheaper to manufacture gramophones, companies began dumping wax cylinders on a market already depressed by a recession, and shellac would rule in record shops for the next half century.

78 Revolutions per Minute

Demand for records – at a time when films remained silent and BBC Radio wouldn't take hold until the mid-1920s – now proved high and 78s were available almost everywhere. Woolworths founded the Crown label to sell cheap 78s in its stores. Marks & Spencer offered the Rex label. Even Currys had its own budget label. Many small record labels set up, aiming to produce only 'budget-priced' records, and Scottish music hall entertainer Harry Lauder sold 90,000 78s in Britain in 1908. That same year found Sydney Dixon, manager of The Gramophone Company's sales branch, reporting, "it is a common occurrence for a small talking machine dealer to sell one thousand records between 2 o'clock on Saturday afternoon and closing time".

The public clamoured for music and 78s were available almost everywhere: street markets; hardware shops; sporting goods stores; tobacconists; and newsagents. With many men cycling, bicycle shops became shellac hubs. At 67 High Street, Camden Town, London, A. Selinger boasted on the sleeves of their 78s 'The Brilliant Incandescent & Cycle Accessory Store'. Classical 78s were priced high, music hall low, lots were in between and everyone involved made money.

Long before 78s were a glimmer in Emile Berliner's eye, the UK had hundreds of musical instrument shops, having a sing-song at home being a nineteenth-century phenomenon. These ranged from huge department stores that housed grand pianos to little shops dedicated to selling cheap pianos, banjos, guitars, harmonicas and fiddles. Most pubs had a piano and many households took pride in owning one – making music was a pleasure many enjoyed. Instrument shops became an increasingly important factor in the dissemination of popular music and led to huge sheet music sales for popular songs, with ditties about mothers doing exceptional business. Inevitably, many of these shops began selling gramophones and/or records, with such notable emporiums as Manchester's Forsyth Brothers Ltd (opened 1857) and Glasgow's Paterson, Sons and Co.'s two-storey 'Music Warehouse' gaining renown for their selection of classical, opera and dance band records and multiple listening booths.

Then and now, Newcastle's J. G. Windows and Cambridge's Millers served as their respective city's foremost musical instrument shops. Back then, Windows announced that they stocked a copy of every 78 released in the UK, while Millers of Cambridge built sizeable soundproofed booths for customers to listen to 78s. In the 2010s, Windows still offers a selection of classical CDs and rock LPs, while Millers stopped selling records in the 1990s.

In Belfast, a wealthy ship building port, Mrs McBurney founded Belfast's Premier Record Shop as a stall in Old Smithfield Market in 1926 (her son Billy went on to develop the shop and a record label, surviving attempts on his life by Loyalist thugs who disliked the pro-Republican records he issued). A more imposing emporium was The Gramophone Shop, which dominated Belfast's city centre from the 1920s until the late 1960s. Founded by Maurice Solomon and Harold Peres, two Russian Jewish immigrants who met selling ice cream and cups of water to sunbathers on Millisle beach resort in County Down, they teamed up and decided to go into "this new-fangled wireless business" in the early 1920s. Immediately successful, the partnership developed The Gramophone Shop into a major part of Belfast lore, with Decca Records trusting Solomon and Peres to handle its Northern Irish interests. Maurice's sons, Mervyn and Philip, went on to be big players in the Irish music business, setting up the Emerald and Major Minor record labels as well as managing Van Morrison, The Dubliners, The Bachelors and Phil Coulter.

The rise of record shops coincided with the shorter working week (between 1914–38 the average working week fell from 54 to 48 hours), paid holidays and increases in real income. By the outbreak of the First World War, one-third of all British households possessed some kind of gramophone and 13 million 78s had been sold across the previous decade. Record sales spiked during the First World War, with John McCormack's 'It's a Long Way to Tipperary' becoming the biggest selling 78 of the war era. The war proved a boost to the UK record trade as it led to a ban on German gramophones and record labels.

Peace in 1919 sparked a major post-war consumer boom, and The Gramophone Company sold some 60,000 gramophones and 6 million 78s over the next few years. Sales were boosted by the 'dance craze' as ragtime, then jazz, introduced a frantic African-American dance music, one that encouraged an outpouring of joyous behaviour amid so much loss. The UK establishment predictably raged against this American invasion, using the language of the Empire's henchmen – "barbaric", "savage", "orgiastic" – but, as would be played out again and again across the century, the youth ignored them, being too busy dancing. With the flapper now spotted on every high street, 1921 saw the most famous British record shop of the era opening.

Nipper in neon: 363 Oxford Street, London W1, 1936.

His Master's Voice

The opening of The Gramophone Company's first HMV (His Master's voice) department store on 20 July 1921 found Sir Edward Elgar conducting his orchestra in a former gents' outfitters reconstructed with an elegant art deco design. A select audience of the great and good were suitably awed. On the pavement outside 363 Oxford Street, London W1, the public oohed while the hacks aahed. Here was the record shop as spectacle, a retail cathedral selling 'albums' (these consisted of a bound folder containing a series of 78s that gathered the likes of Mozart symphonies and Gilbert and Sullivan's comic operas). Its mission statement was "To place before the intending buyer everything that the buyer's particular musical taste requires."

The genesis of 363 Oxford Street is due to The Gramophone Company realising how, if the company owned the shop that sold the records and gramophones they manufactured, then profits would be even greater. And so it proved. Before 1920, both the Columbia and Gramophone Companies each had retail outlets, but they formed a marginal part of their business: records, gramophones and graphophones were sold primarily through a network of dealerships and wholesalers. The Gramophone Company's decision to open a high-profile shop where it could sell company products was hailed by commentators as a talisman for the brave new world of technology and entertainment.

The shop at 363 Oxford Street was described as "something beyond an ordinary merchandise emporium", and the sound of the store was extraordinary: upon entering and hearing Beethoven's 5th or Wagner's Valkyries slice through the air, certain customers felt faint, were left gasping for breath, so intense was the experience. Nothing like it had ever existed before and the store's exterior – with a 15-metre by 9-metre neon sign adorned with the HMV trademark image of Nipper, the nation's favourite dog, and the outline of a man placing a record on a revolving turntable – displayed a retail modernism unmatched elsewhere.

In-store concerts were held to promote important releases, white-gloved commissionaires held the entrance doors open for customers, staff were immaculately dressed and musically literate (having undergone rigorous training at HMV's school for dealers) and so could answer questions about the records on offer – selling classical music was a serious business. Customers had to request a specific title: it would be decades before HMV allowed the public to browse freely through the records stocked. Once a clerk had selected the record, customers could listen to it in one of 25 soundproofed 'audition' rooms (stand-alone listening booths). Purchases would then be charged to accounts and dispatched to homes. This palace of music became a London landmark, with visitors marvelling at the elegant design, high-tech goods and remarkable array of music on offer.

The HMV store did good business from the off, surviving the Depression and rising from the ashes after it burned down on 26 December 1937. Still, for many music fans, 363 must have been seen as a fortress of denial, stocking as it did only 78s issued on The Gramophone Company's labels (or subsidiaries such as RCA, which it held the UK licence for).

"The ring of forts is pretty strong"

Then as now, London had the UK's foremost record shops, and in the May 1928 issue of *The Gramophone* a gushing editorial celebrated such. The anonymous author of 'The Virtuous Circle' noted: "The London Office [of *The Gramophone*] in Frith Street has for a long time been a good centre from which to make a tour of gramophone strongholds. From Keith Prowse in Coventry Street, the Pathé-Actuelle shop in Piccadilly Circus, up Regent Street by Edison Bell, H.M.V. and Columbia, along Oxford Street to Imhoff's, round by Foyle's in Charing Cross Road to the Gramophone Exchange in Shaftesbury Avenue … the ring of forts is pretty strong, and the recent addition of Gordon's shop in Great Newport Street and of Rimington Van Wyck (in the old Edison Bell premises) in Cranbourn Street has filled admirably a rather dangerous gap. But if Imhoff's were not so redoubtable and up-to-date we should feel inclined to advocate a further gramophone shop to cover the ground between Oxford Circus and Tottenham Court Road."

Selfridges department store on Oxford Street doesn't get a mention – it hosted a very elegant gramophone department – and neither does EMG whose 'handmade' gramophones won many awards: the firm's wind-up acoustic model was widely used across the British Empire where electricity was rare or non-existent. EMG's gramophone salon on Grape Street stocked a selection of classical and opera 78s and Francis James, who wrote a history of EMG (1998), noted of the Grape Street 78 department, "anyone who dared to ask for a record of jazz or light music unwarily, was discouraged by a supercilious raised eyebrow, or an expression of great pain, but if they were insensitive enough to insist, reluctantly, the record could be ordered". The snooty record shop clerk having existed since the dawn of dealers.

The 78s were fragile, and customers had to ask shop assistants for access to records, and then ensure that people treated their disc collections carefully. Owning music came to stand for many things, not least sophistication and success; gramophones, with their solid chestnut cabinets and curling brass horns, stood as an emblem of modernism, creations worthy of Brancusi. Listening to shellac discs on a gramophone represented the finest home entertainment available, especially after electrical recording techniques came of age in 1925 (they captured bass frequencies, allowing for a brighter, fuller sound to leap forth). When listening with my friend, the 78 collector Chris King, I'm often shaken by the charged intensity, a sense of occult forces, that bursts out of fragile blues and Balkan 78s. If they can move me today, well, imagine how these records must have been heard almost a century ago. No wonder listeners invested a totemic worth in the music they contained; the world, familiar and strange, beautiful yet unsettling, could now be marvelled upon in your own home.

Record companies created demand by keeping new releases secret so the public would turn up at the shops on specified days each month to see what had come in. Shops served as conduits for customer information and advice, while sending back customer complaints and wants to the companies. The intense passions that records generated saw London publishers launch *The Gramophone* (1923), the first serious monthly discussion of classical records, and *Melody Maker* (1926), the first weekly music magazine devoted to UK dance bands and American jazz musicians. Records enchanted and seduced listeners, and the shops that sold them quickly became secret places where those under the spell could gather.

Levy's of Whitechapel

If HMV ruled the West End of London, then Levy's were masters of East London. This Solomonic music temple was one of the UK's foremost independent record oracles. I once asked Steve Bronstein, a veteran London record man well into his ninth decade, why so many of the city's pioneering record shops were run by Jewish families and he replied, "It's a yiddisher thing, innit?" *Oi va voy!*

The first family of London record retail were Levy's of Whitechapel – or Aldgate, to be exact – their entrepreneurial efforts holding enormous sway across the first six decades of the twentieth century. Levy's started in 1890, initially a market stall selling sewing machines and bicycle parts. The East End in which

they lived and traded hosted the most densely populated ghetto in Europe, one packed with Jewish immigrants who had fled pogroms across the Russian Empire, along with many other migrants and an English working class who existed in near destitution. Infamous due to its poverty and 'foreignness', haunted by the spectre of Jack the Ripper and Fagin-style criminal gangs, Whitechapel also hummed with enterprise and activity: radical political groups gathered, music, art and literature found visionary exponents and plenty of new Londoners settled here. "The word 'multicultural' didn't exist back then," says Bernstein of the Whitechapel he knew as a child, "but the East End was just that. All kinds of people from everywhere. And very Jewish!"

Among this milieu, the Levy family saw a business opportunity: a Levy's advertisement in a 1949 issue of *The Gramophone* states, "For nearly 60 years Levy's have been serving the lovers of music – from the days of the old 'cylinder' record to the modern era of electrical recording, and the marvels of radio and television." This remarkable shop was trading at the dawn of the wax cylinder era before it became the foremost shellac store in London, going on to sell 45rpm singles and LPs up to the Beatlemania era. From 19–20 Whitechapel High Street, Levy's would proclaim itself 'The House of Music' and boast of carrying 'Over 100,000 Records Always in Stock. All Leading Makes and Languages.' As record industry veteran John Jack notes, "That is a lot of shellac on shelves. Imagine the weight of all those records!" Could Levy's record shop have been the first great record emporium in the UK? In Europe? Its 78 sleeves proudly proclaim "London's most popular Gramophone & Record Store", and as record labels began venturing far and wide to record all manner of music, Levy's must have been a vivid, exciting place to visit, pulsing with sound and thronging with ebullient Cockney energies.

Yiddish music hall tunes and ballads nostalgic for lost East European shtetls ('My Yiddishe Momme' was a huge international hit), alongside cantorial records, would have sold well to the Jewish community. As would music hall 78s to the Cockneys who loved the cheeky chappies of Wilton's Music Hall – just a brisk walk from Levy's – while Russian and Polish 78s would have appealed to customers nostalgic for sounds from 'back home'. Soho was dotted with Spanish and Italian, Greek and French neighbourhoods, and 'The House of Music' would have stocked their records. The docks were nearby, with Whitechapel offering myriad seamen's hostels. Levy's would have stocked the new music coming out of the USA and from across the Empire, bought records from sailors and travellers needing to raise a few shillings, taken samples from visiting entrepreneurs hoping to enter the London market – a shellac synagogue for those who worshipped music.

For those who worshipped Yahweh, Levy's made sure their record shop and record labels conveyed kabbalah's esoteric doctrine, both through selling cantorial records (alongside Yiddish folk songs and music hall 78s; surviving examples often wear a Levy's sleeve) and the belief that all music allows for a personal engagement with God. The 'House of Music' also functioned as a sonic salon – the sounds and ideas pouring forth from here helped to shape the UK as an inclusive and progressive society. Did the likes of David Bomberg and Lionel Bart shop here? I like to think so. Randolph Turpin and Alfred Hitchcock? Jack Cohen and Jack London? Rudolf Rocker and Milly Witkop? Well, why not? As the twentieth century began taking spectacular shape, Levy's operated as a place where dreamers and anarchists, Rabbis and ruffians, artful dodgers and dockers all rubbed shoulders as they came in search of a song.

Levy's next opened a showroom and mail order department at 94–8 Regent Street. They then set up two record labels, Levaphone and Oriole Records (a US budget label the Levy's began licensing in 1925, taking ownership of the name after the American label closed in 1937). From 1925, Levy's operated as British licensee for Vocalion Records, an American independent label that released many fine blues and jazz titles. As their record shops and labels prospered, the family built recording studios and pressing plants and released all kinds of music – from Django Reinhardt's 1930s recordings through Patti Page's lush ballads to Joe Meek's early efforts.

John Jack, who first started visiting the Whitechapel shop as a teenage jazz fan in the early 1950s, recalls, "Levy's was important – I remember going in there once and the bloke working there telling me he recalled Sidney Bechet hanging out in the shop in the time before he was thrown out of the country." Bechet, the Creole clarinet genius, got deported from London for assaulting a prostitute in 1922.

The Levy family's many achievements in the London record trade are discussed in later chapters (Chapters 3, 9 and 16). What happened to their Whitechapel 'Home of Music' shop? Its closure appears to have gone undocumented. Blues and jazz collectors were still perusing Levy's basement in the 1950s, hoping to find mint Vocalion 78s from decades past, but no one seems to recall when the shop ceased to exist. No matter, this Whitechapel family demonstrated a route out of the ghetto via selling records and taking control of the means of production. Many others would later to attempt to emulate their strategy.

"Civility, courtesy and satisfaction guaranteed"

Apart from HMV at 363 Oxford Street and a handful of musical instrument shops, all the pre-Second World War original record shops have vanished, swept away as the high street adapted and changed (Spillers in Cardiff continues to trade but has changed location several times over the past century). Most of these shellac outlets attracted no documentation – even Levy's survives in London's

Jewish Museum only as a cardboard 78 sleeve – and it is these sleeves that now whisper of what, before the Depression, must have been a glorious record shop epoch. The surviving sleeves are often more interesting than the 78s they house and document many things: striking graphic design, details of social mores and, in many cases, shops long since turned to dust.

Peter Burton, when we were perusing his 78 collection, picked up a sleeve and noted: "Rimington Van Wyck Ltd's appear quite highbrow. Their pale blue, good quality sleeves announce they deal in 'Gramophone Music for the Connoisseur', and are 'specialists in unique recordings'. Further, they claim 'no record is ever touched with a metal needle' (obviously fibre needles were used for demonstrations) and state 'Music – the only universal tongue' can be bought from them 'in the heart of the West End', where they could be found at 42/3 Cranbourn Street, London WC2. Telephone Gerrard 1171. With a pomposity typical of the time, the sleeve declares, 'To be served intelligently is to be served well'"!

"Just glancing at my collection, I see 'The A1 Gramophone and Radio Stores' at 281 Walworth Rd and 1 East Street SE17 had a sleeve picturing sophisticated 1930s nightlife, and make the extraordinary claim that the music from a gramophone (an HMV cabinet model is depicted) is "better than an orchestra"! They also boast "Civility, Courtesy and Satisfaction Guaranteed". Interestingly, the other side of the sleeve pictures a deco lampshade and a light bulb, on the basis that as well as having "complete stocks of His Masters Voice, Columbia, Parlophone, Decca and Regal-Zonophone records", they are also "Experts in Electric, Incandescent and Gas Lighting Accessories" and that, "All pendants fixed free of charge by experienced workmen".

I pause and have a lightbulb moment: *I know A1*. Or, more accurately, *knew*. When I first moved into Camberwell in 1994, A1 Records was my local record shop and, I tell Burton, even then they still sold lamps and light fittings in the front of the store with a record bar out back. A1 closed in the late 1990s after more than 80 years of service.

"That just demonstrates how long many local record dealers lasted," notes Burton as he sifts through a variety of sleeves bearing addresses from across Britain, some listing all kinds of goods stocked on the sleeves, others emphasising musical instruments. "There must have been thousands of such shops," he adds.

We study these 78 sleeves, remarking on how striking they make the establishments sound, guessing about emporiums that, in their day, existed at the forefront of technology ("Far more exciting than a bloody Apple store," says Burton). We were certain of only one thing: these lost shops sold plenty of Jack Hylton records.

Happy Feet

After the First World War, some 11,000 dance halls and nightclubs opened between 1919 and 1926, and newspapers coined the "dance craze" phrase. These weren't teenagers – that demographic hadn't been invented yet – but young adults who found music and dance a joyous release in a society still run along extremely Victorian principles. And, of course, it was a great chance to connect with the opposite sex. By 1938, it was estimated that 2 million people went dancing every week.

All kinds of dances won popularity but it was jitterbugging (American jazz dances) that set UK dance floors alight. Here dancers learned all manner of American 'jazz age' dances, some straight from the ghetto, others designed by dance instructors for entertaining customers with novelty steps. People danced the slow drag and the Charleston, they did the Georgia Crawl and the Lindy Hop too – many of which upset moral commentators (too sexual, too American) – while the likes of the Turkey Trot enraged those who care to be enraged. "What kind of person impersonated a barn yard animal?" they shrieked. Lots, it appears.

Some danced to dance bands employed by hotels. Others in halls and clubs to gramophones. Most dancers said they liked jazz, although back then 'jazz' was often taken to mean any kind of dance music. Dance music records were popular home listening too, as anyone engaged in 78 crate-digging will confirm after struggling though boxes of foxtrots, waltzes and such. Among the many dance bands working around the UK it was Jack Hylton and his Orchestra who were the genre's superstars, with some 7 million 78s sold between 1923 and 1933.

Songs in the key of Peckham: SE15 Gramophone Store 1933. Courtesy of Science & Society Picture Library

Lancashire pianist Hylton learned his trade in pubs and vaudeville theatres and, like many a young musician, he loved hot American jazz. Yet he valued money more than music and developed a band that swung sweetly, not 'jazz' as fans of the music emanating from New Orleans and New York knew it, but pleasing to Brits who liked a melody they could hum and a tepid rhythm. Tunes like 'Happy Feet' and 'Jeepers Creepers' sound impossibly tame today, but their warmth and optimism provided the public with what they wanted. Hylton happily accommodated them: in 1931 Jack and his band were recording and releasing on average 18 new titles every month.

Jack the lad carved out an archetypal pop star template: acquiring vast wealth, squiring beautiful women, driving fast cars and, on occasion, paying homage to his influences – in the 1930s he brought Duke Ellington and Coleman Hawkins to the UK, these gestures making British jazz fans forever doff their caps in his direction. Hylton's appeal lasted right up until the outbreak of the Second World War (seven members of his orchestra were drafted on the first day of fighting). He then went on to pursue holdings in Decca Records and West End theatre, dying aged 72 in 1965.

In contrast to Hylton's ersatz jazz, Louis Armstrong was the only African-American jazz musician to sell any number of 78s in the UK. On 24 February 1934, Armstrong visited The Cowling Brothers record shop in St Nicholas Street, Leicester. This is known due to the shop's autograph book being auctioned on eBay in late 2015: Armstrong and his then girlfriend (later wife), Alpha Smith, signed the book alongside the British musicians who were accompanying him on tour. Did Armstrong visit Cowling Brothers to do some promo? Possibly, seeing that he had his band with him. Considering how Louis liked to refresh his ears, he might have requested a visit to stock up on fresh 78s for the rest of the tour. Little is known today about Cowling's – surely they had a decent stock of jazz 78s if King Louis came visiting! – but Leicester resident Ron Lambwell recalls they had two shops and says, "Cowling's were well known for their Accordion Band which was very popular before and just after the Second World War."

"I can't afford records so I'll just listen to the radio"

In 1934, no one predicted that the UK would, by the end of the decade, be at war with Germany. But then no one had predicted the Depression, least of all the record industry. In 1927, the industry journal *Records* reported, "The output of records has been trebled and quadrupled; profits and dividends are steadily rising." The peak year for British record sales proved to be 1929. Demand was so strong that HMV's Hayes factory worked around the clock, producing some 25 million 78s (only 12 million of which were sold in the UK; much of the rest were for export to the British colonies and other nations – Italy imported more British records during the 1920s than Italian labels produced). The portable gramophone was designed to be taken on holiday and to picnics – caravanning in Great Yarmouth in 1933, Kate Meyell recalled George Formby's 'Trailing Around in a Trailer' floating across the sands as her father played his favourite 78 over and over. Then, as the 1920s came to an end, the Depression hit and sales crashed.

Columbia Records slashed the price of its 78s, while countless letters to *The Gramophone* stated, "I can't afford records so I'll just listen to the radio." This must have been punishing as the fledgling BBC programmed an extremely conservative remit of dance bands, 'light' classical and other 'non-obtrusive' music. That noted, the UK record trade did not fare as badly as the US, and British record buyers became increasingly cosmopolitan as people embraced all kinds of music. Along with the popular American singers (Bing Crosby, Rudy Vallée) and British music hall stars (George Formby, Gracie Fields), there was a smorgasbord of music now being appreciated: Latin American rumba, American swing, Central European Gypsy rhythms, French chanson, Spanish flamenco and Italian tenors. In the 1930s, people categorised their musical tastes more selectively, and many 'fan clubs' for individual genres and artists sprang up.

Then, as the Depression faded, Hitler came into view. With the severity of the Second World War, records were deemed to be a luxury item and taxed punitively. Many shops closed, HMV's Oxford Street store's record basement was co-opted into serving as a bomb shelter, and the government encouraged people to hand in records (shellac being useful as a machine insulator). The arrival of US servicemen in Britain saw tastes changing, and the dance bands were now deemed old-fashioned. As the sun set on the British Empire, a new generation of UK jazz and blues, pop and rock 'n' roll musicians, all disciples of record shops, would emerge. And they would go on to conquer the world in ways previously unimaginable.

Chapter 2

Dobell's and All that Jazz: Soho's Hot Music Temples

Doug Dobell, war hero and gentleman, pioneers the specialist British record shop, inspiring devotion from music lovers across the decades. Vogue Records and James Asman Record Centre follow, while communist book shop Collet's opens a record bar offering jazz, folk, blues and Soviet 78s. Soho in London is Europe's jazz epicentre and the West End gets very hot. Cameos from Bob Dylan, Richard Farina, B. B. King, Chris Barber, Janis Joplin and David Bowie.

Hitler was dead, Europe liberated and Britain shattered. Nothing would be the same again and many returning soldiers, after living so closely with death, were determined to ensure their lives counted. Londoner Doug Dobell, having worn uniform from 1939–45, decided he would open a record shop – *a jazz record shop* – where he, his friends and like-minded individuals could gather to bathe in the beauty of fragile 78s made by American musicians with names like Kid Ory and Jelly Roll Morton. However, opening this trading post would not be easy.

Dobell's

The UK was broke, near broken and bomb pocked. Food remained rationed, spam and lard were kitchen staples and 'luxuries' – as records were regarded by the government – endured heavy taxes. No bank agreed to underwrite Doug Dobell's dream: jazz may have inspired fierce passions in the young but record shops were still viewed by many as gramophone salons dominated by classical music. Moreover, who could afford American records? Going to work at Dobell's, his family's antiquarian bookshop at 77 Charing Cross Road, London WC2, 28-year-old Doug felt the past weighing heavily on his slender shoulders.

Dobell's first opened in 1877 when Bertram Dobell – Doug's grandfather – set up at that address. Bertram's sons, Percy and Arthur, continued to run the shop after his death, and Arthur, entertaining his son's passion, allowed Doug to set aside a small space in the shop to display 78s he had for sale and exchange. Immediately successful, Doug began liberating book shelves to make more space for 78s and, month by month, tomes lost space to records while music lovers gathered to shop and gossip. In 1955, Arthur Dobell retired and Doug completed his transformation of Dobell's into the UK's foremost musical oracle, a record shop that served both as Aladdin's cave and philosopher's salon, albeit a salon where the gnomic utterances and activities of mythic New Orleans musicians like Buddy Bolden and King Oliver carried more weight than those of Aristotle and Socrates.

Around this time, Soho entered its most celebrated phase, an era where all that appeared urbane and risqué in contemporary Britain seemed to emanate

Jazz pop art: Dobell's iconic record bag as designed by Bill Colyer. Courtesy of Leon Parker.

from the square mile. Dobell's, alongside Ronnie Scott's Jazz Club, helped Soho become a centre for post-war British jazz – not just a record shop but a salon of sorts where youths could clash over whether 'hot music' ruled, as exemplified by Louis Armstrong and Sidney Bechet, or whether the modernists, Bird/Miles and Monk/'Trane, were running the game ("Monk eats shoes" was written on the wall of one of Dobell's listening booths).

British jazz fans took their musical passions very seriously and the youths divided into two distinct camps – mouldy fygges and modernists – with the fygges championing local heroes Chris Barber and Humphrey Lyttelton, while the modernists favoured rising Soho stars Joe Harriott and Ronnie Ball. That the musicians often got on, even played together, was ignored. A decade later youths would argue over blues (acoustic or electric) and guitarists (Clapton or Beck) and, again, Dobell's acted as a church of sorts for the devotees to congregate, discuss the true faith, declaim heretics and ponder those elevated to sainthood.

Dobell's blossomed in a dirty old town where smog led to winter pea-soupers and an omnipresent haze of tobacco smoke permeated all public spaces. Consumer goods were frugal, expectations limited, class divisions rigid and the rights of women and ethnic minorities pitiful. In opposition to this, Dobell's record shop provided a democratic space where race, class and gender were ignored as everyone gathered to celebrate jazz (and its siblings blues and folk). Upon entering you were likely to be struck by a clarinet solo so seductive that everyone in the shop nodded along, many dreaming they were in steamy New Orleans not smoggy London town. To some observers, Dobell's helped build a post-war society where artistry and inclusivity served as unacknowledged legislators. To others, Dobell's might just be remembered as a place where people gathered for one 'helluva' good time: *drinking wine, feeling fine, listening to Louis blow his horn!*

The passion for collecting jazz 78s that inspired Doug to open Dobell's infected many, but this was not easy to pursue: during the war few records were pressed in (or imported into) the UK, while surplus 78s had been recycled, so sending 'junkers' – youths who scoured junk shops for jazz 78s – on obsessive treasure hunts. When aspiring jazz trombonist Chris Barber arrived in London from Cambridge in 1946, he quickly located Dobell's. He recalls: "There were very few outlets for jazz and blues at the time. The English branches of the American record labels tended not to bother bringing over the blues and jazz releases. If you knew someone fortunate enough to be visiting New York City you could direct them to Harlem where there was a record shop with a lot of blues and jazz 78s. Some blues did come out here but it seemed that the only place you could find these 78s were in college towns – because of student interest.

"During World War Two, Royston, where I was born, was evacuated and I got sent to live in a town outside Cambridge. I would cycle into Cambridge every week and go to Millers where they had a record bar. They had very few jazz or blues records and the girls working there had no idea of what I was asking for so one of them said to me 'come behind the counter and have a look' and I found some of the music I was looking for and went through their catalogue and ordered

Sharp dressed men: jazz vocalist Joe Williams drops into Dobell's (Don Solash, Joe Williams, Mick Brocking, unknown, Doug Dobell). Courtesy of Brian Peerless.

more. At the time shellac was being used for the war effort so records really were difficult to find. I bought my first Leadbelly and Sleepy John Estes from Millers. For quite a while after World War Two finished there was a real shortage of records in the UK. Meat was rationed and, so it seemed, were records.

"To my mind, Dobell's was the first record shop that was really special. Doug Dobell had a real understanding of how to do this. The other shops tended to be all the same but Dobell's really set out to get jazz and blues. It knew what music we wanted and how to get it. In 1946, when word got out that Doug was selling jazz 78s, it immediately became the centre for jazz fans and record collectors. It was there in 1948 that I met clarinettist Alex Revell and we decided to form a band. I might also have met a couple of the other musicians who joined what was my first band at Dobell's."

It was Barber who brought a jazz loving youth named John Jack to Dobell's for the first time. More than 60 years on, Jack still recalls the encounter: "I'd joined the London Jazz Society in 1950 and we would meet in The Porcupine pub on Charing Cross Road. There were a network of record clubs before there were a network of record shops. They were the backbone of record collecting as it is now. I met Doug through that and one day Chris said, 'Doug's just got some Sam Morgan 78s!' so we scampered down there and purchased our Sam

Morgan 78s. I was ducking and diving, putting on jazz gigs – sometimes with Doug – for which we'd end up with about five bob to share between us. Doug was beginning to expand. He had already taken on Brian Harvey and one day he said, 'Do you want to come and join us?'

"Everybody was in and out of the place all the time. In the '50s and '60s pubs still shut 3–5 p.m., but one or two places opened at 3 p.m. for members. So, when we got visiting bands in we would be back and forth across Charing Cross Road to get the day's drinking in. Back then a very much sought-after job for musicians was to get into Geraldo's Navy and work on the transatlantic liners playing in the band. You would get 48 hours in New York so people would rush around the shops and clubs and certain guys would bring us back suitcases full of LPs! We had to be careful as Customs and Excise would raid us from time to time to see if the taxes had been paid on the records!"

Doug Dobell, flush with success, opened a branch of Dobell's in Brighton in 1955. The son of the late bandleader Glen Miller hosted an autograph session at the opening of the Brighton shop, attracting much publicity. Yet here Dobell's lasted only 18 months, the seaside city lacking the jazz fans to keep the shop afloat. Doug licked his wounds and launched the 77 record label in 1957 – to avoid the luxury tax that used to apply to UK record releases only 99 copies were initially pressed for each release. He released new recordings by British jazz and blues musicians, licensed American blues and folk recordings and welcomed visiting musicians: Ramblin' Jack Elliot, fresh with tales of Woody and Cisco, cut a notable session, while exiled South African jazz musicians also did recordings.

In November 1960, British jazz saxophonist John Dankworth officially opened Dobell's Folk and Blues Shop at 10 Rathbone Place, London W1. Doug also used Rathbone Place as a base for Agate & Co (the mail order company that handled Dobell's many UK and international orders) and Central Record Distributors (distributors of 77 and specialist US record labels). During this time, the iconic Dobell's record bag was created (along with the slogan 'Every true jazz fan is born within the sound of Dobell's').

In 1965, 75 Charing Cross Road became available and Doug Dobell relocated Rathbone Place's stock here. Jesse Fuller, the African American one-man blues band, played at the opening of what would be known as the 'Folk-Blues' shop. Together, the two shops served as a musical Mecca. On any given day, Dobell's clientele might include local and international musicians eyeing one another up, anarchists rubbing shoulders with cabinet ministers as they dug through orange crates full of rare 78s, and fresh-faced students and grizzled war veterans discussing the merits of recent releases on Blue Note or Savoy.

The beauty of the music and the remarkable selection of records – "Sir Doug Dobell forgot more about music than most people have ever known," states Soho veteran Steve Bronstein – made sure a babble of languages could be heard there as Dobell's fame spread and sailors, tourists, diplomats and other visitors to London headed there. Such activity found working girls touting for business, while their pimps and the shadowy characters who haunted Soho's clubs and private member's bars used the shop as a daylight hours hang-out. Among this flotsam were those who visited simply because they were enamoured with music, and deep friendships were forged. Errol Dixon, the exceptional Jamaican blues/ska pianist, and Charlie Gillett, the preternatural writer and broadcaster, met here and enjoyed a strong bond.

Dobell's reputation ensured that when skiffle awoke British youths to the delight of bashing away on washboards and string bass, Doug served up generous helpings of blues and country records to the teenagers who came in search of songs to add to their skiffle repertoire. Imports of American blues and R&B (rhythm and blues) also found Dobell's helping to kick-start the UK's nascent blues scene: Alexis Korner and Cyril Davies, the godfathers of London's blues bands, learned much of their repertoire via Dobell's, and both recorded for 77.

As the 1960s got under way, long-haired youths would enter Dobell's to soak up the atmosphere, hoping not to get a tongue-lashing from some of the fiercer denizens behind the counter. A teenage Charlie Watts hunted for jazz 78s here and thinks he saw Phil Seamen, the British jazz drummer all others aspired to, huddled in a corner. Watts' soon to be bandmate, Brian Jones, arrived in London from Cheltenham and headed straight for Dobell's. Not long after, a fey folkie from St Albans, Donovan Leitch, also arrived in London and headed to Doug's shop, having heard about it from the older youths he met in pubs and folk clubs. Brian Case, later one of the UK's foremost jazz critics, hitched from Hull to Dobell's as a teen simply to buy Johnny Griffin's *The Congregation* LP. What they all recall is a sense of excitement, of wild possibilities in this jewel of a shop overseen by a prince of a man.

Dave Peabody, then a Southall schoolboy, now one of Europe's foremost acoustic blues musicians, says: "I discovered Dobell's in 1964. Back then I had a weekend job in an ice-cream parlour and all the money I earned got spent at Dobell's. Once you discovered Dobell's you really didn't need anywhere else. It fulfilled every wish, every need. I got to know the little guy behind the counter, Ray Bolden, and he always pretended to be grumpy but you'd pull out a Blind Blake LP and ask him to play a track and he would. I got the basis of my record collection – blues, jazz and folk – from Dobell's."

Are You Being Served? B. B. King, Bowie, Coleman Hawkins and Rory Gallagher at Dobell's

It wasn't just suburban British youths who frequented Dobell's: Mississippi blues seer B. B. King recognised Dobell's as oracle, visiting the shop every time he was in London. In a *Melody Maker* feature on King in June 1971, the journalist Max Jones wrote, "I was surprised to find him [King] almost literally knee deep in books and records. It was the result of a shopping expedition." "Well I took some time off and went to see Ray [Bolden] in Dobell's shop," said King to Jones when quizzed on what he was doing in the Charing Cross Road store. "I remember him from before and it's always nice to talk to him. Whilst I was there I bought some books and records."

It wasn't only Jones who encountered King – over the years many a Dobell's customer would be pleasantly surprised to enter and find B. B. there, chatting or browsing. Jazz saxophonist Coleman Hawkins would sit, sip Scotch and tell tall stories of sessions he had blown on. By the late 1960s, Bill Colyer was managing the blues section of Dobell's and, on returning from the pub one afternoon, he found two hairy young Americans waiting for him. They announced themselves as Alan 'Blind Owl' Wilson and Bob 'The Bear' Hite: these two youths were leading the popular blues rock band Canned Heat and, they informed Colyer, had been purchasing blues records by mail from Dobell's for several years. As with B. B. King, Canned Heat found the Soho shop's stock of rare 78s superior to those of most American stores. Janis Joplin arrived at Dobell's on her sole visit to London and presented the staff with a bottle of Southern Comfort. What, I wonder, did Doug Dobell make of these American rock stars who came to pay tribute to his enterprise? I imagine he smiled and pondered on music's magical qualities and how it managed to inspire and unite all manner of people.

In the pre-internet era, record shops like Dobell's acted as a one-stop search engine for anyone with the slightest interest in music beyond the Top 40. As Londoners mingled with those from distant lands, the shops functioned as epicentres for news and knowledge, a place where, among the fog of cigarette smoke, loud voices and louder jazz, teaching in the Sufi sense of the word went on. That American icons such as Louis Armstrong, Ben Webster, Slim Galliard, Stan Kenton, Horace Silver, Errol Garner, Julian 'Cannonball' Adderley, Brownie McGhee, Muddy Waters (with his guitarist Jimmy Rogers) and Stan Getz dropped in when they were in town suggests the totemic energies that the Charing Cross Road shop exuded.

Along with the US heavyweights, many aspiring British and Irish musicians, both celebrated and unsung, proclaimed Doug Dobell's shop as somewhere special. Lonnie Donegan, jazz drummer John Stevens, youthful folkies Wizz Jones, Bert Jansch and Martin Carthy, and a fresh-faced Irish teenager called Rory Gallagher, were regulars in both the jazz and folk shops. Gallagher first came across Dobell's when in London as a teenager playing with the Fontana Show Band. Coming from Cork – not a city noted for its record shops – Gallagher inhaled the sound of Dobell's and smiled that gentlest of smiles.

A similar epiphany engulfed the teenager who would become David Bowie. Back then humble David Jones carefully purchased jazz, blues and folk imports as he sought his own sound, noting in a 2013 interview: "By 1963 I was working as a junior commercial artist at an advertising agency in London. My immediate boss, Ian, a groovy modernist with Gerry Mulligan-style short crop haircut and Chelsea boots, was very encouraging about my passion for music, something he and I both shared, and used to send me on errands to Dobell's Jazz record shop on Charing Cross Road, knowing I'd be there for most of the morning 'til well after lunch break. It was there, in the 'bins,' that I found Bob Dylan's first album. Ian had sent me there to get him a John Lee Hooker release and advised me to pick up a copy for myself, as it was so wonderful. Within weeks my pal George Underwood and I had changed the name of our little R&B outfit to the Hooker Brothers and had included both Hooker's 'Tupelo' and Dylan's version of 'House of the Rising Sun' in our set."

Even David Essex, dreamboat pop icon of stage and screen, declared in his autobiography: "My musical Mecca was a specialist record shop called Dobell's in the Charing Cross Road and I made regular pilgrimages. In addition to my jazz idols, I would head home with records by venerable blues men such as Muddy Waters, Howlin' Wolf and Memphis Slim. If it looked black and obscure, I would buy it."

Dylan at Dobell's

Among the many Dobell's stories, none matches the time a young Bob Dylan, who sought out the shop during his first visit to the UK, joined a recording session in the basement. This came about on 14 January 1963 when American folk musicians Eric von Schmidt and Richard Farina agreed to record an album for the 77 label.

Even by the fierce standards of that winter, 14 January 1963 was a bitter night. Yet four young Americans didn't let the elements concern them as they gathered for a recording session in Dobell's basement. The sessions found Farina and Von Schmidt, then touring UK folk clubs, taking advantage of Doug's offer to cut an album in London. They were joined by Ethan Signer, a US fiddle player then living in Cambridge, and Bob Dylan. Dylan's debut album had received good notices in the USA, yet he remained largely unknown in the UK; his London sojourn had come via the BBC bringing him over to participate in the recording of the television play, *Madhouse on Castle Street*. To anyone then interested in the US folk scene, Richard Farina, with his movie star looks and a Beat novel to his name, would have appeared the star of the sessions, with Dylan as court jester, the sardonic runt of the litter.

Dylan, under contract to Columbia Records, could not officially join the sessions. However, being a Greenwich Village buddy of Farina and Von Schmidt, he wanted in. He didn't add greatly to the evening's proceedings – occasional backing vocals, a little harmonica – but got into the spirit of things. For this Bob was credited as Blind Boy Grunt. For Dylan obsessives, the album issued on Doug's Folklore label as *Singing Shouting and Playing American Ballads, Worksongs and Blues* (circa 1963) and credited to "Dick Farina & Eric von Schmidt with Ethan Signer & occasionally Blind Boy Grunt", is something of a holy relic, featuring Dylan on the verge of stardom yet at his least guarded.

The set-up for recording was very simple: a ferrograph recorder and microphone were set on the counter of Rathbone Street's basement while the musicians sat on chairs. Events proceeded at a relaxed pace and Dobell's employee Ron Gould remembers his wife being sent out several times to buy booze. At one point, Farina passed Dylan an open bottle of Guinness and Dylan, after taking a large swig, gagged and spat it out, seemingly unacquainted with stout. Doug Dobell, unimpressed, reprimanded the future superstar.

Gould recalled all participants growing drunker as the session progressed and Dylan, while not playing much music, appearing uninhibited and very confident. Von Schmidt later admitted they were all stoned on strong marijuana. Once the session finished, everyone headed down to The Troubadour on Old Brompton

Road in Earl's Court. At London's foremost folk club the Americans drunkenly commandeered the stage. For some in the audience it was a treat, seeing rising stars of the USA and UK folk movements loosely jamming together. For others, it was disrespectful. When Scottish folk singer Nigel Denver took the stage, he became agitated at the hoots and hollers coming from the Americans and directly asked Dylan, who was talking louder than everyone else, to be quiet. Bob replied, "I don't shut up for anyone." This aggrieved Denver who shouted, "I don't give a fuck who you are. Shut *up*!" Dylan, small and skinny and hungry for fame, would soon upset many British folkies on a far more personal level: he transformed several of the songs they sang into his own songs and then embraced rock, so splitting an insular scene. Yet, on that fateful, freezing January night, no one could have imagined such.

Dylan's performance on Folklore is a minor note in his discography, yet his time in London proved important as he developed several songs that would appear on *The Times They Are A-Changin'* (1964) from British folk songs. Quite possibly he heard some of the songs during his regular visits to Dobell's: his anti-war ballad 'With God on Our Side' was a rewrite of Dominic Behan's 'The Patriot Game' (which appeared on Behan's 1961 Folklore LP *The Irish Rover*). *Singing Shouting and Playing American Ballads, Worksongs and Blues* is not difficult to find on vinyl. This suggests that Doug Dobell, over the years, pressed up considerably more than 99 copies.

West End Blues

Cecil Gee, the visionary tailor who started out on London's Charing Cross Road in the 1930s, observed that, "the war changed everything. Before they might have been conservative but now there was no stopping them". Gee was describing the British approach to clothes but could just as easily have been discussing music, and many record shops followed in Dobell's wake. HMV's Oxford Street flagship store increased its basement jazz department while Keith Prowse Music began advertising that their Coventry Street branch was a 'jazz specialist'. Yet it was the specialist shops that ensured jazz was heard.

Jazz Collector

Based in Kensington, London, Jazz Collector Records was opened during the Second World War by Colin Pomroy to sell 78s (including many bootlegs that Pomroy made of rare jazz and blues records). In December 1945, 12-year-old Reg Hall visited and purchased 'Potato Head Blues' (1927) by Louis Armstrong. Hall recalls: "Jazz Collector was situated on a corner and occupied half a shopfront – it was very narrow and got smaller as you walked in. Pomroy was posh and snooty. I've never forgotten how he spoke to me all these years on! He started doing dubs off 78s of Bessie Smith and King Oliver and issuing them on his Jazz Collector label. He later did a folk series where he issued Dominic Behan, Joe Heaney and other Irish singers. His assistant was Paul Carter. He [Paul] married a young writer he met in the shop called Angela who went on to become the famous Angela Carter. The end of Jazz Collector came about when bailiffs came into the shop around '61 and the staff rushed all the stock they could grab to the pub across the road!"

Vogue Records

Vogue Records, a British division of the Parisian jazz record label Disques Vogue, started trading in the UK in 1951, opening a Vogue Records shop. As a record label, Vogue proved a revelation for British jazz and blues fans, issuing as it did high quality 78s by leading jazz musicians (Dizzy Gillespie, Kid Ory, George Lewis, Charlie Parker) alongside a series of blues 78s – Big Bill Broonzy, John Lee Hooker, Muddy Waters and horny jump blues shouter Wynonie Harris all received their initial UK releases on Vogue. Vogue's 100 Charing Cross Road record shop stocked plenty of the label's releases – all extremely collectable today – as well as a select number of other jazz and blues releases, often imports. Anyone old enough to remember the Vogue shop speaks of it with affection but it only existed for five years, closing when Decca bought the rights to Vogue UK in 1956.

James Asman Record Centre

James Asman's huge build, deep voice and goatee meant he commanded a room and, as *The Mirror*'s jazz critic, he was one of the first UK music writers to be widely read and discussed. Asman (1914–97) made it clear that he was firmly in the traditional camp and loudly dismissed music he disdained and those who disagreed with him: notoriously waspish, he fibbed about how Muddy Waters' electric guitar playing was so loud during his debut UK tour in 1958 that audiences fled screaming. This fib has solidified into spurious fact in histories of blues in Britain.

Then, as now, writing about music did not pay well and Asman relied on working in record shops to supplement his writing. He got started in the 1940s when British jazz trumpeter Owen Bryce hired him to run the jazz basement in his Farley Radio Services shop in Woolwich. Asman liked the job and, when offered the capital to start his own record shop, he opened James Asman Record Centre in a tiny space on New Row, Covent Garden.

Asman's bulk and demeanour meant people would visit his shop simply to stare at this Herculean figure, and he made enemies easily – admitting to liking modern jazz often brought on a tongue-lashing. Still, his friends speak of him with affection and he was no fool, managing four James Asman Record Centres across London from the 1950s to the 1980s. While Asman was proud that his shops were stockists of early jazz records, he also, at times, sold soul, country, blues, calypso, ska and pop.

Collet's

Piecing together the history of Collet's finds the London book/record shop serving as both oracle and tidal marker for radical activism across the twentieth century. In 1934, Eva Collet Reckitt (1890–1976), heiress to the Reckitt's Blue and Starch Company business, bought Henderson's, a renowned radical bookshop at 66 Charing Cross Road, London WC2, that had already been nicknamed the 'Bomb Shop'. The shop's basement served as a recruiting centre for the Republican effort during the Spanish Civil War and, in 1936, Collet's acquired the stock of the London–Soviet trading agency Arcos. Reckitt's strong links with the Communist Party and the USSR meant Collet's would import Melodiya recordings and art books from the Hermitage collection. After the Second World War, Collet's expanded by opening branches in Manchester, Glasgow, Moscow, Prague and New York. Reckitt was a devout communist – born into extreme privilege, she would devote her adult life to left-wing causes – and MI5 considered the heiress to be working for 'an espionage organisation'.

Collet's actively supported those involved with publishing and recording, and one of the initial beneficiaries of Reckitt's largesse was the Workers Music Association (WMA), a communist group aimed at getting propaganda songs to the people. In 1939, the WMA formed the Topic Record Club through which it published such noted songbooks as *Popular Soviet Songs* (1941) and *Red Army Songs* (1942). The WMA began using Collet's to distribute its sheet music, both British and imported from Russia, in 1948 and enjoyed brisk sales for 'Pity the Downtrodden Landlord', a satirical ditty regularly used in leftist theatre groups of the time. While I've no figures to rely on, I imagine such WMA sheet music titles as 'Strike While the Iron Is Hot' and 'Unity March' may not have set the Collet's cash registers ringing. Post-Second World War Topic Records developed from sheet music into releasing 78s of UK, Irish, American and Russian folk music, inadvertently developing into the UK's foremost folk music label.

It was in Collet's International Bookshop at 52 Charing Cross Road that a jazz record department was established in the 1940s (likely after the war ended). Trad jazz trumpeter Ken Colyer was one of many musicians who worked behind the record department counter at Collet's when paid gigs were thin on the ground. In 1952, shop manager Ken Lindsay corresponded with Woody Guthrie, praising his music, writing and activism, and Woody replied, expressing a desire to visit the UK, stating that he could write for workers' papers there.

Collet's became the first European distributor of Moses Asch's Folkways record label, ensuring UK listeners got their hands on records by Guthrie, Leadbelly, Pete Seeger and *The*

Anthology of American Folk Music (1952). Collet's also stocked the books of folk songs that US folklorists John and Alan Lomax published and, when Alan Lomax landed in London in late 1950, fleeing the USA for what would be a decade because of the witch hunt for leftists then under way, he could often be found holding court in Collet's. Lomax made his mark on young British folkies, none more so than Ewan MacColl, the Scottish folk singer-songwriter and communist activist who made good use of Collet's whenever in Glasgow, Manchester or London.

Shifting the record department to 70 New Oxford Street in the mid-1950s, Collet's became beatnik central. Here the record department was run by Ray Smith (1934–2011), a gifted jazz drummer, and Gill Cook (1937–2006). They were extremely different personalities (he loved jazz and whisky, she folk and pot) but together Smith and Cook established Collet's as one of Britain's most vital record shops.

Smith's many close friends included Peter Blake and David Hockney, Chris Barber and Charlie Watts, and he rarely ventured outside Soho. Cook befriended musicians young and old, famously providing accommodation for many who were passing through London. The most celebrated of these was Bert Jansch, the whippet-thin Scottish guitarist and singer who cast a huge shadow across the British folk scene. Cook not only secured Jansch a recording deal, in 1965 she had his child. Jansch noted: "Gill was head of the Collet's folk section and ran a few clubs herself. If you wanted to know anything about clubs or singers or wanted to contact someone from that scene, that was the place you'd go. It was through her that I met Bill Leader. Bill was a field recorder, recordist or whatever who was working for Transatlantic Records at the time."

When not playing London's most celebrated folk clubs – The Troubadour (Earl's Court) and Les Cousins (Greek Street, minutes from Collet's) – many folk and blues musicians hung out at Collet's record bar, it being cosy during the winter and a hub for like-minded musicians. One such musician was aspiring singer-songwriter Ralph McTell, who would venture from Croydon into the West End. He says: "The two shops that meant the most to me were Collet's in New Oxford Street and Dobell's on Charing Cross Road. Collet's record bar was run by a guy called Hans who was extremely knowledgeable – he'd tell you who played bouzouki on what record! Collet's had a great blues and folk selection. Dobell's was more sophisticated, more jazz oriented. The people in there seemed to know everything. They wouldn't just sell you a record but tell you what recording you should buy as to who was on trombone on that specific session! I often think people who know too much about records need to get out more."

As the UK shook off wartime privations, hot music began to roar from basement clubs and South London pubs. Jazz was akin to religion, waking UK youth to a wild, lascivious America, and several disciples, stretching from Plymouth to Belfast, followed in Doug Dobell's wake, opening jazz and blues shops. A brave new UK was taking shape and these tiny record shops would play many roles in shaping it.

Chapter 3

Sounds that Swing: Record Shops Rock the UK

Jazz, blues and folk record shops open across Greater London, Birmingham, Plymouth, Liverpool, Nottingham, Sheffield, Scarborough, Manchester, Bristol, Cardiff and Belfast. Skiffle and rock 'n' roll create a teenage market. Woolworths, WHSmith and Boots record bars do record business. Things get very hot indeed. Cameos from Van Morrison, Stan Kenton, Mike Westbrook, Peter Guralnick, Brian Jones and John Peel.

As the 1950s began, old warriors found themselves empowered with the British electing Winston and Americans liking Ike. Reds were under beds, nuclear sabres rattled, the carrot of consumerism dangled. *Don't worry, be happy!* Conservative times ensure music takes on an added urgency, and the likes of Dobell's and Collet's were part of an underground empire for those who railed against what Vladimir Nabokov characterised as his essential loathings: *stupidity, oppression, crime, cruelty, soft music.*

The jazz and folk shops existed as marginal operations, odd little oracles sharing little with the high-street record shops, bars and stalls that survived by selling a mix of balladeers, novelty songs and light music to customers who didn't wear CND (Campaign for Nuclear Disarmament) badges or care about trad versus modern. Liverpool's The Musical Box supplied the local cinema with new releases to be played before the evening's film, and employee Diane Cain remembers one evening in late 1952 when they played for the first time the 78 of American crooner Al Martino, 'Here in My Heart'. The audience around the ice-cream concession fell silent before unanimously asking, "Who's that singing?" Martino's 78 became the first ever UK No. 1 song: sheet music sales having accounted for the Top 10 prior to the *New Musical Express* (*NME*), then a struggling weekly, starting a sales chart by ringing 20 London record shops and asking for their weekly sales figures. The chart made the *NME*, and it was soon ringing 53 record shops (in London, the home counties, Liverpool and Manchester) for sales figures. Record shops would go on to command all kinds of dark powers over the UK charts, while Al Martino went on to play Johnny Fontane in *The Godfather* (1972).

Among the cinema crowd wowed by Martino might there have been a 13-year-old John Ravenscroft? Ravenscroft, later to win adulation as John Peel, never mentioned such but did recall buying his first record "with my own money and without outside assistance" that same year at Liverpool department store Crane's. Peel would later describe Crane's as being a furniture and musical instrument shop with a record department, noting, "despite the well-established popularity of the gramophone, there were, even then, very few shops which traded exclusively

NOTTINGHAM
JAZZ 'n' SWING
COLLECTORS

It certainly is a drag thinking up clever ads.

So we won't bother.

We'll just say—do yourself a favour and drop in sometime.

We've plenty of red-hot discs, including a goodly stock of Blue Notes.

We welcome orders by mail.

PAPWORTH'S

Music Inn

32 ALFRETON RD. NOTTINGHAM
Phone 77248

in records". The 78 that the young Ravenscroft purchased was Ray Martin and his Concert Orchestra's 'Blue Tango' (1952). This slice of light music isn't a particularly auspicious start for the DJ who would later command huge influence in UK music – and record shops – but things were about to change.

Cut to 1954: in a London recording studio, Chris Barber, trombone master blaster and secret hero of British blues, unintentionally sets the future in motion. Barber is recording an album of trad jazz for Decca, and to fill it out he switches to double bass, puts his banjoist Lonnie Donegan upfront and they record an up-tempo rip on Leadbelly's 'Rock Island Line'. They called this turbo-charged sound 'skiffle', and synchronicity finds Donegan cutting 'Rock Island Line' the same month Elvis made his recording debut, with a similarly ferocious reinvention of country blues in Memphis. No one knew it then, but these two dark-haired, garrulous youths would soon have the Western world wobbling on its axis.

'Rock Island Line' was initially recorded to fill out an album and, until well over a year later when a sharp-eared BBC DJ started playing it (so making sure the Beeb's phone lines lit up with youths wanting to know what it *was* and where to *get* it), it stayed that way. Rushed out by Decca – who had never imagined that within Barber's trad jazz band resided a musical missile primed for stardom – Donegan's debut 78 entered the charts in January 1956 and became the first debut UK record to sell gold (500,000+ copies). Skiffle pre-dated Elvis, Fats Domino and Little Richard, all of whom would hit the UK charts later that year. Admittedly, Bill Haley and His Comets, had scored four big UK hits across 1954–5. While establishment commentators might have dismissed rock 'n' roll and skiffle – *The Daily Mail* shrieked and described the new music as "the Negro's revenge" and "jungle music" - those who worked in record shops, milk bars and Italian style cafés saw how the sounds possessed teens: *things, they realised, have changed.*

Teen Tunes

'Haley's 'Rock Around The Clock' became the first single in the UK to sell a million copies (on 78 and 45) as it kept returning to the charts – first in January 1955 and then October of that year, twice in 1956 and twice in 1957. January 1958 registered the greatest 'disc sales' in British history, spurred on by Elvis's 'Jailhouse Rock', which was released that month. This steamroller of a hit sold more than 500,000 45s in the UK. Record labels were experiencing boom times like never before, and the shops and stalls that sold the records enjoyed the financial benefits.

The likes of HMV and Imhoff's, formal stores whose record departments prided themselves on the seriousness of their stock of classical and Broadway show albums, found groups of youths packing their listening booths and openly contemptuous of everything except the raw new music they craved. Independent record shops – then still relatively scarce across the UK – noted more and more customers popping in not just for the latest hits but hungry for records, knowledge and kindred spirits.

HIS MASTERS VOICE . BRUNSWICK . MERCURY
CAPITOL . VOGUE . PYE . DECCA
PHILIPS . COLUMBIA . PARLOPHONE
LONDON AMERICAN . RCA

DAVIDS RECORD SHOP

ROCK'N'ROLL TOP TUNES
JAZZ . CALYPSO . CLASSICS

1 Chalton Street, Euston, **London, N.W.1.** Tel. Euston 8651	**26 Wardour Street,** **London, W.1.** Tel. Gerrard 4924	**20 Covered Market,** **Slough, Bucks.** Tel. Slough 24310
2 St. Johns Parade, High Street North, East Ham, London. Tel. Grangewood 8909		**2 Market Place,** **Bracknell, Berks.** Tel. Bracknell 2395

The tiny amount of airplay that the BBC gave to rock 'n' roll and skiffle, blues and jazz, bottled up desire and led to jukeboxes becoming sonic shrines: at the end of 1945 the UK had 100 registered jukeboxes; by the end of 1958 it had 13,000. US-styled milk bars, with their signature black and white chequered floors, bar stools, jukeboxes and gleaming chrome, were where teens gathered to slurp milkshakes and listen to the hits. Meanwhile, white goods stores (fridges, cookers and other electrical goods including radios and gramophones) and department stores with record bars became improvised youth clubs, teens huddling together in listening booths or sharing headphones on listening posts. David Lands, born and raised in Herne Hill just after the end of WW2, says: "The record shops of Brixton were our haunts. In 1957 I was 12 and bought my first 45, 'Whole Lotta Shakin' Going On' by Jerry Lee Lewis. My favourite shop was Chip's Music Box in the Granville Arcade. It had a sloping counter that displayed around twenty 78s. This was a period when 45s were becoming more popular but this shop sold only 78s. It was an odd record shop with the whole counter covered in 78s. My mum took me there to buy me a record for my birthday. I chose Lonnie Donegan's 'Backstairs Session' EP. And I later found 'I Put a Spell on You' here.

"The other record shop in the arcade was L&H Cloakes, a popular shop run by a Jewish family. It was a large unit with the counter some 12 feet from the entrance. The walls were adorned with album covers and record company advertisements and chart information. I bought 'Heartbreak Hotel' here on 78. Cloakes was well established so I presume it had been there for a few years. Chip's was a couple of years older. Chip looked like a bit of a hipster. I think jazz was his main stock. Prior to these two shops the main place to buy records in Brixton was British Home Stores. I used to go there too. Again, loads of 78s on a vast counter. You picked the one you wanted and handed it to the assistant. And Morley's department store on the high street, where they sold radiograms and furniture, had a counter with the rack of records behind. I bought Gene Vincent 'Dance to the Bop' there."

Irish music and country music both sold strongly and many shops initially ordered Elvis 78s believing he was a new country singer. At The Musical Box, Diane Cain recalls her mother unpacking the Elvis 78s, putting needle to 'Heartbreak Hotel' for the first time and, as Presley moaned and groaned about being "so lonely, babeeeeeeeee", exclaiming, "It's *terrible!* We'll never sell this!" In Sheffield, Cann The Music Man, established in the 1920s, had a little more warning when it came to the Memphis Flash. "A woman who worked there told me how in 1956 teenagers started coming in asking if they had any records by someone called 'Elvis Presley'," recalls local music historian Simon Robinson. "They ordered 200 78s of 'Heartbreak Hotel' and sold them all on the first day."

In Scarborough, local teenager Pete Stellings bought records by Tommy Steele, Lonnie Donegan, Guy Mitchell and Elvis from Gray Radios. He says: "The record shops in Scarborough were two, Gray Radio and Deans. Gray Radio did indeed sell just that, radios, radiograms, record players – my Dansette record player came from their first-floor showroom – while the basement was the record department and for 6/6d [6 shillings and 6 pence] you could purchase a 78 record. EPs and LPs first came on sale in 1955. The record department featured a counter, a Top 10 chart adorning the wall, two turntables and two booths at the side with earphones where you could listen to the record of your choice – it was always only a maximum of three you could listen to before making your purchase."

Stellings then chanced upon Alfred Headlam's Golden Record Shop in Golden Lion Bank, Whitby, a shop that specialised in country music. "From here I bought Skeeter Davis, Jean Shepard, Kitty Wells and many others and learned that anything published by Acuff/Rose was well worth a listen."

The British Blues Boom

Even before Donegan and Presley blew things wide open, British youths were developing a taste for African American blues. Wizz Jones, today one of the UK's foremost folk musicians, frequented Kennards, a large Croydon department store, in the early 1950s. His first purchases in the record bar were Smiley Lewis's 'Shame Shame Shame' (1957) and John Lee Hooker's 'Hoogie

Boogie' (1949) 78s. Jones says: "Years later I became friendly with Davey Graham and he played this piece, 'Davey's Boogie', and it sounded very similar to 'Hoogie Boogie' so I mentioned it to him and he replied, 'Yeah, I bought that record' so blues records were not that rare here in the 1950s. And that was before rock 'n' roll took off. How Kennards came to have blues 78s I'm not sure but the demand must have been there."

Liverpool's foremost specialist record shop following the war was Hessy's on Manchester Street, which billed itself as "The premier store in the North for the collector and musician" and "The rendezvous for jazz collectors". The youths who would become The Beatles were regular, rowdy customers.

Down in Portsmouth, the teenager who would become Paul Jones, vocalist on Manfred Mann's greatest hits and the voice of Radio 2's Blues show, entered a record shop and found the owner offering him T-Bone Walker's 1960 album *T-Bone Blues*. "I was surprised to find Junior Wells playing harmonica on it," says Jones. "T-Bone didn't normally record with Chicago musicians. Anyway, I bought it, went home and listened. And then I thought, 'that's what I want to do with my life'."

In Birmingham, Morris Hunting opened The Diskery in 1952 to service his love of jazz, but this soon developed into the city's main retailer of rock 'n' roll, blues and calypso.

In Manchester, a teenage John Mayall began collecting blues 78s in the early 1950s, many purchased at The 78 Record Exchange at 21 Marsden Square. This small shop was set up by two record collectors, Peter Howarth and Bill Kloet, who met as they dug through the city's junk shops looking for old records.

Also in Manchester – and of use to Mayall – was Barry's Record Rendezvous at 3 Blackfriars Street, a shop that boasted in ads how it was "The North's only jazz specialist". Shop owner Barry Ancill kept his ears open to prevailing trends and, once blues and R&B caught on, he began importing releases from Chess, Arhoolie, Atlantic and other US labels and advertising as "The only specialist Rhythm and Blues Record Shop in the North". Ancill put on blues and jazz shows at Manchester's Free Trade Hall and this meant the musicians who performed could often be found on the afternoon of the concert hanging about the Record Rendezvous.

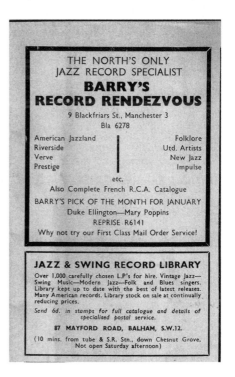

City Radio in Cardiff advertised that it stocked a huge selection of blues and jazz records – "The best in Wales and the west" – while just over the border in Bristol, Stan Strickland opened The House of Sound and encouraged youthful jazz and blues fans to come in and listen, even if they could rarely afford to purchase a record. Record stalls operated in markets, selling new and used discs. While Scottish record collector Ray Templeton recalls, "The Barrows, Glasgow's massive street and indoor market, had record stalls – probably still does!"

An intense passion for jazz and blues found remarkable record shops opening in the decade following the Second World War. The following all served with honour.

Foxley's

Ray 'Professor' Foxley was born in Birmingham (1928–2002), and played powerful stride piano with the likes of Chris Barber and Ken Colyer before, in 1955, setting up Foxley's on the Kilburn High Road. Foxley's sold all kinds of music (it had a 'Symphonic' section), but having a jazz musician owner ensured a strong selection of jazz and blues. Growing up nearby, Paul Vernon – now a noted blues historian with vast experience in buying and selling old records – says Foxley's played a formative part in his musical education: "I bought most of my Django vinyl not from Dobell's, but from a small independent record shop nestled behind the Kilburn & Brondesbury tube station that sat at the gateway to the Kilburn High Road, just four traffic lights from home. It took about 20 minutes to get there, and it was always worth every second. It was called, simply, 'Foxley's' and was run by the thin-haired, wiry and very pleasant Ray Foxley.

"My mother began to buy her records from him and I have dim memories of accompanying her into the shop as a child. Now, however, I discovered it for myself and every visit was an education. The shop sat in an extraordinary shaft of natural light that squeezed its way down into the choked urban mash that was lower Kilburn. Ray surprised me one morning by nodding his head vigorously to Lowell Fulson's 'Talking Woman Blues'. He then said to me, simply as one fan to another; 'What a GOOD little record'. From that moment, I began to understand just what an extraordinary breadth of knowledge he possessed. As I was a younger brother retailer he would share with me his views on how a record shop should operate; how stock control and display should be handled, where to look for bargains, who the good and not so good wholesalers were, how to handle a naked record to keep it mint. I listened to every quietly delivered word like a student in the presence of Einstein."

More than just a good record man, though, Ray had tales to tell, and perhaps the most fascinating was this one. Responding to numerous local requests from recently arrived Jamaicans, he privately pressed 50 copies of an Amos Milburn Aladdin 45 he happened to have. It sold out in one morning. Realising the potential, he contacted a friend who worked the passenger lines sailing from Southampton and arranged to have him buy a regular selection of new R&B records in New York. These would then be copied and cut onto metal acetate singles, which he sold across the counter. News quickly spread and Saturdays at Foxley's became famous inside the Jamaican community. He presided over what was, to all intents and purposes, a regularly scheduled record party. People came from all across London and further – Birmingham, Manchester and Bristol – to talk, listen and buy. It served as a meeting place for fans and musicians alike. So, that nice Mr Foxley turned out to be a proto bootlegger. Well, well … good for him.

The Swing Shop

In south-west London, a similarly themed shop to Foxley's existed. The Swing Shop on Mitcham Lane, Streatham, initially opened in 1939 but proprietor and trad jazz drummer Dave Carey (1914–1999) quickly had to close once hostilities broke out. Carey served in the RAF (Royal Air Force) and survived to reopen in 1946. The Swing Shop offered musical instruments, accessories and a selection of jazz 78s. Carey played with Humphrey Lyttelton and, via The Swing Shop, spread the jazz and blues gospel. An extremely gregarious man, Carey's musical enthusiasm led to him regularly jamming with the teenage wannabes in the shop and giving out advice on records and musical technique.

Thirteen-year-old Val Wilmer bought her first ever jazz 78 at The Swing Shop in 1954. Wilmer found the shop somewhat intimidating – its customers appearing to consist solely of earnest men in raincoats smoking pipes – but the staff encouraged her musical education and she went on to become the foremost British photographer of jazz and blues artists, as well as a noted critic. A young American blues fan also found himself impressed by Carey: Peter Guralnick, now biographer of Elvis, Sam Cooke and Sam Phillips, then lived in London and loved The Swing Shop, saying that "you could buy rare transcriptions by Barbecue Bob and Kokomo Arnold there and engage in conversations with someone who knew and loved the music".

Not long after Wilmer and Guralnick made use of Carey's shop, Streatham schoolboy Jon Newey came upon it: "L&H Cloake was the main record store in Streatham during the 1960s. They had two shops, both on Streatham High Road. WHSmith had a record department upstairs opposite the Odeon cinema with a reasonable selection of Beatles, Merseybeat, Rolling Stones, R&B and such. But the shop that really had an impact on my future was The Swing Shop. I used to peer through the window and wonder about entering. I could see it sold LPs, guitars, banjos and sheet music but no pop music. I was later to learn this was one of the UK's foremost jazz and blues record shops – the likes of Jimmy Page, Eric Clapton and Jeff Beck would all travel to Streatham to purchase records as it had blues imports they couldn't find elsewhere. The Swing Shop became the centre of the Streatham blues scene of the mid to late 1960s with people such as guitarists Tony McPhee, Dave Kelly, Martin Stone, blues singer Jo Ann Kelly, and blues duo Simon Praeger and Steve Rye amongst the many who would hang out there."

Chris Wellard's Jazz & Blues Record Shop

While The Swing Shop served south-west London, Chris Wellard's Jazz & Blues Record Shop enriched the city's south-east. Now in his late 80s, Chris Wellard is the last of the pioneering jazz record shop men still standing. He says: "I grew up in Greenwich and the first record shop I ever visited was run by Mrs Furlong on Deptford Bridge. It was a very old shop, went right back to the 1800s, a big shop, double-fronted and long and inside it was an enormous area racked up with 78s. She was wizened even when I went in there as a child, and had run it for decades.

"I did an engineering apprenticeship at Woolwich Polytechnic. We were all being trained to be factory fodder for the factories that used to run from Deptford to Kent along the Thames. At seven in the morning it was like some dystopian picture of people going to work – trams were packed! – and Woolwich Arsenal was the biggest, quite immense. I didn't start buying records until I was at Woolwich Polytechnic when I was 15. Owen Bryce, the trumpet player in George Webb's Dixielanders had a Woolwich shop called Farley Radio Services that sold radios and TVs and gramophones and records. Owen opened the basement of his shop as a jazz record shop in the late 1940s and this was really important for South London. That said, he charged ten shillings for an imported 78 – incredibly expensive! James Asman worked there and he attracted a lot of custom because he used to write a jazz column in *The Daily Mirror*."

Another early south-east London record shop Wellard recalls is Payne's, a jazz specialist that set up in suburban Catford in the late 1940s: "This was a marvellous shop placed in the middle of a dispiriting row of other shops. Completely positioned wrongly. The area was 'boredom personified'. But, once inside the shop, there was the whole world of jazz, curated by the charming and very knowledgeable Pete Payne."

Inspired by the aforementioned record shops and the music men and women who ran them, Wellard decided he too would prefer the vagaries of selling shellac and vinyl rather than the certainty of a factory engineering job: "My

The New Cross jazz nucleus. Courtesy of Chris Wellard.

father offered to lend me the money to set up a record shop as he received his war credits pay and knew this is what I wanted to do. I came across this record shop in New Cross that was for sale. It was run by a woman – a lot of women used to run record shops – who stocked pop music 78s and a few LPs. She was very sharp and stayed to help in the shop initially so I got to know how to order and such. She said, 'If business is a bit slow put Vera Lynn's *Hits of the Blitz* in the window'. I said, 'Why?' She said, 'You'll see!' And she was right! We sold many copies of that record."

When Wellard opened on 6 Lewisham Way, London SE14 in 1955, New Cross was a mess of dilapidated housing and ruination left over from the war: the local Woolworths had taken a direct hit by a V2 one lunch time, killing 168 people. Wellard's Jazz & Blues Record Shop brought a brilliant splash of beauty and creativity to the area, and Wellard quickly became something of a local hero. Appropriately, a huge superhero was painted out front, with Wellard's name in large, bright letters, so ensuring the shop existed as a South London landmark. Wellard says: "We stocked the Top 50 and lots of calypso and Blue Beat records that were popular with the local West Indian community. As Goldsmiths [University] was nearby the lecturers would come in and buy classical LPs. But I always wanted jazz so we set up a jazz section. I remember putting the Lee Morgan *Sidewinder* album cover in the window and a West Indian guy coming in pointing and saying, 'I want that record!'

"I was crazy about jazz so I started doing lists of all the jazz records we had and giving them out and putting them in *Jazz Journal* and this attracted lots of mail order business. It led to me doing the yellow book where I listed all the jazz releases over the past eight months and writing reviews of each one. I was never a good businessman but I was good at publicising jazz records.

"I started importing a few things from Jack's Record Cellar in San Francisco. They sold quite well and one day the postman came with a big parcel of 50 LPs of someone that I had never heard of. One of the shop assistants, Chris Trimming, had ordered John Fahey. I said, 'We'll never sell that!' Chris said, 'We'll sell them all by the weekend!' And we did. We had the Goldsmiths students queuing to get them. After that Chris ran the imports. At that time, when John Peel was broadcasting and talking about the shop, we'd get a queue outside up to the pub on Saturday to get into the shop. It was an extraordinary experience. People used to smell of marijuana!"

With Wellard's droll personality, he ran advertisements in *Jazz Journal* at the height of the Cuban Missile Crisis, guaranteeing that his records came in "sealed, radiation proof bags" while setting up a mock display of the 'saints' in his shop window: "Sonny Boy's harmonica, Bix's Cornet, Cripple Clarence Loftin's Boot and LuLu White's Red Light! This idea came from my cousin John Wellard during a refreshing evening at Bernard's, a great pub near the shop. I thought it hilarious but like all satire it risked backfiring as people were coming and taking photos of the window!"

Wellard's shop became a south-east London meeting place where hot music and CND activism, bottles of bitter and much laughter were shared, and relationships that have lasted a lifetime were forged amid a fog of tobacco smoke and Ornette Coleman LPs. Yet, in 1975, the New Cross shop went into liquidation. Wellard says: "The reason it closed was we weren't getting any customers. As the docks started closing we got less and less customers and then they knocked down all the slums and all the people moved away. So, the whole of New Cross died. It was a minor tragedy. A very difficult time. I ran jazz mail order from home and did distribution, driving around all the jazz shops in London."

Chris made many friends while running the Jazz & Blues Record Shop. Most memorable was Miss Stella Williams – an employee whose beauty impressed all who visited – and she became Mrs Wellard. "I couldn't have done it without Stella," says Chris. "She was essential to the shop." As at 2016, they still live locally. "It was a great experience," he says of his record shop. "I'm pleased Stella and I got to do it!"

Peter Russell's Hot Record Store

In Plymouth stood a record shop that served the south-west of England. Pete Russell (1925–2014) first began working for a record shop in Nottingham when they wanted someone to help out in the jazz department. "The pay was a pittance but a nice chap ran it and I loved it," he told *The Plymouth Herald* in a 2012 interview. Wanting to open his own shop but not wishing to compete with his employer, Russell chose Plymouth as suitably far away.

Russell opened the only jazz record shop in the south west in the mid-1950s, quickly realising there was little interest among Devon's habitués in the music he loved. Determined not to quit, Russell shared premises and survived by developing a mail order business that sent jazz records around the world. By and by, his monthly newsletter, *The Good Noise*, and excellent service would build him an international customer base. Russell's electrical engineering skills came in handy when he set up Pete Russell's Hi-Fi in 1963 as part of the record shop: "People used to say the records didn't play well and I realised why. This was a prehistoric city and many people still had wind-up players. So, I started selling hi-fi and built it up from there."

Mike Westbrook, the now renowned jazz pianist, was studying at Plymouth Art College and says Russell's shop changed his life: "Peter's arrival in Plymouth in the 1950s was a turning point for those of us who were struggling to play jazz. He had a major effect on the subsequent careers of musicians like myself,

John Surman, Keith Rowe, Stan Willis, Ron Hills and many others. Peter's Hot Record Store in Union Street became our Mecca. He opened our ears to the new music coming out of the States at that time as well as to the rich history of jazz. He never imposed his taste, but had subtle ways of making us aware of things we needed to hear. I first heard Duke Ellington's *Blues in Orbit* there and it is one of the sounds that changed my life."

Jazz may have been Russell's passion but it never made him much money. When his second wife, Betie, began working in the shop she insisted on selling pop and rock records and this quickly improved fortunes. Russell recalls: "She said one day, 'People keep coming in and asking for The Beatles and Elvis, not the jazz that we're selling' (*The Plymouth Herald*, 2012). I told her that they were rubbish and would never catch on! I was worried we would be left with a lot of unsold stock. But Betie was right: she doubled the turnover in about two months. In those days we didn't have much competition."

Russell remained in the record and hi-fi trade until his retirement in 1991, a man admired by many for his kindness, musical knowledge and determination not to quit.

Atlantic Records

Atlantic Records opened on Belfast's High Street in 1953. Run by Solly Lipsitz (1921–2013) and Tom Cusack, these jazz fans (Lipsitz played trumpet; Cusack published the first Jelly Roll Morton discography) kept an extraordinarily well-stocked shop that served Northern Ireland's jazz fans when no one else did. The proprietors were very much in the trad jazz camp but stocked modern jazz and, Lipsitz noted, on Saturday afternoons arguments between trad and modern fans could get heated. This seems appropriate as Lipsitz himself was a feisty character, once punching out American jazz musician Eddie Condon after the banjoist suggested Solly, being from Belfast, must support the IRA.

Atlantic Records has now entered popular music lore not for its jazz records, but because this is where a young Ivan 'Van' Morrison found the blues, country, R&B and skiffle records that shaped his muse. Morrison has openly praised Atlantic Records while dismissing Belfast's oft-remarked-on port status as playing any role in making available the music he loved. Morrison told journalist Gavin Martin: "There was a guy called Solly Lipsitz and he had a record shop called, believe it or not, Atlantic Records. This was in the high street in Belfast and my father used to go there. He got all his records at Solly's place. He had the records and he wasn't a sailor (grins), so, no – I don't get that one."

Morrison would accompany his father George on trips to Old Smithfield Market, home to the Premier Records (run by the McBurney family since 1926) and a number of record stalls where, as he recalls, "You'd go for a certain R&B side and they'd already have it out for you. They knew what you were coming for." The pair would then head for Atlantic Records. Lipsitz noted how he and Cusack: "… started out with collectors' records, both jazz and operatic, and at that time there were a lot of embryonic jazz collectors. Van's father used to come *every* Saturday.

He was more interested in the blues side of things, Howlin' Wolf and Little Brother Montgomery. I remember Van very well in a grey school cap."

When he died at the age of 92, Lipsitz was widely mourned in Belfast. His obituary read: "Solly Lipsitz is one of those extraordinary figures around Belfast who always seems to come at things from his very own angle – one of those essential citizens who has consistently let the light in." Indeed, he helped Van Morrison and others to shine.

Eric Rose's Music Inn

At the start of the 1960s, Nottingham's longest established record shop, Sanders Papworth Music Company, changed its name to Eric Rose Music Inn and began to emphasise the proprietor's passion for jazz. The name change came about as Rose felt a more contemporary name suited the shop his grandfather had opened in 1919. Rose also expanded, shifting the musical instruments the shop had always stocked into the retail space next door. Rose's shop stocked all kinds of music but jazz was his passion, especially the American swing bands that had achieved huge popularity during the 1930s and 1940s. Music Inn continues to trade in the 2010s, with Eric's son David, who started here aged 15 in 1965 and has never worked anywhere else, continuing to run the family business as a specialist jazz shop. This makes it not just one of the very few surviving jazz shops, but the oldest family-run record shop in the UK. David Rose says: "Dad developed a strong connection with the big band jazz musician Stan Kenton. Stan set up his own record label Creative World and, initially, ours was the only shop that stocked them. I remember dad saying once he had placed an order, 'Once we have taken freight and tax into the equation we will have to sell these for £2.70' – this is when a new UK LP sold for £1.50! He was worried that we would not be able to sell them but by the time the package arrived by surface mail – it took six weeks – he had sold those albums ten times over! We ordered so many albums from Kenton that we became the official UK distributor for Creative World. Back then importing records was difficult, you had to fill in so many forms and go and explain to customs that you weren't smuggling drugs. These days it's so easy.

"Dad sold the musical instrument shop off to its manager and we shifted to our current location in the West End Arcade as there simply wasn't enough footfall where we were based for a record shop to survive. The instruments shop continues to trade in our original 1919 location! By not having to run the musical instrument shop we could really concentrate on developing as a jazz shop and this is how we came to go on tour with the likes of Stan Kenton and Buddy Rich. We would set up each night at their concerts to sell their albums and, also, during the daytime, we would visit the local record shops and offer them the albums we distributed. The Music Inn got very well known amongst the British jazz community and this has served us well as we always did a lot of mail order and continue to do so. You have to duck and dive to survive these days. I'm fortunate that because enough people still value personal service we can continue to exist. Right now I'm just focused on keeping going until 2019 so we can celebrate the shop's centenary."

Woolworths, WHSmith and Boots

The Poundland of its day, Woolworths (fondly known as Woolies) initially excelled at selling cheap goods and these included records released by budget labels. In 1954, Woolies entered into partnership with the Levy family whose Whitechapel shop had, for more than half a century, dominated London's East End record retail (see Chapter 1). The Levys, having run record labels since the 1920s, came to a specific agreement with Woolworths: their Embassy label would record and manufacture cover versions of chart hits that only Woolies would stock (selling them at half the price of the original hit). Cheap and nasty as this was – and many a music lover of a certain age will recall the severe childhood trauma caused when given for a birthday or Christmas present an Embassy record after having specifically requested the hit – it proved profitable, shifting vast numbers of records (Woolworths opened its 1000th British store in 1958), and employed many struggling British musicians as session hacks.

WHSmith and Boots, Menzies and Currys, even Marks & Spencer, all operated record bars in many of their outlets. If they largely stocked a smattering of Top 40, light music and perennial best-sellers, these stores would order in records if requested. Or, if overseen by music loving managers, they made sure 'jazz' titles were available. In the late 1950s, a Cheltenham teenager managed to purchase several jazz and blues LPs at his local Currys. Having studied said discs intensely, young Brian Jones ran away to London, girlfriend and baby in tow, and set about forming a band who would soon be upsetting almost everyone over 21.

Chapter 4

Rudie Can't Fail: Ska Shops Surge

Ska shops are kick-started via a CIA operative, Rita & Benny rule Stamford Hill, Joe runs Brixton, and Island Records sell ska door-to-door. R&B Records, Muzik City, Joe's Record Centre, Desmond's Hip City and Webster's Record Shack. Cameos include Emil Shalit, Charlie Harper, Prince Buster, Chris Blackwell, Bunny Lee and Paul Simonon.

The HMT Empire Windrush's docking at Tilbury Dock, Essex, on 22 June 1948 is now recognised as a hinge that UK society swings upon. Prior to that liner docking, black musicians had, on occasion, thrived in the UK – American vaudeville stars Turner Leyton and Clarence Johnstone became music hall stalwarts; Ken 'Snakehips' Johnson led London's foremost jazz band before a Nazi bomb silenced the music – but the Empire Windrush's passengers included four noted Trinidadian calypso musicians. Lord Beginner, Lord Kitchener, Lord Woodbine and Mona Baptiste disembarked without fanfare but, as members of a West Indian community determined to find its place in the UK, they initiated a brilliantly fecund era.

Today, calypso is largely ignored (outside Trinidad), but in the years following the Second World War it served as the ruling tropical exotica. Harry Belafonte's 1956 LP *Calypso* became the first album to sell a million copies while everyone from The Hilltoppers to Frankie Laine scored hits employing calypso rhythms. Trinidadian calypso never saw such popularity; no matter, on the streets it ruled and in Notting Hill, London, the Calypso Record Shop opened on the corner of Portobello Road and Blenheim Crescent. The Calypso Record Shop was owned by two brothers, Michael and David Tobin and, during the Notting Hill race riots of summer 1958, it served as headquarters for those fighting gangs of racist Teddy Boys. The Tobins' shop was an anomaly at the time, most retailers having no concept of calypso, while West Indians tended to shop at street markets and general goods stores. Thus, calypso records were more likely to be found alongside plantain and goat meat – or in barber shops – than in a high-street record shop. Emil Shalit, an Austrian-born US citizen, observed this and saw only opportunities.

Mr Blue Beat
Short and portly, foreign to the UK, and elusive, Emil Shalit (1909–83) may appear an unlikely nominee for Great British icons but, to my mind, he deserves a statue. Shalit was one of the UK's foremost record men and did much to open up the local music industry to Caribbean artists, independent labels and the

Speakers oppose Tory Housing minister Henry Brooke's Rent Act on Portobello Road, 1958. Calypso Record Shop provides moral and musical support in the background.

hustle and flow that ensures the music of the marginalised gets heard.

Being an Austrian Jew likely taught Emile early on that his survival depended on remaining opaque; understanding far more than he ever let on while seeking out talent and money where others failed to look. He claimed to have worked as a spy for the Allies during the Second World War (and been lucratively rewarded for his services) before setting up Melodisc Records in New York City in 1947, and some believe he remained a CIA operative for many years.

Independent record labels were the lifeblood of the US R&B and jazz industry, and often cut-throat in their dealings. Shalit, finding the US independent record label sector overflowing with men similar to him (entrepreneurs out to make a buck from black music), chose to run Melodisc in less ruthless climes, first settling in France then, by 1949, London. Here, Shalit developed into one of the great (if unsung) heroes of the British music industry. Ironically, he claimed to have no interest in music and saw selling records as akin to selling potatoes. For a spud salesman, Emil certainly had a good ear and remarkable instincts, recording, licensing and releasing fabulous music.

Back then the Big Four – EMI, Decca, Philips, Pye – had a stranglehold on the UK record trade and only a brave man would have attempted to set up as an independent. Having outwitted the Nazis, Shalit had no fear of the British establishment, and set about trading in music that the Big Four had little interest in: licensing Woody Guthrie, Charlie Parker and Leadbelly recordings, Irish and English folk, Hungarian Gypsy music, even early Bill Haley. Hiring Trinidadian musician Rupert Nurse in 1952 helped Melodisc take control of the fledgling UK West Indian record trade. Launching the Kalypso label, Emil sold 78s by the likes of Lord Kitchener and Mighty Terror. The calypso connection helped Melodisc export records to the Caribbean and Africa; in turn, Shalit recorded Caribbean jazz musicians Joe Harriott and Russ Henderson alongside London-based African musicians.

When Melodisc released Laurel Aitken's 'Lonesome Lover' 45 in 1960, it sold so strongly that Shalit shifted his affections from Trinidadian to Jamaican music, appointing Sigimund 'Siggy' Jackson, a Polish migrant, to run a new label devoted to this. Siggy, aware Jamaicans described dance music as having "a blues beat", named the label Blue Beat and released hundreds of 45s and a series of LPs, none more remarkable than those licensed from a man known as Prince Buster. Buster was the don of Kingston's sound systems, a gifted producer and an entertaining proto-rapper; his records and 'cool ruler' style would make him a mod icon. Before The Beatles or The Stones, Blue Beat unleashed what would become one of the 1960s' fiercest musical movements.

Shalit's licensing deals made sure new Jamaican 45s were released in the UK, giving Britain's growing West Indian community a voice from home and the youths who styled themselves as 'rude boys' a soundtrack. The rudies, in their flash clothes and disrespect for authority, possessed a feckless cool. Mods emulated rude-boy style and danced to their music, which would soon be known as 'ska'. This new music, then never heard on radio or TV, was largely sold via a network of West Indian hairdressers, barbers, grocery and general goods stores.

R&B Records, a small shop at 282 Stamford Hill, London N15, shared Emil's enthusiasm. There is no plaque to mark where R&B Records once stood. Nor are there books written about this narrow North London record shop. However, to anyone interested in London histories – Jewish and Jamaican, mod and ska – then Rita & Benny's stands as a place of legend.

R&B Records

Saturday afternoons across the 1960s found R&B Records sizzling. Here, in leafy Stamford Hill, London, the rude boys and the mods gathered, feisty clothes horses who puffed on cigarettes, boasted about their tailors and danced across the lino floor as new tunes – 'just off the boat' – blared forth. Ska's energy, optimism and furious dance rhythms brought Jamaican music international attention and it became one of the sounds that got the UK swinging. Ironically, R&B did not stand for Rhythm & Blues but for Rita and Benny Isen, a Jewish couple who anglicised their surname to King around the time they entered the music industry.

As 1960 began, R&B Records stocked lots of Melodisc, Blue Beat and Island

RMS
REGGAE MUSIC SERVICE
TOP 50

Price 10p Issue No. 1
Period ending 17.5.83.

Personality Page

The lady above is NONE other than our own Rita King of R. & B. Records in Stamford Hill. So many of us will never forget the wonderful service given to the record industry by Rita and her dedicated husband Benny. They have decided to give up the retail trade and when they finally do we shall sadly miss them both.

Reggae Music Service wish Mr. and Mrs. King all the good things in life, and thank them for over twenty years of their dedicated service to the Reggae Music Industry.

Queen Rita of R&B Records. Courtesy of Noel Hawks.

releases but, by 1963, they had established their own R&B record label. R&B both licensed recordings and signed local artists: Georgie Fame's backing band The Blue Flames issued a series of 45s on R&B and this only encouraged more sharply dressed youths to head there. The Kings obviously found running record labels profitable as they set up plenty of them: Giant, King, Ska Beat, Hillcrest, Caltone, Jolly, Port-O-Jam and Prima Magnagroove. The last was a label devoted to Louis Prima, the New Orleans trumpeter and Las Vegas showman who achieved immortality by voicing King Louie in Disney's *The Jungle Book* (1967). The Kings issued more than 20 Louis Prima 45s and three albums, Prima's music long being a mainstay of Kingston's sound systems.

R&B issued recordings by Laurel Aitken, Jackie Opel, The Maytals, The Skatalites, Lee Perry, Delroy Wilson, Derrick Morgan, Don Drummond, Stranger Cole and many others. Bob Marley and the Wailers' seminal 1965 anthem 'Simmer Down' came out on R&B's Ska Beat label. Rita King set up distribution networks across the UK, ensuring these releases were widely available in West Indian shops. Jamaican producer Bunny Lee told the Reggae Vibes website that the three people who ran the fledgling Jamaican music industry in the UK were: "Emil Shalit, Mrs King and her husband name Benny. Benny use' to come a Jamaica too, yunno, an' put out – a get record. Him use' to put out anyt'ing Ken Lack [Caltone imprint] make. Rita an' Benny. Them did 'aye a big distributing place from — dem was powerful people inna the business. Mrs King was a force to reckon with. Them use' to have a place inna Stamford Hill. If she na sell the record is better you come outta the business. [He chuckles] When she talk everybody jump! By the way, she a the firs' person whe bring U Roy come inna this country. And Roy Shirley an' Maxie Romeo. Max Romeo did come a'ready with Pama dem but him did go dung back, a Rita did bring 'im back. Yeah."

While the amiable Benny King visited Jamaica to do deals, Rita stayed in Stamford Hill and ruled as only a Queen can, shouting down the phone at both Jamaican producers and the employees of Island, Melodisc, Pama, Trojan and London Records. R&B Records served as a lodge of sorts and, on Friday nights and all day Saturday, R&B was packed with youths – black and white, Jewish and gentile – buying the new releases. A teenage Tony Rounce (writer, DJ and music consultant) was one of them: "R&B Records was a great, great shop run by this very personable Jewish couple selling mostly music that would appeal to Jamaicans. The shop was very long and brightly lit, always with a line of customers the length of the counter. They and their shop manager Barry liked me as I spent a lot of money there every time I went. Some of the young black customers hanging out would get a bit annoyed that Rita, Benny and Barry gave a white boy what they saw as preferential treatment and would frequently complain, but Rita would always reply, 'He buys lots of records every week. How many have YOU bought today?' As well as new and old Jamaican music, they also sold albums by the likes of Jim Reeves, Marty Robbins and other artists that are nowadays classed as 'Big People Music' alongside a lot of Gospel and Christian music, as that's always popular in Jamaica."

By 1984, with Rita and Benny feeling their age and R&B Records having long lost its dominant position, the couple retired. Since then, the legend of the little Stamford Hill store has been enshrined in song and exhibitions, a lost North London landmark akin to Arsenal's original stadium or Walthamstow's greyhound track.

Brixton and Beyond

While Stamford Hill remains an odd place for a ska shop to exist, it's unsurprising that London's Brixton hosted several. David Lands notes: "Towards Tulse Hill a delightful record shop called The Record Rendezvous opened on Water Lane in 1957. The lovely dark-haired lady who ran it first played me Laurel Aitken's 'Boogie in My Bones'. The Record Rendezvous was a general record shop that stocked West Indian records alongside pop, easy listening and jazz. Ska first got sold in a Brixton shop on Atlantic Road. The man running it was Jamaican, a rotund chap and jolly. The shop had no name, just a hole in the wall. He stocked lots of rhythm and blues and Blue Beat – it was the sound of the mods and me and my mates bought quite a few singles. 'Oh Carolina' by the Folkes Brothers. 'Al Capone' by Prince Buster. 'Gypsy Woman'. 'Housewives Choice'. Lots of Eric Morris. I was at work by then and a mod. Blue Beat was king at parties."

Charlie Harper, later to gain a degree of fame as leader of punk band The UK Subs, was a Brixton teenager in the early 1960s: "I was living in a council estate and Prince Buster ruled Brixton back then. I saw him play Brixton Town Hall then bought his album *I Am King* at a record shop on the Brixton Road. It was up by the Oval, a good record shop, sold ska and R&B. As I lived in Brixton I heard a lot of Jamaican music and I just loved Prince Buster."

Buster was the cool ruler of the ska era and, once again, when 2-Tone took off in 1979 with The Specials and Madness championing the Prince. Decades later, at a London music awards ceremony, Buster would thank (the by then late) Emil Shalit for "internationalising my mind" – the CIA's man and King Rude Boy made certain ska gained a global audience.

The popularity of Blue Beat in Brixton found ska records for sale at The Music Box, 37 Granville Arcade (this shop lasted from the 1950s–1980s), and at Nat Cole, a West Indian hairdresser's on Atlantic Road that boasted "Joy, Health & Beauty" on the sign outside while stocking a fine selection of West Indian records across the 1960s and 1970s.

Teenage Balham resident Terry Davinson heard the *Club Ska 67* compilation on Island Records, "a mate at school lent it to me and it blew me away!" He and his friend found that Readings for Records in Station Approach, Clapham Junction, had an excellent selection of ska and rocksteady 45s: "Readings were an old-fashioned record shop run by lovely people and they stocked everything. That was their way. In 1967 I was so into rocksteady that for a year my mate and I would buy the *Weekly Gleaner* to see what was in the Jamaican charts. And Readings started to do pre-releases. No one else was doing that. I got 'Fire in Me Wire' by Laurel Aitken on pre-release.

Readings had great stock – they had a wall of Sue 45s! – and there were lots of Jamaicans in Clapham Junction."

Chris Wellard ensured his Jazz & Blues Record Shop stocked plenty of Melodisc releases: "New Cross was full of working-class West Indian families. It was like a village then although many were forced to live in slum housing with terrible facilities. They were great customers, many characters, and West Indians always wanted to hear the records. They'd say, 'Let I hear it' then say, 'Turn it over' – they were worried it would jump! Some of the West Indians couldn't read so you had to tell them what each record was. That's also why they wanted to hear the records because they knew how the record sounded but couldn't read the record label. We sold calypso and Blue Beat and jazz to them."

Romford mod Steve Barrow recalls that his introduction to Jamaican music came through the West End clubs in the early 1960s: "When I first started going to the West End I went to a club called The Limbo, a basement place where you could score, and I heard my first Jamaican record, 'Humpty Dumpty' by Errol Morris. When that 'whoah' came in the whole club was singing it. I went up and asked the DJ what it was and he said, 'Blues'. I thought, 'Not blues, not Muddy', but later learned that Jamaicans called them 'blues'. I asked him, 'Where do you buy them?' He said, 'Any record shop'. Not true. Jamaican records were impossible to find until I found a little shop in Stratford, Angel Lane, not a record shop, an iron mongers, and you couldn't play the records there, it was just another line the shop had. There was also a stall outside Whitechapel Station, Paul's For Music, and that's where I got 'Hurricane Hattie' and Prince Buster's 'Madness' in 1963. That was the record that busted out Buster to people like me."

Outside London, ska and rocksteady records were popular wherever there were West Indian communities. In Birmingham, The Diskery, then the city's foremost record shop, made sure it had the latest releases on Blue Beat, Island, Trojan, Pama and Pyramid. In Handsworth, Brian Harris Records, which opened as a general record shop in 1964, soon began specialising in Blue Beat, Pama and Island 45s as the neighbourhood became home to one of the UK's largest West Indian communities. Don Christie, situated through the rag market behind Birmingham's main train station, opened in the mid-1960s and quickly established itself as the Midlands' foremost Jamaican music shop. It's remembered by some customers for the "one-legged owner" while others recall it "always smelling of marijuana". In Manchester, Paul Marsh Records on Moss Side stocked plenty of ska and rocksteady 45s. There were many others, some opening and closing seemingly on a whim, but it would be a London-based Jamaican who launched a chain of ska shops where black music was sold to the black community by black staff.

Musicland/Muzik City

If Emil Shalit pioneered selling Jamaican music in the UK, it was Leichman 'Lee' Gopthal (1939–97) who set about opening shops to sell Jamaican records. Gopthal's father, a tailor, had immigrated from Kingston, Jamaica, to London on the Empire Windrush, and sent for Lee when the boy was 13. Trained as an accountant, by his early twenties Lee presided over 108 Cambridge Road, South Kilburn, London NW6. Here, he rented a room to sound system operator Sonny Roberts who built a primitive recording studio in Gopthal's basement and set up his Planetone record label here in 1962: the first UK recording studio and record label with a black owner. Roberts recorded and issued 45s by the likes of Rico Rodriquez, introducing Gopthal to Chris Blackwell (born 1937), a white Jamaican releasing ska records on his Island Records imprint when he settled in London in 1962.

Blackwell started Island Records in 1959 in Kingston. Relocating to London, he initially sold 45s from a stall in Portobello Market. Industry veteran Steve Bronstein remembers watching Blackwell at work: "Blackwell's stalls on Portobello Road market were beneath the flyover, at the poorer end of the antiques market, and they would be full of records he had brought back in suitcases from Jamaica. He'd buy these singles for about a shilling each and sell them for a lot more than that. People crowded around the stall buying and buying – as many white people as black!"

Georgie Fame, the first English musician to embrace ska, also recalls going to Ladbroke Grove in the early 1960s to find ska records. "A great place for music", says Fame. "West Indian record stalls and clubs."

Blackwell joined Roberts in situating Island at 108 Cambridge Road, then invited Gopthal to get involved with the fledgling record label, his accountancy skills being valuable. Gopthal was initially cautious about joining Island – he set up Beat & Commercial in 1963 to distribute Jamaican records – but the huge 1964 success of Millie Small's 'My Boy Lollypop' (a Blackwell production that he licensed to Fontana, correctly guessing demand would overwhelm Island's capacity) enticed him to sign up.

Gopthal's first executive decision was, upon noting how difficult Blackwell found it to get Island's releases stocked by record shops, to insist on door-to-door selling of Island releases in West Indian neighbourhoods: a team of 16 salespeople were recruited. He then decided they should set up a record shop, opening Musicland at 42 Willesden Lane, Kilburn, London NW6 in early 1966. The success of the first Musicland shop – selling ska and soul, pop and rock, Irish and country – saw the chain rapidly expand across London. Gopthal began opening Muzik City shops in London's West Indian neighbourhoods with the emphasis on selling ska and reggae, soul and jazz. Gopthal understood how London's Jamaicans wanted control of their destiny and, by ensuring Muzik City shops employed black staff, made sure they served as community hubs. Immediately successful, Gopthal pushed the chain out across London – the ebullience of records from newly independent Jamaica pulsated across the shops, a roar of youthful Caribbean confidence. "The world is ours" the ska and rocksteady tunes seemed to declare – *no more doffing cap to bossman!* – the singers were tricksters who poked fun at the former colonial master while telling truths from the yard.

Ian Hingle, who worked at several Musicland shops, notes that, "The Blue Beat shops, Muzik City, would sometimes be next to Musicland, side by side with one another, but separate. This is the '60s and if there was a shop with a lot of black people in it white people wouldn't go in there." Hingle also remarks that the Muzik City shops tended to employ only black staff so making them even more distinctive in a London where ethnic minorities were largely invisible on the high street.

Britain's foremost reggae musician and producer, Dennis Bovell, made use of Muzik City as a teenager: "The Muzik City shops were the first ones I knew of that had all the new Jamaican records. They picked them up cheap and priced them up high but Muzik City was where you went if you wanted to get the new tunes. They were an incredible chain."

Likewise, Dennis Morris, a Hackney youth soon to photograph Bob Marley and The Sex Pistols, recalls the Muzik City shop in Ridley Road Market as where he and his friends gathered to get a taste of Kingston, Jamaica.

"Records were really important to the Jamaican community as they let you know what was going on back home. And the Ridley Road record shop was brilliant, you not only got to hear new tunes but could find out all the information about new records and who was coming to town and where the blues dances were."

Morris also notes that he and his mates would hang about outside Muzik City, "trying to look cool and pretending to be rude boys!"

Beyond setting up the Musicland and Muzik City shops, Gopthal's greatest achievement was joining Blackwell in forming Trojan Records. Trojan existed to license and release Jamaican recordings – Island now largely focusing on rock – both in the UK and internationally. Trojan would set about packaging and promoting

Jamaican music in a manner never seen before, scoring many hits and finding a way of selling LPs (the *Tighten Up* compilations of previously released singles) to British youth. As with everything Gopthal did, he ran Trojan in an often haphazard manner but, until it crashed in 1976, the label achieved remarkable things.

Those who worked for Musicland recall the chain opening and closing shops rapidly. Terry Davinson who had a job in Musicland in the late 1960s says: "They'd rent a shop space on Oxford Street just for the summer, things like that. They were a fast-paced, high turnover company and that's why you hear of Musicland and Muzik City shops having opened all over London, even though some of them didn't stay open long. We never met the owners of the shops and I think we felt lucky for that as they were pretty shadowy."

Shadowy but enterprising; Joe Mansano, Desmond Bryan and Webster Schroeder were three such Gopthal acolytes who would go on to run remarkable ska shops.

Joe's Record Centre

Joe Mansano arrived in the UK from Trinidad in 1962, originally intending to study accounting. In 1965, he came to the attention of Len Dyke and Dudley Dryden, two London-based Jamaicans who asked him to work with them at Dyke & Dryden, a shop they were opening in 1965 on West Green Road, Tottenham, London N15. They aimed to sell black beauty products and guessed Mansano could sell records. He did, quickly establishing Dyke & Dryden as one of the UK's foremost ska shops. So much so that when Graeme Goodall, a Kingston-based Australian sound engineer who had helped Chris Blackwell found Island Records, came to London to launch his Doctor Bird record label in 1966, he chose Dyke & Dryden as the place to do so.

Dyke & Dryden's success at selling cosmetics and hair care would lead to a chain that made both men millionaires and, by 1967, Mansano felt cramped. When Island Records offered to set him up in his own record shop, he leapt at the offer.

Joe's Record Centre opened at 93 Granville Arcade, Brixton, London SW9 in 1967 and Mansano's personality – he quickly became described as 'The Boss' – and passion ensured he became an iconic figure. Aware that many Jamaican producers ran record shops, he determined to do the same. Mansano would recall of his Record Centre: "It was not unusual to see record artists in the shop listening to the latest tunes on big, big boom boxes with 18 inch speakers booming. Some of the artists that frequented the shop were Bob Marley, Bunny Lee, Lee 'Scratch' Perry. During some of these visits by musicians they suggested to me that I try my hand at producing. I thought about it and decided to give it a shot. And so, as they say, 'the rest is history'."

Mansano's recording history began in 1968 with 'Life on Planet Reggae', a 45 on Blue Cat Records (a Trojan subsidiary) that finds Joe speaking the praises of reggae and the community who embrace it. It's an offbeat, goofy groove of a record with wild, wheezy organ and it sold well. In 1969, he produced Rico Rodriquez's 45 'The Bullet' on Blue Cat, a trombone-organ drone filled with dread atmosphere, and this won even louder approval. Trojan then stepped up and offered Mansano his own label imprint: Joe Records began releasing 45s by The Boss and anyone else he fancied recording. Mansano had both a feel for the times and a businessman's touch as his records sold well to both West Indians and skinheads (45s like 'Skinhead Revolt' and 'Dracula, Prince of Darkness' were aimed at such), while his debut album *Brixton Cat* (1969) paid tribute to his adopted home.

Gifted as The Boss was, he could also prove very intimidating: Noel Hawks, now a leading authority on reggae recordings, remembers hanging about outside Joe's Record Centre as a schoolboy: "… listening to the music but, if Mr Mansano saw you and thought you were there for too long, he would turn off the music, come out of the shop and 'screw you out' as we used to say … that is to give you a menacing look. Can't blame him really – we didn't have enough money to buy that many records!"

The 1970s would prove harder for The Boss with youths now wanting roots and dub and, by 1976, Mansano had relocated to Trinidad. Once settled there he opened Trinidad's first reggae record shop.

Desmond's Hip City

If Joe's Record Centre waved the flag for Brixton as a loud and proud Caribbean community, the most celebrated record shop in London SW8 was Desmond's Hip City. Situated at 55 Atlantic Road, Desmond's opened in the mid-1960s as part of Gopthal's Muzik City chain under the stewardship of Desmond Bryan. Desmond's had a big, illuminated sign hanging out front proclaiming "BLUE BEAT CENTRE", and many locals took real pride in this black and proud Brixton record shop.

With its pentagon-shaped window, vibrant interior, stock of new ska and soul 45s and atmosphere of untamed, new breed possibilities, Desmond's became *the* place for Brixton youth to hang out. One such youth was Paul Simonon, later to find fame in The Clash, then a teen intent on soaking up rude-boy anthems. Simonon recalls how he would gather with his mates at Desmond's on a Saturday morning but, as his family didn't own a record player, he never made any purchases. Other white youths travelled to Brixton purely to go record shopping. John Slater notes: "I used to go to Desmond's with my mates in 1967–69 to buy imported ska and Blue Beat that had white labels with a stamp on them saying recorded at 'so and so studio, Orange Street, Kingston, Jamaica'. We were white kids from Carshalton in Surrey and we'd get the train to Streatham then bus to Brixton and we would stay in the shop for ages. We loved the music!"

Webster's Record Shack

As with Desmond's Hip City, Webster's Record Shack was bankrolled by Gopthal as part of his Muzik City chain, and Webster Shrowder was one of the salesmen Gopthal had employed to sell Island Records 45s door-to-door. Having demonstrated a talent for selling, Gopthal rewarded Webster with a stall in Shepherd's Bush Market, London. Hingle remembers how, when he worked at Musicland: "… if someone

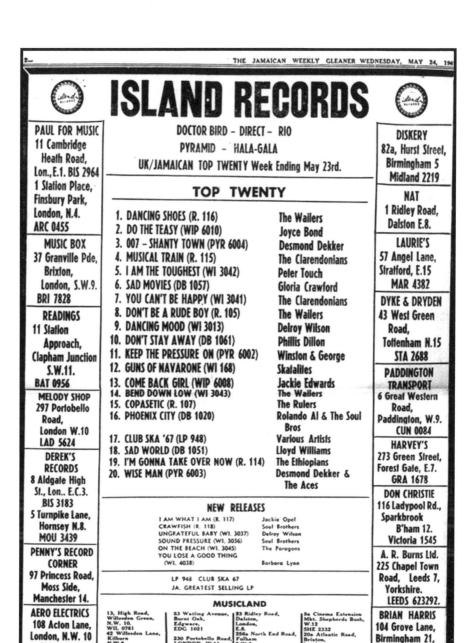

Ska shop directory. Courtesy of Leon Parker.

would come in and ask for a reggae record often they didn't know the title but they would remember the chorus. We would ring up Webster's and ask Shrowder, "What is the record that goes 'my baby loves me'?" and he would say something like, 'It's by John Holt' and we would either have it or order a copy from Muzik City."

Chris Lane, then a teenager who sought out Jamaican music shops, notes that Webster's had a brick wall built around it one night in the early 1970s, "by other market stall holders as it was attracting all these lairy black kids and they were sick of it!" Webster kept his stall going even after he moved into producing reggae. In 2016, he's still at the counter, the last of the original Jamaican record vendors.

Happy Sounds and Soundville

Trojan's main competitor in the late 1960s was Pama Records, a Harrow-based record label run by the Palmers, three Jamaican brothers who started out selling records before moving into running record labels. Their first record shop, Happy Sounds, opened at 827 Harrow Road, London NW10 in 1962 and sold 45s alongside electrical fittings. Harry Palmer spoke to reggae historian David Katz about Pama's early days selling Jamaican music: "In those days you only had three record suppliers: EMI, Decca, and Pye, so we got most of our stock from there, but then we used to get the authentic things from a company called R&B in Stamford Hill, and then Shalit's Blue Beat. Island was just being born about then too. 'My Boy Lollipop' we sold in that little shop some four thousand copies, you know why? We used to put a speaker outside, and it was a bus route on Harrow Road, and that tune went on, every time somebody was not listening to something else, and people would come from all over, not just black people but everybody, they would come because they knew they could get this record there. Every day we used to get supplies of 'My Boy Lollipop', it was the biggest thing. We used to do all sort of music then. The Moody Blues were being born, The Rolling Stones, of course The Beatles, Otis Redding, that type of thing, those were selling."

After Happy Sounds burned down in 1966, the brothers opened another shop in 1967 and set up Pama Records: "We moved from Harrow to Craven Park, not very long, because the space in Harrow wasn't right, you couldn't get to us to buy the product, although by then we had two vans on the road, we still couldn't … we wanted to be among the people. We were hold back by that thing, so in Harrow Road, we had a retail shop, a distribution depot, a recording thing with offices and everything, but everything was there, at 17 Craven Park Road. That became sort of a headquarters for reggae for a while, until Trojan became big, but we were in operation before Trojan."

Chris Lane visited their shop: "Pama Records had its own shop, Soundville, in Harlesden. Lots of stock but no Trojan 45s! The Muzik City shops were all over London and they were great. You used to be able to buy reggae records quite easily in the local shops as it got popular with white kids. People don't realise how big reggae was in the late 1960s. Only a few records got in the national charts because the charts were rigged by the chart return shops (the only shops whose sales counted in the charts). But the local non-chart return shops, and the black shops, were selling tons. Even the Co-Op sold reggae!"

Lane's passion for Jamaican music would eventually lead him to co-found the seminal Dub Vendor stall/shop (see Chapter 13). However, that wouldn't happen for several years and, by then, both Jamaican music and British society were under very heavy manners.

Chapter 5

Hustle and Flow: Long Firms, Larceny and Loot

As the 1960s get under way, four Londoners found record shop chains – Alex Strickland Records, Disci, Harlequin, Musicland – while Manchester's Ali Family create a mini-empire of record shops, pressing plants and cash-and-carry distributors. Money flows and the hustle is on. Cameos from Frank Sinatra, Manfred Mann, The Foundations and Reggie and Ronnie Kray. Also noted: what to do when 10,000 Simon & Garfunkel LPs fall off the back of a lorry.

Never had it so good? At the end of the 1950s, both record labels and retailers would have agreed with Tory Prime Minister Harold Macmillan on that. Lonnie Donegan, Bill Haley and Elvis Presley had alerted the British recording industry – then run along the lines of a minor public school – to the vast profits in singles, while a Brummie orchestra leader demonstrated the loot to be gleaned from LPs: Annunzio Paulo Mantovani, forever in tux, dicky bow and simpering smile, his muzak the aural equivalent of Blue Nun wine, became the first artist to sell a million albums in the UK.

The kids loved rock 'n' roll, their parents appreciated light music, and the music industry counted the loot: farthings, ha'pennies, pennies, thrupenny bits, sixpences, shillings, two bob bits, half crowns, ten bob notes, pound notes and five pound notes rolled in, with 1958 declared the most profitable year in British music industry history. In an exact reversal of today's reality, housing was cheap while records were expensive but, with nothing matching the excitement of a black beauty, people bought more and more records. There was serious money to be made in selling records, but it was the shareholders of Boots and WHSmith who initially enjoyed the benefits that came from stocking the Top 40. With HMV yet to set up a chain of stores and Woolworths completely missing out on Top 40 sales (but finding its ersatz releases on Embassy very profitable), the UK market appeared open for exploitation.

Four Londoners and a Manchester couple, all sensing money to be made in selling music, would revolutionise record retail across the 1960s. This disparate assembly – three London Jews, one Jamaican Hindu, an Indian Muslim and an Irish Catholic – were all outsiders to the British establishment and made their own rules as they went along. Their rush to open record shops involved great personal effort, huge profits, disastrous losses, and encounters with illustrious entertainers and notorious gangsters. Wise to the hustle and flow of the loosely regulated music industry, these adventure capitalists hacked out a road map of sorts for much that was to follow.

Eyes on the prize: Alex Strickland and Bob Dylan survey the '60s. Courtesy of Nigel Strickland.

Alex Strickland (Soho Records, Alex Strickland Records)

Alex Strickland (1930–2009) was born to a Jewish family who ran a tobacconist and sweet shop on Coptic Street, London (near the British Museum), and Strickland, initially, ran his own tobacconist, The Hobbit, on Wardour Street. He started to sell records from The Hobbit's back room in 1957 and then opened the Soho Record Centre on the corner of Old Compton and Dean Streets in 1958. Here, Strickland employed a chic modern décor, specialised in LPs and enjoyed immediate success. Enamoured with showbiz, Strickland used his shop to sell tickets to West End theatres and publicised the visiting crooners and stars of stage and screen.

In 1960, Strickland opened the first Alex Strickland shop, and by 1965 there were 15 Alex Strickland Records from Golders Green to Brixton, the chain specialising in musicals and classy ballad singers. The Soho Record Centre became a hub for entertainers doing public appearances: Frank Sinatra and Johnny Mathis became Alex's personal friends, while he got on so well with Sammy Davis Jr that he became his UK agent. Eartha Kitt, Andy Williams, Shirley Bassey, Perry Como, Glen Campbell, Peter Sellers, Petula Clark, Sacha Distel, Roger Moore, Lena Horne, Rita Moreno, Sonny & Cher and a young tyro called Bob Dylan all appeared too. The public rushed to, and the press gushed at, such events. Strickland, always stylish and smiling, let everyone know that his stores stocked the best mono and stereo LPs available.

There's no record of The Rolling Stones doing an in-store appearance at a Strickland shop but their manager, Andrew Loog Oldham, would reflect in his autobiography, *Stoned* (2000), on "Alex Strickland, the record store owner who gave me good and kindly counsel on my future in the biz". However, it was not the Stones but Barbara Streisand, Andy Williams and Perry Como who sold the most LPs at his stores, as Strickland noted when interviewed by BBC TV in the late 1960s.

Being based in Soho encouraged Strickland to stock jazz LPs but, unlike Doug Dobell and Ray Smith, he had no interest in being part of the milieu who gathered at Ronnie Scott's Jazz Club for late-night jam sessions. Instead, Strickland focused on the stars who packed the Palladium and appeared in the Broadway musicals that always did big business in central London theatres. His shops also supplied LPs to be sold at theatres – and Strickland became almost as famous as some of his artists, forever called on by the London media to comment on popular culture. This surely helped him sell a 51 per cent stake in the shops to Pye Records in 1965 (and then complete ownership in 1969). Pye subsequently rebranded Strickland's shops as Pye Records and ran them into the ground.

Strickland became managing director of Chappell of Bond Street (the musical instrument/sheet music shop that had been trading in London since 1811), setting up a successful record bar on the ground floor. Leaving Chappell in the mid-1970s, he opened two new London Alex Strickland shops in Southgate, Enfield N14, and Temple Fortune on the Finchley Road, NW11. Yet Strickland now found himself a man out of time in the age of disco and punk – he didn't dance the hustle or desire anarchy in the UK – and so sold up and retired to his mansion in the south of France.

Laurie Krieger (Harlequin Records)

Laurie Krieger (1926–97) was a small man with a big smile who loved both people and money. In turn, people loved Laurie and money stuck to him. Krieger's fledgling steps into entrepreneurship involved selling ice-cream cones on Oxford Street in the 1940s. Newspapers and stationery followed, and then music. Krieger founded Harlequin Records in 1961, opening his first record shop in the basement of a newsagent he operated at 96 Berwick Street, London W1. He then opened Harlequins at 116 Cheapside, London EC2 and 36 High Holborn W1. All three made money and Laurie never looked back: at one point he owned some 70 shops across London, the home counties, East Anglia and the Midlands.

Harlequin's Berwick Street shop found Krieger selling newspapers and tourist tat (postcards, souvenirs, etc.) on the ground floor while the records were in the basement. Here the female manager's taste for jazz and R&B ensured many a mod dropped their wages on new Arthur Alexander and Ramsey Lewis import 45s. This initial Harlequin is thought to have been the acorn that made sure this Soho street grew into the UK's most illustrious record shop road. Not that Krieger ever imagined such; he just wanted the records to march out the door as quickly as he could stock them.

By the mid-1960s, Harlequin's flagship shop sat opposite The Prince of Wales theatre on Haymarket where a sign stated "London's original 24-hour record-store". The Haymarket Harlequin's late hours made it a favourite with creatures of the night – musicians (Hendrix was a customer), transients, clubbers, sex workers, taxi drivers and such – and one former employee recalled it having: "… strobe lights and disco lights in the ceiling and a switch to turn off the shop lights to make it into a club. All the guys were gay and DJs. The rent boys used to come in with their box jackets on and clutch bags and everyone would be dancing in the shop. Excellent fun."

A true mensch, Krieger visited his London shops every week to collect takings and engage with staff. He drove either a pale blue Rolls Royce with the personalised number plate LK1 or a large American car that had a plate fitted to it proclaiming the vehicle was made from "recycled jukeboxes". Joyce Lindo, personal assistant to Krieger from 1963–76, recalls him treating Harlequin Records as a family business, even when it consisted of more than 50 shops: "On a Monday morning I would ring all the different stores to take the sales tallies and write them in a ledger – this is before computers took over – and one morning Mr Krieger said to me, 'You're taking a long time today' and I replied, 'Didn't you say Harlequin was a family business?' 'Yes.' 'Then you can't expect me to not ask how everyone is then, can you?' And he agreed with me!"

Lindo confirms that the Harlequin shops across the 1960s stocked and sold every kind of music, select shops featuring managers with specialty knowledge ("the manager of the Oxford store was a classical expert and did very well with classical LPs"), with a vast turnover of Top 40 singles underpinning business: "We would sell all the big names – Beatles, Stones, T. Rex, Doors – and everything else. Mr Krieger would buy bankrupt shop stock so Harlequin stores would sometimes end up with records that had gone unsold elsewhere. Mr Krieger was not really interested in music, it was all about business to him. He was a real wheeler dealer and when he bought a bankrupt store he'd take everything: light fittings, sockets … everything!"

Lindo suggests that Krieger's success at building Harlequin into a chain was due to, "good staff, good managers, good selection" and laughs out loud when recalling the opening of the Canon Street store. "Manfred Mann were bought in to do the honours and we got completely mobbed by teenagers! The police were called to hold them back and we ended up having to smuggle the band out the shop's back door before the windows gave in!" She also notes that Krieger stayed true to his roots, with the Oxford Street Harlequin selling ice creams over summer.

In 1970, Krieger purchased two HMV stores then, in 1972, bought the Pye Records chain of 17 record shops for a reported US$750,000. That gave Krieger a total of 43 shops and, by 1976, he owned some 64 Harlequin Records shops. The ubiquitousness of the Harlequin shops found a shop being used for an amorous tryst in the 1975 British sex comedy, *Confessions of a Pop Performer*.

In 1980, the Our Price chain purchased 58 Harlequin Record shops from

Krieger, quickly rebranding them all as Our Price. Krieger then opened a pool hall and health club in Debenham, Suffolk. Not that Laurie lost his interest in retail dosh: a caller to Robert Elms' BBC London radio show recalled how, as the new manager of an Our Price store, he heard a knock on the shop's back door one morning. Opening, he found Krieger patiently waiting to empty the Space Invader machines of their coins. His pale blue Roller sat in the parking lot.

Barry Class (Disci Records)

Barry Class's multifarious, global business dealings make him appear to be a character worthy of a Bond novel, having fingers in many pies. How he made his fortune and what he did with it must be left for another book. What concerns us here is Disci, a chain of record shops that Class scattered across Greater London.

The Disci stores featured an Olympic discus thrower emblem, and it was through the Westbourne Grove Disci that Class altered British pop history. In 1967, a young band approached Class's wife, Silvia Wolf, in said Disci about getting some music industry help. She mentioned the band to Barry. He dropped in on a rehearsal and decided to manage them. They were The Foundations and when their single 'Baby Now That I've Found You' topped the UK pop charts in 1967, they became the first multiracial group (Afro-Caribbean, English, Sri Lankan) ever to do so. The Foundations scored a slew of memorable pop-soul hits – 'Build Me Up Buttercup' is two minutes and fifty-five seconds of pure joy – but issues of ego and money made The Foundations fragment before they fulfilled their potential. Class went on to manage other bands but none matched The Foundations' success, and his real passion remained that of a 'property developer'. This involved many interests, including owning Westbourne Grove slum housing which he rented to West Indians.

"In essence, Barry Class is like dealing with a hologram. If the angle's right you can see him. If not, you can't. He was very good at disappearing. One week he would be driving a Rolls Royce, the next a Mini," says Steve Bronstein, former manager of two Disci shops on Carnaby Street. Bronstein's London music biz history is fascinating enough for him to get his own separate section below; here I'll keep his quotes to Disci.

"The Disci shops I had in Carnaby Street made loads and loads of money. Barry gave me prime sites and Saturday in Carnaby Street you had everybody coming in – members of The Bee Gees and The Rolling Stones – everyone would drop in and say, 'How's my record doing?' Eric Clapton would come in. Johnny Rivers once dropped in and spent $800 on records – that's a lot now and this was in 1972!"

Bronstein also notes that John Stephens, the pioneering Glaswegian fashion designer nicknamed 'The King of Carnaby Street' and 'The £1m Mod', had "one of his clothing stores inside one of my Discis". Also of note, Bronstein says: "The Disci in Piccadilly Circus, right underneath the Coca Cola sign, was the biggest selling singles shop in the history of music. It was only a little shop but it would stay open until midnight and queues would form outside the shop for new releases. Like Record Store Day today!"

Swinging London: Disci Records in Piccadilly Circus.

Bronstein thinks there may have been fifteen Disci shops in total but, having left London for LA in the early 1970s, he is unsure of the chain's mid-'70s history. Rumour has it that the Disci stores may have ended up being run as a "long firm" - a fraudulent company that gets large amounts of stock on credit then defaults on paying for said stock while selling it off. Whatever the case, the Disci stores had all vanished by the end of the 1970s. Bronstein last bumped into Glass in Beverley Hills in 1978 and, by then, Class was managing an antiques shop and buying up property across Los Angeles. "Barry Class knew how to make money," he says, "and how to make a million pounds vanish faster than you can imagine. He owned property in the Seychelles and lots of other places.

He was one of those London characters that slip in and out of sight when they choose to."

Bronstein has no idea if Class still walks the earth today and an internet search reveals that he last attracted attention in 1994 when a tobacco plantation he owned in the Philippines entered the luxury cigar market. No obituary exists so, perhaps in true Bond character mode, Class will reappear when least expected.

Lee Gopthal (Musicland, Muzik City)

Musicland's main man was Leichman 'Lee' Gopthal, whose origins are outlined in Chapter 4. Gopthal founded Beat & Commercial Records in 1963 to distribute Jamaican 45s before joining forces with Island Records in 1964. While Chris Blackwell concentrated on developing Island Records' artist roster, Gopthal got on with the business of selling records, initially opening a Musicland shop in Willesden Lane, London NW6 in 1966. Gopthal worked behind the counter of this shop, getting a feeling for what customers wanted and, within a year, he had opened London branches of Musicland in Willesden Green NW10, Shepherd's Bush W12, 230 Portobello Road, W11, 20 Atlantic Road, SW9, 53 Watling Avenue, Burnt Oak, HA8 and 256a North End Road, SW6.

Island were importing records from Jamaica and the USA (specifically R&B) and Gopthal stocked his shops with these alongside the UK Top 40. He rapidly opened shops in parts of London with West Indian communities, each shop following the Jamaican tradition of blasting music via speakers placed on the street to attract customers. Noting how rock LPs outsold all others, Gopthal somehow made sure that Musicland's shop at 44 Berwick Street would be celebrated by long-haired youth as *the* London import shop.

Sixteen-year-old Ian Hingle began working at the Musicland in Fulham, London SW6 in November 1967: "I got started the week the Long John Baldry record 'Let the Heartaches Begin' came out – they flew out of the shop! It was tiny. It used to be a baker's and people would come in and ask if they had any bread! We sold everything – it was a pop record shop – but we sold a lot of Blue Beat as there was a big West Indian population back then in West Kensington. We had about three listening booths and a speaker on the street. I worked on and off for Musicland – they had about eight shops – in Fulham, Portobello Road, Willesden, Kilburn, Ealing, Hounslow."

Gopthal enjoyed a great deal of success, yet those who worked for Musicland recall things not always appearing above board; which might explain why the chain that had appeared so dominant rapidly lost its way, finally being declared bankrupt in 1976. Terry Davinson recalls: "I started at the Kilburn High Road branch of Musicland in 1970. Then they moved me to Oxford Street – they only had had this shop on a six-month lease – and then I moved to the Portobello Road shop, quite close to where Honest Jon's is now. I remember selling lots of the Daryl Banks single 'Open the Doors to Your Heart', a great record loved by northern fans and London fans. We never met the owners but heard about them as ghost-like figures you didn't want to mess with.

"Whatever our concerns about our bosses, I must emphasise that Musicland was a great place to work: the stock was fantastic as the area we were in meant you had all kinds of records, no limits to what we could have. Brian Eno was a customer, not that he was famous then, and he really surprised me by buying a rock thing like Steppenwolf and then the Doris Duke album *I'm a Loser* – my favourite album of all time! – and I wondered 'Who is this guy buying Doris Duke?'

"Back then Notting Hill and Ladbroke Grove was pretty rough. Not in a negative way but in a very working-class, market stalls kind of way. I liked it, thought it a great place. And it was always so packed in the weekend! Musicland's head office would buy bulk deletions but that was only 10 per cent of the shop, the rest was new releases. I can still remember the catalogue numbers! I must say that Musicland always felt a bit dodgy – like it might not last into next week – you suspected it might come to an ignominious end! I left Musicland to work at Record Corner in Balham. And I stayed there right until the end decades later."

disci

AMERICAN & CONTINENTAL IMPORTS

records

BRANCHES

BAYSWATER	100 WESTBOURNE GROVE, W.2
HENDON CENTRAL	23 WATFORD WAY, N.W.4
SOUTHALL	84 THE BROADWAY
BLETCHLEY	90 BLETCHLEY ROAD
RUGBY	36 HIGH ST. (Opposite Marks & Spencer)

ADMINISTRATION-117, WESTBOURNE GROVE, LONDON, W.2. PARK 3503 CABLES-"NOTADE" LONDON

Across the 1960s, Alex Strickland Records, Harlequin Records, Disci and Musicland were all inventing possibilities as they went along. Yet by the mid-1970s – with the exception of Harlequin Records – these record retail pioneers had all but vanished. Strickland sold his chain. Gopthal crashed his. Class was pursuing new opportunities elsewhere. Only Krieger, who opened more shops than the combined efforts of the other three (while possessing the least interest in music), would make millions out of record retail. That his legacy would be helping the ever rapid expansion of the characterless Our Price chain is neither here nor there; Krieger ran record shops to ensure that he could drive Rolls Royces. And so he did.

Steve Bronstein

Whippet thin, immaculately groomed and very savvy, Steve Bronstein is one of the last old-school British record shop men. Still active in 2017, Bronstein trades in rare records, so continuing a near 70-year association with the music industry. I initially met Steve at a concert, and as our conversation went from old records to old record shops, he mentioned having managed "a couple of Disci shops on Carnaby Street". This and much, much more: "I grew up in the East End, Vallance Road, Kray Town. Reggie and Ronnie [Kray] were acquaintances. They always treated me respectfully and were known for doing local good deeds – if a pensioner or a poor family's water or gas got cut off they'd pay for it to be reconnected. Back then that meant a lot. But I knew the other stuff they were up to so was aware the twins were a mix of Robin Hood and Dracula. I only ever went into business with the twins once. A long firm operation. They used to ask, 'How does he make money stick to him?' See, I was never a musician but I play the most important instrument in the band: the cash register! I've always been very good at maths and before I did my National Service, between the age of 15 and 18, I ran two jazz clubs. One in Kingston, the other in Surrey.

"I finished my National Service aged 20 in 1953 and went on to manage the basement in the 2i's Coffee Bar on Old Compton Street. There had been a change in the scene while I was in the army – all the clubs seemed to be suddenly owned by Australian wrestlers! It was all very cliquey and we all hung out together. I was booking Tommy Steele at the 2i's, paying him £2 a night. Vince Taylor, Marty Wilde, all those guys would perform there. Larry Parnes – 'Miss Parnes' we called him – was always there checking out the talent.

"Then I got a job running a 2000-capacity club in Wardour Street called La Discotheque. It was owned by Peter Rachman. I had no problem with him, he was only nasty with his tenants. He had a very flash car, a Ford Sunliner convertible with a Polish chauffeur. At night he'd turn up to pick up his money with Mandy Rice-Davies and Christine Keeler at his side. The Bag O' Nails was another West End club owned by a villain. Most of the clubs were owned by villains. Back then the British music industry was centred around Soho and there were so many characters. Flash Ronnie, I bet he's not still with us as he was always having run-ins with people. I had to sort out an altercation between him and the twins. The Maltesers too. Mervyn Cohn was another I had a lot of dealings with. He was connected with Ember Records, the label Jeffrey Kruger, the owner of The Flamingo, set up.

"I came to meet Barry Class at his Westbourne Grove Disci Records headquarters in early 1970. See, as I had all these music industry contacts I used to get a call to come down to the Blind Beggar as someone there would have something they wanted to shift via record shops. Usually it would be a lorry full of albums that had gone missing and the villains would want these records resold through shops – and I had contacts to do this. So one night I go down the Beggar and it turns out that the lorry they lifted this time doesn't have a variety of LPs. Instead, it has 10,000 copies of Bridge Over Troubled Water by Simon & Garfunkel. They were incredibly popular at the time so I didn't doubt I could get rid of them but, still, it's a lot of albums by one artist. So I go to see Barry Class and he knew about me. I told him what I had and he said, 'wow!' He then said he would give me two shillings a record and that's how the deal went down with him and a couple of other record chain owners. Krieger took a few boxes too.

I was still booking bands for clubs at the time but Barry took a real shine to me and said, 'Why don't you run a couple of record shops for yourself? I've got two in Carnaby Street and I'll give you them for a good price'. I considered, thought it a good idea and did very well on them. In the old days, the record companies had van salesmen and the driver would come to the shop and take you to the van and you'd sign for what you got and every single driver would say, 'By the way, I've got a couple of boxes of Led Zeppelin or Cream LPs', and these were records he had lifted from the warehouse and would sell for a low price, cash in hand. There used to be SOR – sale or return – and so you would buy records on the side then send them back to the labels and make money on 'em! But the labels got wise to what we were doing and made you pay for records, no returns.

"Through my level of contacts I had a chart shop list and it was a bloody goldmine as managers of artists would come down and – this was singles, mainly – you'd order 100 singles and list them as sold and charge the manager a plus 10 per cent fee for doing this. We made out like bandits on that. So many records made No. 1 that hardly sold a copy! We were all at it! See, the higher an artist got in the charts, the more they could command for their concerts. And if you got into the Top 5 your fee went through the roof. So, these managers hyping their artists up the charts by buying lots of 45s from us were doing it with the aim of making a lot of money on the live circuit.

'Jeffrey Collins had a shop in Saint Martin's Lane and one on Granton Street off Carnaby. He was, like me, a bit of a flash monkey. We all used to hang out together. He came down and bought boxes and boxes of *Bridge Over Troubled Water*. He was king of the bootleggers and I sold bootlegs. Sold 'em to Branson when he was doing mail order. Got a visit from Led Zep's manager, Peter Grant, once about Zep boots. He's a lot bigger than me but when I let him know who I was connected with he left quietly. We used to drink as a group. Band managers, record shop owners, music people and models – they would hang out with us as we were making money. The inner circle was very tight. They were brilliant times. Back then, owning a record shop, the records did all the work, and Soho was where we all hung out, thick as thieves."

Enter the Ali Family

From the mid-1950s to the twenty-first century, the Ali family were major players in many areas of the independent music business – record stalls, shops, pressing plants, cash-and-carry distributors, labels – yet there is almost no documentation of their invisible empire. In Blackpool, I met Jim Ali, youngest son of Sayed and Margaret Ali. This is his family's story: "My father Sayed Mouzzan Ali is from India: during Partition his family were murdered as they were Muslims in a Hindu area. He fled and made his way to Bombay where he joined the merchant navy. He met my mother, Margaret Brennan, over here [England]. Mum's Irish and worked in a milk bar in Manchester. He was selling fruit on the street and would come into her milk bar to get something to drink and, one afternoon, some local racists attacked him and my mum came out from behind the counter and beat them off with a tray! That's how they met! When they got married her Irish Catholic family disowned her.

"Mum and dad set up together selling stockings in a market stall in 1954. One day a Jewish gentleman came over with a suitcase of singles and said, 'Music is where the future is. Try and sell these and I'll come back and see how you've done.' Well, my dad sold them all in one week and realised the Jewish gentleman was correct and he set up the first record shop in Rochdale. By then he and my mum were running four different market stalls selling records.

"Dad opened a shop in Tib Street, in the heart of the Northern Quarter of Manchester, then a thriving quarter in the old animal market, and that was his main shop, The Record Bar. My mum and dad didn't stick to one name for their record shops – I don't know if this was for tax purposes or whatever – but they had suffered a lot of racism when they got together so they kept things low key.

"Dad's dream was to come to London. Everyone told him this was the place. We moved down in about 1965, first settling in Billericay as everyone in the music business told dad it was a great place to live. But they were all white and we found out that it was very right wing, very racist. We got hounded: my mother was spat on, attacked on the streets, we'd get called 'wogs' and singled out. It wasn't safe for us to be living in Billericay. We had to go live on a farm because it was so rough.

"Dad bought a warehouse in the East End and he set up a cash and carry. People could come and buy records off him. At that time the whole record industry in England was run by Jewish people and it was pretty much a closed shop, not at all easy to get into. Dad bought an old textile mill in Royton, a textile town in Greater Manchester, and he turned it into a record pressing plant. He got a contract with Decca and was pressing Tom Jones, The Rolling Stones, all the big names. Obviously, because of the records he was pressing he wanted to set up shops. He met Lee Gopthal and, they both being Indian, got on well. So, they went into business together. Lee started using dad as a one-stop and he proved vital to Musicland and Muzik Zone getting going. Dad was the secret financier – the deals mainly were between Lee and dad.

"Lee was a ruthless businessman. He never paid the artists properly and got threatened so many times. Once we were in the pub with Lee, he was playing pool, and Dandy Livingstone came in demanding his royalties for 'Suzanne Beware of the Devil'. Lee ignored him, kept playing pool, so Dandy slammed Lee down on the pool table, got his belt off and started whipping Lee!

"Laurie Krieger was a brilliant man. He started to buy records off my dad in Harlesden as dad had opened a big cash and carry called 12 Grades Records. When we had a shop that didn't perform as well as it should have he'd give it to Laurie Krieger and he would turn it into a Harlequin and make a deal and it was brilliant. Our family and the Krieger family were incredibly close, both in business and personally. Back then no one cared that we were Muslim and they were Jewish.

"My mother bought Keith Prowse's seven record shops in 1971. Mum was always the most down-to-earth person and a very hard worker. Even when we had lots of money she never changed, she'd be working in the shops or packaging records in the cash and carry, no airs or graces about her. Dad and mum were brilliant together. Dad had lots of nice motors including a red Rolls Royce with the number plate SMA3.

"When Trojan was having difficulties, we took over all the Musicland and Muzik City record shops. I remember we went into the warehouse in Neasden Lane and

we had to shovel all the 45s into a truck. Bamboo and all those labels. They'd be worth a fortune now but were unwanted back then. At one time my parents owned Musicland, Muzik City, Keith Prowse and Music Scene – a bunch of little shops – and Scene & Heard, a big record shop on Oxford Street. The manager changed its name to Pearson's Records when dad sold it off. Fifty-two record shops. We bought chains when they were in trouble. Bought the Sounds Unlimited chain of nine shops. Dad became the biggest independent distributor in the UK. He was a partner in Record Merchandiser, a racking company that sold records to Tesco's and WHSmith.

Ironically, by doing this he helped set in motion what killed record shops.

"At that time, lots of things happened. Dad had a very big fire in his warehouse in Chelsea Road, Harlesden. Dad's distribution was in tatters and, due to the fire, he had lost his computer records so he got rid of a lot of shops to Harlequin along with unloading some to my brother and sister. Jeffrey Collins had a big shop in King Street, Hammersmith– there was all kinds of ducking and diving going on – and he sold his shop and warehouse to my dad. Dad also set up Deacon Records, a budget label, to sell to Woolworths. This is the early 1970s and I'm just starting by now, working in wholesaling, working in the Shepherd's Bush shop for a long time. I also had a shop in Aldgate East, Austin Records, in the Petticoat Lane market side.

"Around the time we had the fire, we suffered a home invasion robbery. It was very violent. Me and mum were put on the ground with guns to our heads. Someone knew that mum and dad kept a lot of money at home – I think it would be the equivalent to about £2 million today – and they organised a gang to rob us. I got totally immersed in what happened, obsessed with finding out who had robbed us. I joined criminals and did a lot of bad things. I ended up finding out that it was the police who robbed us. We got harassed by the police when we went searching for justice. My mum died of stomach cancer nine months after the robbery. I'm sure it was the stress of the robbery, the trauma, that brought it on. And the robbery, my mum's death, it just destroyed dad.

"Dad got out and went to America. He wanted a fresh start. That's when our own record shop identities came about: Jolly Jester, All Ears, Centrepoint Records in Tottenham Court Road, Bargain Records was a little chain I had. Every shop was different. I never kept to a formula. My main shop was 245 Portobello Road and this was under the control of Joe Sinclair of Trojan. It became Klik Records and Joe ran his Klik label from there. Tappa Zukki and Dillinger would hang out in the shop when they were on the Klik label. I bought that one off dad. When I took over 245 Portobello, reggae and punk were what we specialised in but we also did rock as French Italian tourists came in wanting Beatles and Doors and stuff like that.

"I even ran a record shop in Bangor, Northern Ireland: Cheeseburger Records. It was hard, the Troubles were still on. Sold lots of Country and Western and showbands. I owned Wavelength Music in Wembley, sold tapes, some CDs, VHS. I kept the Portobello Road shop going as Bargain Records, but closed the others. During this time, I worked for Charlie Grech – the Maltese Soho gang boss – for a number of years. I'd run my records shops during the day and then go into Soho and run one of his sex shops.

"Black Dog Music in Berwick Street was my last record shop. I had a basement doing rock music and upstairs was mainly doing all the latest soul and hip-hop, good reggae. Black Dog closed because of the lease. Most of the Soho record shops had peppercorn rents, not real leases, so when the property values went up they got priced out. They were great times. It's all changed now. Which is why I live in Blackpool and run a big men's outfitters."

Chapter 6

The Beatles, Bowie, Bassey and HMV: Shops of the Stars

Brian Epstein begins managing his parents' Liverpool record shop, discovers The Beatles, turns to HMV's Oxford Street store for help and changes the world. Shirley Bassey and Kenny Lynch open branded record shops in London. The teenager who would become David Bowie learns the record trade in Bromley. A very young Morrissey gains wisdom in Moss Side's Paul Marsh Records. HMV Oxford Street is a swinging London hotspot. Cameos from Jimi Hendrix, Dusty Springfield, Pete Townshend and Vera Lynn.

Brian Epstein and NEMS

The North End Road Music Store (NEMS) of Liverpool is the record shop that changed the world. If there had been no NEMS then, quite likely, there would have been no Beatles. No Beatles, then no British invasion. No British invasion, and the UK music scene would have remained a backwater akin to, say, the French music scene (with better singers if none quite so chic). And, without the phenomenon that The Beatles unleashed, rock music and British culture (as well as tax revenue, tourism and national self-esteem) would all be irredeemably poorer. As far as retail achievements go, this is not insignificant.

Such speculation could be dismissed as wrongheaded due to the fact that, if NEMS had never opened, John Lennon and Paul McCartney would still have formed the group, played at The Cavern Club in Liverpool and Hamburg's the Star Club, written songs, rocked hard and commanded devoted fans in Liverpool and Hamburg. But would they have got any further? The Beatles had talent and character in spades, but so did many musicians who never achieved success. What the band needed was a record deal, and no one was giving those out in the port cities in which the band worked.

Music fans all have their stories of artists with huge potential/great performances/fabulous songs, and so on, who never achieved any real level of recognition. It wasn't the lack of talent that stymied them – it was the lack of *luck*. Luck goes way beyond talent in establishing who tastes success. Effective management comes a not too distant second.

Anyway, if it had not been for Harry and Queenie Epstein's son, Brian, and his success at turning the family's musical instrument shop into a thriving record shop, there is a strong possibility that The Beatles would be just another band that a handful of people who were at The Cavern and The Star Club fondly reminisce about. This, then, is the story of how a Liverpool record shop served as a launch pad for The Beatles and much that followed in their wake.

Nineteen-year-old Isaac Epstein fled Lithuania in 1896, one among the 2 million Jews who fled the violently anti-Semitic pogroms sweeping Slavic

Liverpool calling: The Beatles command NEMS' stairs, 1962.

lands. Epstein landed in Liverpool and, by 1900, was the owner of a Liverpool furniture store on the Walton Road. This store served the city's impoverished northern suburbs and Epstein's fairness and business acumen established him as a trusted retailer. Success ensured that, in 1929, he purchased The North End Road Music Store next door. His son, Harry, took over managing both stores that year, developing NEMS's stock of instruments, sheet music and 78s. Highly regarded – McCartney and Cilla Black's families bought pianos there on extended-purchase plans – NEMS proved a success. As business grew post-Second World War, Harry decided to expand into downtown Liverpool. He wanted his oldest son, Brian, to run the new store.

Brian Epstein had different ideas. Born in 1934, the dreamy, gay youth flunked out of public schools, got discharged from National Service, and demonstrated very little interest in joining NEMS. Instead, he wanted nothing more than to flee Liverpool and his loving, if confining, Jewish family for the anonymity of a bigger city. Initially, the teenage Brian had told his father he wanted to be a dress designer, but Harry angrily refused to consider the idea, putting Brian to work in the furniture store. A gifted salesperson, Brian made it clear that this was not where he wanted to be, instead enrolling at the Royal Academy of Dramatic Art (RADA) in London. Harry always felt his son should be working in the family business and, each time Brian returned to Liverpool, Harry would ask, "When are you going to come to your senses and come and work for the family?" In 1957, during his third year at RADA, Brian admitted he hated being a student and agreed to manage a branch of NEMS that Harry planned to open in Liverpool's Great Charlotte Street.

Brian set up the Great Charlotte Street NEMS with his younger brother Clive, whose role it was to manage the white goods (fridges, cookers) and furniture-based electrical goods department on the first floor. Brian insisted that the firm expand the ground floor's stock from pianos and radios to include a far greater range of records (popular on the ground floor; classical on the first). This achieved, the Great Charlotte Street NEMS opened on 7 December 1957 with an appearance by Anne Shelton (a singer popular with British armed forces in the Second World War), and a large crowd turned out for the occasion. On the first morning, the record department took over £20; in Walton, the record department took £70 in a good week. Brian Epstein had found his forte.

Get your 'BEAT' and 'Rhythm & Blues' Records at . . .

NEMS

Whitechapel & Gt. Charlotte St.
Largest Selection of Popular Records in the North

Brian's eye for detail, constant desire to improve stock, and success in tracing hard-to-find recordings won NEMS acclaim, and the shop

Mr NEMS: Brian Epstein displays his favourite stock.

gained further renown for being the first in the city to stock OST (original soundtracks) and West End and Broadway cast albums. Market trader Mick O'Toole remembers purchasing records from Epstein on Saturday evenings after working at St John's Market: spotting Brian behind the counter of the (by that time closed) NEMS store, Mick would knock on the shop door and Epstein would let him into the shop informing him to: 'Always give a knock on the door – if I am there doing the books, I will open up.' Mr Epstein, as everyone knew him, would always be helpful. It wasn't like other shops where the record racks might be just an add-on to a TV shop and you were considered to be a bit of a nuisance. He genuinely cared about music and would not hesitate to order something for you.

With records sales rapidly escalating, Brian engaged in the thrill of making sure that NEMS provided a service second to none. Epstein said, when reflecting on NEMS' success with Hunter Davies for The Beatles' official biography (1968): "Most record shops I'd been in were lousy. The minute a record became popular it went out of stock. I aimed to have everything in stock, even the most way-out records. I did this by ordering in triplicate any record that anyone ever wanted. I reckoned that if one person asked for something, there must be others who would want it too. I even had three copies of the LP *The Birth Of A Baby*, just because one person had wanted it."

Customers were encouraged to leave an order for a record if NEMS failed to have it in stock and stock was checked religiously throughout the day. Brian also worked out his own top 20 sellers in the shop, checking this twice daily. Having a NEMS Top 20 worked both as a gimmick for customers and to let Epstein know what he should be stocking up on. Two years after opening, NEMS in Great Charlotte Street employed 30 staff, and its extensive pop and classical department covered two floors. Business went well and, in 1959, Harry decided to open another store at 12–14 Whitechapel, right in the heart of Liverpool's central shopping district.

Again, Brian took control and the shop's opening found movie star/singer Anthony Newley doing the honours. Newspapers reported that crowds comparable to a cup final turnout surged around NEMS, excited by both Newley's appearance and how the new record shop represented a magnetic triumvirate of showbiz, technology and rock 'n' roll. Epstein loved the glamour and clamour surrounding his new shop; in selling records he had found a passion that, for the time, supplanted his love of theatre and the yearning of a lonely heart. As a gay man in the UK, where homosexuality remained a criminal offence until 1967, Epstein had found himself harassed by police, thugs and blackmailers – to counteract this he used NEMS as a safe space of sorts for Liverpool's gay community, with many of the male employees having a similar sexual preference (record shops across the UK were known for often being gay-friendly workplaces). The new NEMS store continued to offer white goods on the ground floor, but its basement was what generated all the excitement: here a 13-metre, U-shaped counter faced racks and racks of records. Above which, a suspended ceiling decorated with a thousand LP sleeves attracted much attention. The floating ceiling was Brian's idea and many shops would subsequently copy this.

The Whitechapel branch quickly went on to outperform every other record shop/bar across the north of England. Having the pre-eminent record shop outside London was not enough for Brian, and he constantly aimed at improving NEMS, devising a string system to ensure the staff were aware when stock got low. He scouted for talented employees, notably hiring Peter Brown from Lewis Department Store (Brown worked in Lewis's music section; George Harrison would later reveal that, pre-fame, he shoplifted 45s from here) with an offer of a higher salary and a commission on sales. The NEMS stores remained paragons of department store service with the male staff in suits and the female in dresses with NEMS embroidered on the breast pocket. Customers were addressed as "Sir" and "Madam" while Brian and Clive were "Mr Brian" and "Mr Clive".

The record business was booming across the UK – a *Melody Maker* headline in the 8 April 1961 issue proclaimed "Disc Sales Climb To Record Peak" and noted that the sales tally for January of that year had grossed £1,643,000. This was 20 per cent higher than the previous January and 3 per cent higher than the record set in January 1958. Experts quoted in the feature put the sales boom down to teenagers finding nothing of interest on TV and so were turning their passions to music. How passionate these teens could be the UK would soon find out but, back then, no one expected anything like Beatlemania. Especially not Epstein, whose Whitechapel NEMS stood near a dingy basement club called The Cavern.

The Beatles

Brian Epstein's listening tastes rarely extended beyond show tunes and light classical music, but he studied the charts and made sure NEMS began selling local music magazine *Mersey Beat* from its first issue on 6 July 1961, guessing it would be purchased by teenagers. Proven correct, Brian then asked *Mersey Beat*'s editor Bill Harry if he could contribute a record column. Brian's first column appeared in the third issue of *Mersey Beat* on 3 August 1961 and was called "Stop the World – And Listen To Everything In It: Brian Epstein of NEMS". In August 1961, Brian took out an advertisement in *Mersey Beat* proclaiming that NEMS hosted "The finest record selections in the North" – EMI had confirmed that NEMS was their best customer outside the capital. *Mersey Beat* was the first publication to champion local band The Beatles, yet Brian would claim not to have heard of them until that fateful day in 1961 when a youth called Raymond Jones came into NEMS asking for a 45 of 'My Bonnie'.

Epstein had no record of the single being available and, in his autobiography, *A Cellarful of Noise* (1964), he states how Jones taunted him, "You won't have heard of them. It's by a group called The Beatles..." *Beat on the brat!* 'My Bonnie' turned out to be by Tony Sheridan and The Beat Brothers, and Epstein, who ordered at least one copy of each new record released in the UK, was frustrated to find that NEMS had no stock of said 45 (because it had only been released on a German label). Even more humiliating must have been learning that The Beat Brothers were actually The Beatles, Liverpool's No. 1 band. As the North's No. 1 record dealer, Brian felt slighted to be unaware of this.

Interest piqued, Epstein – accompanied by NEMS employee Alistair Taylor – went to a lunch-time performance of The Beatles at The Cavern Club. The dank, smelly club wasn't to Epstein's taste but he keenly watched the future of popular music perform and then dropped into their cupboard-sized dressing room to say hello. The Beatles recognised the smartly suited Epstein because they regularly visited NEMS, crowding into the store's basement's listening booths where they studied the new US 45s ("Play the other side" being their frequent request) and attempted to chat up the female staff, much to Brian's annoyance. When he asked whether the 'yobs' actually bought any records, his staff replied that they did: R&B. Indeed, The Beatles used NEMS listening booths as audition stations for songs that they could add to their set and, when one member thought the tune then playing was suitable, he'd shout "I'm gonna do this one!" Epstein's initial misgivings were forgotten after visiting The Cavern that lunch time, and he would later invite the band to visit him at his NEMS office where he would offer to manage them. Quite a risk for this cautious man, especially as their previous manager Alan Williams had warned Epstein, when he enquired about whether the band were still contracted to him, "not to touch them with a fucking barge pole".

Yet Epstein, bored after having launched two successful shops, wanted to engage in the creative arts again. Fortune would have it that he came across the most creative artists in Liverpool. Brian's role as manager of The Beatles is beyond the realm of this book, but I'll note that when he offered to manage the band they truly got *lucky*. Without his belief, dedication and contacts with London record labels (via NEMS), it is unlikely that the band would have won a record deal. In 1961, as a valued retailer, Epstein was invited on a Hamburg retail management course run by Deutsche Grammophon, Here, he met Bob Boast from HMV's flagship Oxford Street shop. This meeting would prove fortuitous: on 8 May 1962, a flustered Epstein visited Boast at HMV, complaining of being turned down by everyone at British record labels (even freelance producer Joe Meek dismissed The Beatles' demo as "just another bunch of noise, copying other people's music"). At that time, HMV had a small recording studio on the first floor where budding artists could make 78 demonstration discs. Boast took Brian there and introduced him to disc cutter, Jim Foy, who, impressed by the original songs on Epstein's tape, introduced him to Sid Coleman of Ardmore & Beechwood, one of EMI's top publishing companies. When Epstein made it clear he was looking for a recording deal, Coleman called George Martin, head of A&R (artists and repertoire) for Parlophone Records, an EMI subsidiary. And so the future of popular British music was under way. (EMI then owned HMV, and a bronze plaque honouring said meeting is fitted outside 363 Oxford Street.)

What did four Liverpool urchins make of having a manager who ran the best record shop in the north of England? Like bees to pollen, The Beatles swarmed through NEMS' stock, listening to whatever took their fancy, studying both British and American releases and learning new tunes for their live performances from newly released records that had not been hits. "Exciting little black moments" was how Paul McCartney described the 45s they devoured in Epstein's basement, NEMS serving as a finishing school for The Beatles, allowing them access to far more records than almost all of their contemporaries. Before the Parlophone deal, NEMS boosted the band's local popularity by selling dozens of copies of the imported 'My Bonnie', concert tickets, and ensuring shop assistants were au fait with all the news and gossip concerning the band.

Roger Armstrong of Ace Records observes: "I always wondered how The Beatles got hold of some of the songs they covered, as several of them were virtually unknown in the UK. For a long time the story went that Liverpool seamen brought back R&B records from America and this is how the local musicians got to hear them. But I'm sure that's a myth. See, it turns out that every song The Beatles covered was released in the UK. Often only in very small numbers. But NEMS was one of the record shops that ordered a copy of every new release so The Beatles would have found those records in NEMS. My guess is that Brian Epstein let them have free run of the shop and they listened to everything and anything. So, The Beatles found obscure gems by digging through NEMS stock and taking them home to learn – all with Brian's blessing".

Prior to NEMS' rise, Liverpool's foremost specialist record shop was Hessy's on Manchester Street. Hessy's had a well-stocked record bar alongside gramophones, TVs, sheet music and musical instruments: Lennon bought his first electric guitar here for £17 in 1957 and the other Beatles would follow, the shop's lax hire purchase arrangements allowing budding rockers to get their hands on otherwise unaffordable equipment. When Epstein began managing The Beatles, his first task involved covering a debt of £200 that the band owed to Hessy's. Poetic justice of sorts, seeing that NEMS' success had shut down that shop's record bar.

Being managed by Epstein didn't just enrich The Beatles' repertoire and cover their debts; his professionalism and understanding of rock 'n' roll as part of the entertainment industry ensured the band became a less raucous, more amenable unit. Brian was bright and bright-eyed, a man of considerable personal charm, and this helped the band throughout. Initially, he focused his energies on The Beatles, while continuing to manage both shops, combining both jobs when he made certain that NEMS' position as a chart return shop listed thousands of sales of The Beatles' debut 45 (so it crawled into the Top 20). Founding NEMS Enterprises, Brian handed day-to-day running of the shops to a manager, and when The Beatles shot to UK No. 2 in early 1963 and initiated Beatlemania, Epstein lost all interest in retail. Not that he forgot his NEMS staff – many of whom went to work for Brian at NEMS Enterprises (including brother Clive). By June 1964, Harry Epstein, realising his sons had moved into a more lucrative area of the entertainment market, decided to sell NEMS. Long-term staffers like Peter Brown stayed on for several months but, disliking the new owners, left to join NEMS Enterprises, now based in London.

The Beatles signalled not just a revolution in popular music and fashion, they also indirectly shaped a demand for record shops, specifically those that catered to a passionate youth fan base. This change in UK record retail wouldn't get going until the mid-1960s, with Boots and WHSmith enjoying the vast record sales being clocked up. The chain that missed out was Woolworths: selling only Embassy records, Woolies issued imitation Beatles 45s before quitting selling records altogether when the Levy family sold their labels (including Embassy) and studios to CBS in 1965. Woolies then chose to sit out the 1960s selling Fab Four dolls, wigs and lunch boxes. If the 1960s were swinging, Woolworths appeared unaware of this.

HMV: Big Boss Shop

At the dawn of the 1960s, HMV's store at 363 Oxford Street, London W1, remained a formidable, if staid record emporium. Having survived the Depression and the Second World War, the flagship central London record shop continued to sell large numbers of EMI and RCA records (which EMI held European rights for), but success had made the shop complacent and archaic. Managed by Robert Boast – an employee since the 1930s and white goods specialist – HMV emphasised classical and show records.

Things had begun to change in HMV's parent company when Sir Joseph Lockwood took over as EMI chair in 1954. One of his first initiatives was to loosen the hold on what accredited HMV stockists could offer the public, removing the restrictions that had stipulated they only sold EMI and RCA records. In 1964, Lockwood appointed Ken Whitmarsh as manager of 363 and commissioned extensive remodelling to the interior. Whitmarsh proved both capable and affable, his light touch ensuring 363 embraced the spirit of the 1960s as a paragon of modern technology and design.

Entering Whitmarsh's 363, you would have found the ground floor stocked with classical LPs while on the mezzanine there was Cosmopolitan Corner, specialising in records from foreign lands. Everything else – pop, rock, blues, jazz, easy listening, country, folk – sat in the basement where staff were corralled in a large central enclosure. Company policy was to stock one copy of every UK record release still in catalogue, and this meant HMV had stock dating back to before the Second World War.

Two teenage music fans who worked at HMV were Bill Holland (started 1961) and Cliff White (started 1964). Both loved the idea of working in the famous record temple. Holland recalls: "£9.12s.6d were our starting wages. HMV was very formal. We had to wear the store jacket and tie and address one another by our surnames. Bob Boast was really out of touch with modern music so when he retired and Ken took over it was a huge relief. Ken was a great guy and huge jazz fan and the store began to feel more alive, less like a museum."

White agrees that Whitmarsh made 363 London's foremost record emporium with a vast stock and a real sense of excitement: "Ken, being a jazz fan, ensured we had a strong stock of jazz albums." Both White and Holland chuckle over the class divisions then evident in store, with a noticeable difference between the toffs in classical and the plebs in the basement. Yet, they note, everyone shared a passion for the area of music they loved and this meant a real sense of bonhomie existed. White says: "Back then all the records were displayed as cover only, so a customer would come up to the counter and bash me around the head with the cover while saying, 'I want this one,' and I would have to get the actual 45 or LP out. I remember older staff talking about how 'Rock Around the Clock' had been the first time that a record had been stacked by the till as there was so much demand for it. And that proved true for new records by The Beatles and Stones – demand was so huge you had them stacked up by the cash register, none of this fussing about finding the vinyl to fit the sleeve."

While HMV now stocked releases from non-EMI labels, some things didn't change. "Every morning we had to go around the record racks and move the EMI releases to the front of each rack," says Holland. "We were instructed to bump up EMI record sales," adds White. "As EMI had acquired the Motown franchises and also launched its Stateside label this didn't conflict too much with my sensibilities."

In 363's basement there were two listening rooms ("for the more serious customer") with rows of listening posts built down the left wall and around the back wall. These allowed dozens of people to listen to different records at the same time, standing as they did with their heads encased in wooden hubs. White notes: "Each listening post had a separate record player connected, so you would get a customer saying, 'Can I listen to this record at booth number 9?' and I'd put the record on No. 9 record player. Most people were quite decent about it but some were obviously taking the piss and you would end up saying, 'That's enough. Have you come here to shop or just to listen?' We were always polite but we had an ex-sergeant major on the door to sort out troublemakers."

In 1965 HMV trialled a self-service department on the ground floor – a

Dig those open spaces,
    get your records fast.
Don't be keen for queues man,
    you'll end up being last.
Pick your records easy,
    slip into a booth.
Listen at your leisure,
    nice and cool and smooth.

THE WORLD'S LARGEST
RECORD STORE
OPEN TILL 8 P.M.
MONDAY TO FRIDAY
EARLY CLOSING SATURDAY 1 P.M.

DIG THIS JAZZ SERVICE!
★ Huge stocks from the available catalogues ★ Every new release ★ Specialist items on independent labels ★ The pick of the importations ★ Wide range on 45 singles. We have *everything* from Oliver to Monk and Coltrane—and all points farther out.

TOP FACILITIES!
★ Separate display sections for all types of Jazz and Blues ★ 37 browser boxes ★ 12 audition rooms ★ 26 listening booths ★ Hi-Fi playing equipment ★ Expert advice on all aspects of Jazz records.

HIS MASTER'S VOICE

363 OXFORD STREET, LONDON W.1. MAYFAIR 1240

25

browser box that had records in sleeves – for the first time, and as records were expensive back then this really encouraged shoplifters. There used to be a bloke who ran a record stall just off Cambridge Circus and he'd come in and select a handful of albums then take off up Oxford Street with the sergeant major after him. But the sergeant major had a gammy leg so he never caught him!"

Both Holland and White recall 363 heaving with customers. White says: "Especially at lunch time and after people got out of work. Being such a famous shop we'd get not just people from all over the UK but from across the world coming in. I'd regularly have blokes from Germany and France coming up and waving a fistful of money in my face and saying, 'Please sell me the top 250 hit singles for my discotheque!' I'd make sure they got the latest Guy Stevens releases on Sue, the new James Brown and whatever else I fancied. I offered across-the-spectrum service with a smile!"

363's EMI connection and status meant that plenty of famous musicians made use of the shop: "There was a small recording studio on the first floor where the likes of Cliff Richard and The Beatles would go to make floppy disc records for their fan clubs, so we'd see their like. But I was an R&B fan so got a real thrill when Betty Everett and Charlie and Inez Fox dropped in. The Who came in one day wearing all their Union Jack regalia and their manager Kit Lambert once bribed me with lunch so he could use one of the listening rooms to promote an acetate of 'I Can't Explain' to likely takers. He can't have had an office at the time!

"My most memorable day was the one where I served both Vera Lynn and Jimi Hendrix. Separately, not together! This was early on in Jimi's career but I recognised him immediately. He came in with two other guys who might have been his bandmates, and bought several soul records. I insisted he buy 'The Whammy' by Screaming Jay Hawkins – I was a huge fan of Screaming Jay! Jimi was very pleasant, a really nice guy."

Beatlemania helped establish 363 Oxford Street as the UK's most successful record shop: at one point 2.5 per cent of all recorded music sales in the UK went through 363's tills. The now London-based Beatles were regular customers, with Lennon purchasing *The Freewheeling Bob Dylan* (1963) here. This retail largesse found Lockwood determined that HMV should exist as a chain of London record shops and, in 1966, HMV purchased the Saville Pianos Ltd shops that had existed in North London since the nineteenth century. Saville's sold pianos, sheet music and records but, like the Keith Prowse chain of theatre tickets and record outlets, struggled to comprehend the huge demand for pop and rock. White recalls: "There were six or eight Saville shops, and I got assigned to help de-clutter the Tottenham shop before it reopened as an HMV store. In the stockroom they had lots of unopened boxes of records. I reached in one and found a dozen mint copies of 'Be Bop A Lula'! A couple may just have fallen into my bag."

White and Holland moved on to other areas of the music industry while Lockwood continued to expand HMV: by 1970 London was home to 15 HMV shops. Other cities soon found HMV stores opening as this archaic institution rapidly morphed into the most powerful record retailer in UK history.

Shops of the Stars: Bowie, Bassey and Co.

The biggest retail beneficiaries of Beatlemania were WHSmith, Boots and Menzies, chain stores with prominent record bars that stocked the UK Top 40. More independent shops began opening on high streets, but record bars in department and white goods shops continued to do plenty of business, and many who worked and shopped in them had their eyes fixed on future prizes.

Out in leafy West London, a teenage Mary 'Dusty Springfield' O'Brien worked in Squire of Ealing, a shop on Ealing Broadway that sold radiograms and hosted

a record department in the basement. I wonder if Dusty ever served young Pete Townshend. He lived nearby and bought blues albums from Squires: "There was a very good record shop in Ealing where I lived called Squires," Townshend told BBC Radio 6 Music. "They had a great selection of folk blues and I bought Big Bill Broonzy and Sonny Terry and Brownie McGhee albums from them." Jon Savage, the writer later to serve as punk's premier biographer, recalls buying Del Shannon's 'Hey Little Girl' at Squire's in 1963 when he was a child.

Among the new record shops opening were two that attracted plenty of tabloid attention: Shirley Bassey and Kenny Lynch, two very popular singers, both launched personalised record shops in the early 1960s. That these young singing stars – then two of the UK's most prominent black Britons – opened branded record shops reflects the status record shops now possessed: alluring, youthful and cutting edge – this was retailing with a hip, exciting cachet. The wonder is that far more pop stars did not follow Lynch and Bassey's example and engage in this early form of celebrity branding. Admittedly, several Jamaican singer-producers would follow Kingston practice and set up a UK record shack, but the stars' reluctance to open branded shops may have come from management spelling out the hard, daily grind that running a shop involved.

If famous entertainers only owned a few shops, they certainly liked to be seen in them and, as the 1960s progressed, record shops became increasingly chic. Once dismissed as places where teenagers gathered in excited huddles after school, these retailers of plastic magic were now seen as trading in stardust. Understandably so: The Beatles, The Rolling Stones and The Who represented cutting-edge British pop art, while Matt Monro and Shirley Bassey embodied a suave British glamour. Who wouldn't want to partake in this? Popular music held a brilliant confidence and creativity that crossed class and race and gave the British a renewed sense of themselves as world beaters when the Empire had gone.

David Bowie: Bromley Record Shop Boy

Born in Brixton, David Jones would move, aged six in 1953, with his parents to Bromley, the Kent suburb that is now part of Greater London. Here, David developed a strong attraction to music at an early age and would frequent London record shops throughout his adolescence, regularly buying blues and folk at Dobell's. Soho's Musicland and One Stop Records provided import LPs by The Stooges and Velvet Underground (among others) that would influence Bowie's sound and vision. Yet, before Jones had ever explored Soho, before he ever sang in a band, he was a regular customer at Medhurst's, a Bromley department store based in a vast Victorian building that sold furniture and furnishings and records. Medhurst's record department was overseen by a discreet gay couple, Charles and Jim, and as well as sheet music, chart LPs and 45s, it stocked a selection of modern jazz and other contemporary tunes. Here the thin, white youth would check out the latest records, regularly popping in after school to soak up new tunes in the shop's listening booths. "There wasn't an American release they didn't have or couldn't get," Bowie recalled 53 years on. "Quite as hip as any London supplier. I would have had a very dry musical run were it not for this place."

Young Jones was such a regular Medhurst's customer that Charles started giving him a "huge discount" on purchases, "enabling me to build up a fab collection over the two or three years that I frequented this store. Happy days." Among the many records Bowie bought at Medhurst's was Charles Mingus's 1961 opus *Oh Yeah*, "recommended to me by Jimmy". If Charles and Jim helped broaden Bowie's musical appreciation he, in turn, made an impression on shop assistant Jane Green. Bowie told *Vanity Fair*: "She took a liking to me. Whenever I would pop in, which was most afternoons after school, she'd let me play records in the 'sound booth' to my heart's content 'till they closed at five thirty. Jane would often join me and we would smooch big-time to the sound of Ray Charles or Eddie Cochran. This was very exciting as I was 13, 14 and she would be a womanly 17 at the time. My first older woman."

Bowie recalled that in 1959 Jane sold him *The Fabulous Little Richard* LP "at a discount".

SINGER David Bowie has been touring the country visiting leading record stores to meet the staff and distribute publicity material for his first record, "Can't Help Thinkin' About Me." Here he is seen autographing a copy of his disc for Pauline Williams and Mary McGuckin at the record department of Cranes in Coimore Circus, Priory Ringway, Birmingham.

Bowie in Birmingham: 1966 in-store record signing.

Jones then got a Saturday job at A. T. Furlong & Sons, a small music shop on Bromley's High Street that sold records, sheet music, radiograms and TVs. As he was happy to relate many years later: "So, aged thirteen, maybe fourteen, I got my first real big break. Saturday mornings and sometimes Wednesday after school, I would dress to impress and style my hair just right before making my way to Bromley South. It was at Furlong's I got my first real taste of how things could be. Furlong's was owned and run by the pipe-smoking Vic Furlong, an intense man in his forties who was the perpetual jazzer/college type. New Orleans was his thing. Furlong's was *the* record shop. For absolute integrity and a huge stock of jazz, R&B and pure blues, there was nowhere else like it until London itself. It was here that the power of recorded music struck home. I don't mean it was where I discovered music (I had already discovered that power through Little Richard and Elvis), no, it was more how those bits of black plastic could affect other people's behaviour. Getting a job behind the counter at Vic's place, albeit part-time, was enough to boost my cred a hundredfold. It had an effect on the girls … an effect I liked… and, erm, another effect on the boys … quite a different effect."

And at Furlong's the boy who would be Bowie experienced what he calls the "intoxicating power" of recommending music. Perhaps it was the intoxicating effect of the music that led to the teenager being fired for "daydreaming". Or

99

maybe he was actually daydreaming about the records he would make and how, one day, they would be stocked in A. T. Furlong's and most everywhere else.

Shirley's Record Shop

Dame Shirley Bassey (born 1937), the mixed-race girl from Tiger Bay in Cardiff, grew up experiencing the kind of social deprivation generally associated with African-American blues musicians: born into absolute poverty with her father absent (or jailed) and her mother turning tricks, Shirley became, aged 16, a solo mum. From this milieu, the young Shirley used her powerful voice, strong personality and considerable beauty to rise to the very top of British

Shirley and friends (Danny Williams, Shane Fenton, Jess Conrad) in her West Hampstead record shop, 1962.

entertainment. Alongside thirty Top 40 hits, three James Bond theme songs and vast international fame, Bassey should also be noted for opening Shirley's Record Shop at 172 West End Lane, West Hampstead, London NW6, in 1962.

In November 1962, Bassey hosted a star-studded opening of the shop and signed copies of her own LPs for an adoring media and fans. Shirley's Record Shop was an extension of Books Unlimited, a shop owned by Bassey's first husband, Kenneth Hume. Today, little information is available on Shirley's Record Shop but I imagine Mr and Mrs Bassey stocked it with lots of easy listening, show tunes and jazz vocal LPs and Top 40 singles. Moreover, for Bassey fans, it surely had her complete catalogue. If nothing else, Shirley's Record Shop made for some fine Bassey photo sessions with the singer striking poses against a wall of records.

However, Bassey and Hume's relationship proved anything but easy: he was a gay film producer and so Bassey might have simply been a 'beard' for him at a time when homosexuality remained illegal. The couple separated in 1964 and divorced in 1965 with Hume citing Bassey's affair with the film star Peter Finch as the reason. Hume committed suicide in 1967 and, not long after, both Shirley's Record Shop and Books Unlimited closed.

Kenny Lynch Record Centre

The esteemed Kenny Lynch OBE (born 1938) bears comparison with Shirley Bassey, having risen from hardscrabble origins to become one of the first black British entertainers to command a large audience. Lynch was born in Stepney, London, and grew up ducking and diving, serving in the army (where he became regimental boxing champion), working both as an East End barrow boy and petty criminal: "I used to do fly pitching on Oxford Street," Lynch recalled. "We'd get arrested almost every day. Start the morning in the magistrate's court then back to Oxford Street. We'd earn about £60 a week and end up with maybe £15 left after paying all our fines."

"Kenny ran with a really bad crowd," notes Steve Bronstein, a Soho nightclub and record shop manager of that era, "and it was when he was locked up and someone heard him singing in his cell that he went on to get his first break."

Singing gave Lynch the break he was looking for and he would pepper the charts from 1960 until 1965. Earning a small fortune, Kenny took to swanning around London in a chauffeur-driven Rolls Royce, entering pop history when he became the first artist to cover a Lennon-McCartney composition ('Misery'), having met The Beatles when booked on the same tour as the rising Liverpool band. Ironically, Lynch's chart career would be cut short by Beatlemania, but Kenny is one of life's survivors and he became a gifted songwriter and all-round entertainer.

One of Lynch's early investments was the Kenny Lynch Record Centre in Walker's Court, a historic thoroughfare between Rupert Street and Berwick Street in Soho. When Lynch first opened the Record Centre, he would likely have found legacies of old Soho still operating nearby, Walker's Court being home to an eel pie shop, a horse butcher's and Isow's Kosher Restaurant. The new Soho quickly swallowed these traditional businesses and TV footage of Lynch wandering down Berwick Street to the Record Centre makes it clear that the sex industry now dominated the junction – Raymond's Revue Bar, then a new and highly controversial enterprise, being very close by while various 'non-stop striptease' clip joints operated alongside. The footage shows Lynch entering his shop – a large, framed black and white photographic portrait of Kenny dominates one wall – while modish youths bop in listening booths. LPs on the walls include Fats Domino (*Getaway With*), Chuck & Bo's first Chess dual album, an early Bob Dylan effort, Nat King Cole, Buddy Greco, Sandy Nelson, The Waikikis (*Hawaii Tattoo*), Judy Garland, the *Gigi* show's soundtrack, Tom Paxton, Dean Martin, Tony Bennett, Sylvie Vartan and others. A printed-out listing of the Top 50 is on display for customers to browse. In the film, Kenny is asked by a female customer to sign an album (not one of his). It's very urbane; a hip place in which to be seen.

Appropriately, mod DJ Jeff Dexter worked at the Kenny Lynch Record Centre and remembers it fondly: "At the end of 1963 Kenny opened a shop in Walker's Court and I would work in there a few days a week. It was right next to the Raymond Revue Bar and had two brothels next door and London's newest shoe store across from it. It was just brilliant!"

Lynch closed shop in the late 1960s, and the premises became one of Soho's most prominent 'bookshops' run by Fat Bill, a notorious pornographer. Thus, the American R&B and French ye-ye albums were replaced by stroke magazines and 8mm films. Dirty old town? So it must have seemed.

Morrissey: A Moss Side Shopper

In 1965, the infant Steven Morrissey first ventured into Manchester's Paul Marsh Records, experiencing something akin to epiphany. "The Paul Marsh record shop on Alexandra Road had been my Eton, a temple of Holy Scriptures and evangelical hope. Paul Marsh is revelation and prophecy and every effort is made to invoke enough pity from anyone with cash to take me along Alexandra Road and to pause at the temple,' Morrissey wrote in *Autobiography* (2013). When the singer appeared on *Desert Island Discs* (2009), Kirsty Young asked him to tell her about Paul Marsh Records.

Morrissey: Is that really a serious question? Good grief, yes. Well, any education that I now presently have was gained at this record shop in Moss Side in Manchester in the sixties, where I was raised. I was fascinated by this little record shop with wooden floorboards exposed, with sawdust on the floor. And I would go there as often as I could as a five-year-old, six-year-old. And I would simply stand and examine everything, and read everything.

Kirsty: What did you like about it?

Morrissey: I was completely entranced by the song, recorded song, and the emotion that came from people singing. I found it so beautiful and the recorded noise, the recorded song, I thought was the most powerful, beautiful thing. And I still believe that.

What is fascinating about Paul Marsh Records – viewed from this century – is that it largely catered to Moss Side's burgeoning Jamaican community.

Therefore, the young Mozza is likely to have heard lots of ska and rocksteady there. In the twenty-first century, Morrissey would revive the Attack record label (back then a subsidiary of Trojan Records) on which to release his own albums, inspired by the memory of a record shop with sawdust-covered floors.

Chapter 7

Maximum R&B: Mods Get Soul

R&B soundtracks the mod clubs. Transat Imports inspires The Rolling Stones and Small Faces. Dave Godin helps launch Tamla-Motown in the UK then founds Soul City. DJ culture begins with Jeff Dexter, Ian 'Sammy' Samwell and Guy Stevens. Northern soul starts to take shape. Cameos include Georgie Fame, Berry Gordy, Mick Taylor, Viv Stanshall and Pete Townshend.

Out with the old, in with the new: as the 1950s ended, a new tribe of London teenagers embraced schmutter and song with fierce intent. Emerging just as 78s stopped being manufactured, these council estate dandies focused their worship on US R&B 45s and LPs. Mods, as they were soon tagged, set a template for youth tribes to follow: wear the gear, dig the tunes, head to where the action is.

Dig the New Breed

As the 1960s got under way the rock 'n' roll stars who had experienced sensational success were now dead or derailed while such glossy US folkies as The Kingston Trio and The Brothers Four failed to win UK hearts or minds. Making inroads was an African-American music full of swagger and lust (but wise to heartache and loss) called R&B. The mods swore allegiance to this blend of church and brothel that insisted dancers shake a tail feather and everyone get out on the dance floor.

The high priest of R&B was Ray Charles, and his 'I Believe to My Soul' (1959) helped christen R&B as *soul*. Throughout the 1960s, soul would turbocharge British popular music and serve as *the* soundtrack to Saturday night. Nothing packed a dance floor faster than the new sides issued on Atlantic, Chess, Modern, King, Fury, Fire, Enjoy, Imperial, Ric, Vee-Jay, Satellite, Sue, Hi, Duke, Tamla, Motown, Gordy, V.I.P., Excello and other pioneering independent American labels.

London Records set up licensing deals with several US indies and, as well as releasing plenty of pop and country 45s, ensured new releases by Ray Charles, Bo Diddley and other mod icons could be purchased in the UK. However, they couldn't be heard on UK radio: the BBC's unwillingness to give airtime to raucous American music found listeners tuning into Radio Luxembourg and US forces radio stations (pirate radio would change everything when Radio Caroline came into existence in 1964). Or, if staying in didn't appeal – and Radio Luxembourg was more pop than R&B oriented – select DJs were beginning to spin the new tunes in clubs and Mecca dance halls.

The book *Absolute Beginners* was Colin MacInnes' 1959 attempt at teen Beat lit, and follows the adventures of an unnamed 19-year-old as he pursues kicks and girls in Soho basement jazz and jive clubs. MacInnes' narrator describes himself as a "modernist" and distances himself from Teddy Boys (by then associated with rock 'n' roll and racial violence: the book touches upon the Notting Hill race riots of 1958). *Absolute Beginners* is slow in many places, but it effectively documents the birth of the Soho mods – distinct from the Stamford Hill mods who acquired the tag and togs around the same time – as they congregated at Soho's The Flamingo Club and the Lyceum Ballroom, just off The Strand. Here, British DJ culture took embryonic shape and the tunes that were spun in these smoky clubs helped shape 1960s pop and rock.

"I had an eye for sharp tailoring from the age of nine," says Jeff Dexter, both DJ and 'face' on the London scene, "and I liked to dress up!" Dexter also liked music: "I first bought a pop record in 1955, a 78 of Tennessee Ernie Ford's '16 Tons', from A1 Records on the Walworth Road, Elephant and Castle." After initially working as a dancer at the Lyceum, a Mecca ballroom, Dexter joined Ian 'Sammy' Samwell as resident DJ: "The Lyceum is the ancient Greek and French seat of learning and it certainly was for me. I was dancing and DJing with Sammy. Rhythm and blues is what we played as it got people dancing. The Lyceum was a great venue. Amazing music, beautiful women, smartly dressed crowd, it really was special."

Mod music: HMV's listening booths.

"Because the records we played were what the kids liked we were suddenly getting given new music by every record label and publisher in London. We had the records before everyone else. We'd still go out shopping for imports as lots of the best American records didn't get released here. Mecca had an account at Imhoff's on New Oxford Street and the new release records would be delivered on Tuesday afternoon. Sammy and I would go in and listen to all the new records. I'd go into one of the listening booths with a big pile of new releases and listen to them one by one. I was firstly looking for how good they were to dance to. Secondly – if they weren't dance tunes – how they worked for the dreamtime snogging.

"Alex Strickland first set up the Soho Record Centre in 1958. I used to go there. In 1962 an electrical store opened in Lisle Street and they had Transat Imports in the basement. The guy running Transat would, initially, open only on Friday morning. Then it became Friday and Saturdays. He had great US imports. We'd get there early and grab everything good."

Soul aficionado Dave Godin noted, "in some ways, the Lyceum was the first place

People all over the world buy records from Imhofs

Imhofs export postal record service has been operating for over sixty years, improving all the time. Indeed, even before the gramophone had been invented, Imhofs were sending through the post supplies of the steel discs which operated the musical boxes which delighted the mid-Victorians. Today, there is no better record service, no easier way of buying your gramophone records.

All you need to do is to fill in one of our simple order forms, giving your choice of records, and post it to us. We do the rest. You need not even send any money if you have a credit account with us.

We inspect all the records you have asked for, pack them carefully in special cases to withstand the long journey, take out insurance on the parcels, handle the shipping and customs documents and send the records off. All this is done by our own staff here at New Oxford Street, the most experienced staff you would hope to find.

If any of your chosen records is unobtainable, even from the manufacturers, we will gladly choose alternatives for you if you make a note on your order.

that could merit the name discotheque", while East London mod Steve Barrow regularly attended The Flamingo where Georgie Fame was King Mod. Barrow says: "He had a hot band, sounded like one of the US black bands, not a beat combo, and was a great organ player. Georgie said people would bring him records and say, 'You should do a version of this' – that's how he came to play so many great R&B tunes. The clubs were black and white, straight and gay, all mixing together."

In 1963, the President of Chuck Berry's UK fan club, Guy Stevens, got a Monday night DJ gig at The Scene in Ham Yard, Soho, London W1. Stevens, an insurance clerk by day, was an obsessive record collector who, at The Scene, spun many a record that later would be declared a mod 'classic'. Among the audience were members of The Beatles, The Rolling Stones, The Kinks, the Small Faces, The Yardbirds and The Who. The latter's manager, Peter Meaden, paid Stevens to tape songs to enrich the band's repertoire: their debut 45 (as The High Numbers) 'I'm the Face'/'Zoot Suit' were Meaden rewrites of Slim Harpo and Dynamics songs provided by Stevens. While 'Daddy Rolling Stone' – a mod anthem due to Stevens' incessant spinning – became the B-side for The Who's second official 45, 'Anyway Anyhow Anywhere'.

Chris Blackwell of Island Records hired Stevens to run Sue Records, a label that Island Records set up to license R&B. Back then, when getting your hands on new music on US independent labels was often extremely difficult, Sue Records provided a great repository of music for young Brits. Stevens was the mod magus, obsessed with clothes and music and (to his eternal detriment) amphetamines. A contact in Louisiana would regularly send him out parcels of new 45s, but even these weren't enough and Stevens kept hunting for records, hitting London shops and market stalls regularly, alongside setting up his own record stall.

"Guy used to have sales of US records on a Saturday morning in Lisle Street or Newport Court," says teenage mod David Lands. "He used to flog albums for £2.00 and 45s for ten shillings." Pete Townshend also noted: "We would buy records from Guy Stevens and learn them as no one else in the UK had copies so that made us popular with the mods. But it wasn't just that. We wanted to share the music. And you want to share it with like-minded people. Because you don't want to be alone in your room listening to the music. You want to find other people who shared your passions."

R&B, with its sanctified groove and sexual knowing, made pop music sizzle, and bands like The Beatles, The Rolling Stones and Dusty Springfield all swore allegiance, regularly recording their favourite soul tunes. At this time, Motown Records, the foremost US R&B record label, had cracked the US charts but could make no headway in the UK. Motown had tried UK distribution deals with the London American and Fontana labels to no avail; when label boss Berry Gordy cut a deal with Jacques and David Levy – of Levy's of Whitechapel record shop (see Chapter 1) – he must have hoped that their Oriole label would launch Motown in the UK.

Although Berry might hope, Oriole failed to break such classics as 'Do You Love Me' (1962), 'Fingertips' (1963), 'You Really Got a Hold on Me' (1962) and 'Stubborn Kind of Fellow' (1962). All told, Oriole released 19 Motown singles on their black and white Oriole American label (and several albums), none of them making any impression. After 18 months of Oriole failing to break through, in 1963 Gordy took Motown to EMI and, with the support of pirate radio and ITV's *Ready Steady Go*, Motown entered the British charts.

Overexcited, Gordy believed British teenagers had followed America and capitulated; in March 1965, the 'Tamla-Motown Revue' brought The Supremes, the Miracles, Stevie Wonder, The Temptations and Martha Reeves & The Vandellas to the UK. London mods were ecstatic, but ticket sales elsewhere were so poor that the organisers had to add Georgie Fame to the bill. Gordy painfully learned that the British public preferred Cilla to Dionne and the Moody Blues to Bessie Banks. Godin, then employed by Motown as its UK adviser, had forewarned Gordy of his folly and lost his staff position for speaking truth to power. No longer at the label, Godin did the next best thing: he opened the Soul City record shop. However, several years before Soul City there existed a mysterious shop in Soho that played pied piper to the mod scene: Transat Imports.

Transat Imports

Buried in a Soho basement, Transat Imports at 27 Lisle Street in London (a narrow street navigating the spine of Chinatown) opened for only a few hours a week across a handful of years. Yet the fortunate few who got to enter this airless cellar speak of it in a manner akin to those who accompanied Howard Carter into Tutankhamun's tomb.

With no photos, record bags, advertisements or press clippings to document Transat, the mod shop has taken on a mythic sheen, a retail ghost from when Soho existed as a free state of sorts. Even more unbelievable than its invisible existence is how this tiny retailer played a major role in shaping the sound of London as the city began to swing. Transat was the first British record shop specialising in selling imported soul 45s and LPs, supplying mod DJs and dancers with the hottest new tunes and providing many soon to be celebrated British rock bands with material that enriched their repertoire. This was where the hip headed for American hot wax.

So good was Transat's stock that Jeff Dexter, Sammy (Ian Samwell) and Guy Stevens were customers, Transat getting records they were unable to source elsewhere. Barrow recalls Transat as: "Just a basement with a few record sleeves on the wall and a couple of boxes of new LPs and singles – only American imports of soul and R&B. They had all the stuff on labels like Duke, Chess, King, as well as music on a label from, say, New Orleans as well – that basement was where I saw Barbara George's album on AFO. He didn't even have a sign outside, just Transat Imports painted on the wall with an arrow pointing to the basement. I bought The Impressions' LP *It's Alright*, Bobby Bland's *Call on Me* and James Brown's *Showtime* on Mercury there a week after it came out in the US. This music was the new thing at the time in the US R&B chart, which you could read in *Billboard* magazine, available at all the import newsagents shops in Soho."

Transat's creation myth begins in 1961 with Richard Hyde writing a letter to Stax Records in Memphis telling them how much he liked their records: they wrote back expressing amazement that anyone in England knew of their existence and then asked if he wanted to sell their records. Yes, please. If only life were so simple: Hyde worked for Imhoff's department store on New Oxford Street, London W1, managing the Melody Bar. Imhoff's seemingly allowed Hyde to run Transat Imports as a part-time offshoot: possibly because the department store had such an impressive stock of imports that having a specific outpost to unload new soul and blues imports every weekend made business sense. It also served in keeping youths of a certain class away from the department store where the British royal family reportedly brought their hi-fi equipment.

Imhoff's certainly were noted for regular supplies of imported records: a teenage Eric Clapton used to take the train from Surrey to London to visit Dobell's and Imhoff's, recalling of the latter, "the whole of ... [the] basement was devoted to jazz", while a young David Lashmar, later to found the mighty Beanos record store in Croydon, recalled how, in 1962, much to his amazement he came across Imhoff's window ablaze with a selection of Bo Diddley LP sleeves. Blues historian Paul Vernon got a job as a teenager in the Melody Bar in the late 1960s: "We got all the crazies coming in asking the usual nonsense record shop employees endure, alongside lots of very reasonable people looking for the week's number one 45, or the current hit LP or an oldie they had missed out on: Imhoff's had an extraordinary 45rpm back stock that would be worth a fortune on eBay today. I played willing fisherman for serious soul and R&B freaks with carefully researched lists of obscure 45s they were trying to track down.

"We also served the needs of Viv Stanshall [of the Bonzo Dog Band] the oddest fish I've ever encountered. He was genuinely, wholly, completely and wonderfully eccentric. He would appear in a baby blue crocheted one-piece jumpsuit with huge bright orange octagonal specs and a clockwork laugh machine in a knitted bag. His wants were simple: 'The Laughing Policeman' by Charles Penrose. We had that. He then told me the tragic tale of how Penrose came to obtain his wonderfully infectious laugh. It had been bestowed upon him by trauma, following the accidental drowning of his son. Stanshall often came at quiet times when he could listen to arcane recordings for whatever project was cooking inside of him, and we gave him the attention he deserved. He was a lovely man and a gentle soul with true wit."

Vernon arrived at Imhoff's after Hyde's departure, but agrees that the connection is likely to explain how Transat Imports managed to have new blues and soul records the very week they came out in the USA. Richard Williams, later to edit *Melody Maker*, visited Transat Imports as a teenager on a trip to London and recalled: "You have to remember that back then British fans of black American popular music still felt like members of a secret society. On a visit in 1964, during a day trip down to London, I remember seeing boxes full of stuff I wanted so badly that I could hardly breathe. I could only afford one 45, so I bought the Mar-Keys' 'Bush Bash'."

R. W. HYDE *Melody Bar Manager*
a jazz enthusiast with a wide knowledge of jazz and popular recordings. Once you have seen him performing on the bongos, you will know what we mean by 'enthusiast'.

Transat first began trading in late 1961, word of mouth letting the right people know it existed. Based in the basement of a store selling electrical goods (Chinatown then largely consisted not of restaurants but cheap electrical goods), Transat initially traded on Friday mornings only. Demand meant Transat soon began opening on Saturdays. And then Thursdays. At its peak, Transat may have, quite possibly, opened four days a week. Yet Transat always existed as something of a secret society, not easy to find, often closed and aimed at serving a cognoscenti who shared arcane knowledge surrounding records made by black Americans.

As word got out, the city's young rockers could soon be found there: Steve Marriott and Ronnie Lane made good use of Transat, while Keith Richards and Mick Jagger were such regulars that they would discuss what the best new 45s were with any fellow R&B fans who dropped in. The Savoy Brown Blues Band formed through its core members meeting at Transat, and Tom McGuinness, guitarist with Manfred Mann, recalls finding a John Lee Hooker LP there that he had long been after. He memorably described Lisle Street as, "lined with shops selling ex-army surplus electrical stuff. There would be all these men in grubby brown macs gazing longingly into the windows at radio valves and cathode ray tubes. The sort of men who a generation later would be looking in the porn shops".

Mick Taylor, the teenage guitar slinger who replaced Peter Green in John Mayall's Blues Breakers and then Brian Jones in The Rolling Stones, recalled a shop that was surely Transat in a 2015 interview: "There was a record shop in Lisle Street in Soho, near the old Flamingo Club. All the guitarists used to go there on a Saturday morning – Jeff Beck, Eric Clapton, loads of people. They used to import American blues albums and singles. One of the very first albums I ever bought (there) was B. B. King's *Live at the Regal*. That was very influential and an album that's dear to my heart."

Tony Russell, now a blues historian, went along as a youth and bumped into John Mayall while browsing, noting: "For someone just entering the secret world of blues fandom it was a revelation. Transat stocked many Chess, Excello and, I think, Vee-Jay 45s and LPs. I remember the impression made on me by the fiery red-and-yellow Lightnin' Slim *Rooster Blues* LP, a sleeve of which was mounted on the wall by the stairs down to the basement. On my next visit, in December, I succumbed and bought it."

Transat Imports appears to have operated for around five years, its closure possibly brought about by Hyde's liking for a drink. Brian Crane recalls Hyde openly drinking beer behind the counter on Saturday mornings and suffering from delirium tremens. So much so that some customers would whip records off the wall – the majority of stock being kept behind the counter – and hide them in their jackets, Hyde being too drunk to notice theft going on in front of him. Ian Saddler, later a record dealer himself, remembers how, when arriving to find the shop closed, he would go and seek Hyde out in a nearby pub: "Back then you had the afternoon closing of the pubs, and, if you wanted to drink between 3 p.m. and 5 p.m., you had to belong to a drinking club. Well, Hyde belonged to all of them and I would wander around them until I found him. There was a lady called Ann who ran a little record stall in Newport Court and, after Transat closed, I found a lot of their albums on her stall."

By 1967, when Godin opened Soul City in Covent Garden, a short walk away from Transat, this tiny basement record shop no longer existed, Hyde and the legend of Transat having vanished into the London ether.

Soul City

A quintessential British eccentric, Dave Godin (1936–2004) served as high priest to the British soul scene, his intense belief in R&B and animal rights marking him out from a Soho scene where fashion and hedonism ruled. Born in Peckham, London, the Blitz forced Godin's family to flee to Kent where he, a milkman's son, won a scholarship to Dartford Grammar School. As a student in the mid-1950s, he first heard R&B when Ruth Brown's 'Mama He Treats Your Daughter Mean' got played on an ice-cream parlour's jukebox (acquired, it seems, from a nearby US air force base).

The Ruth Brown record affected Godin deeply and he immediately set about sourcing this music and sharing it with others. One of these 'others' being fellow pupil Michael Philip Jagger. Godin did sit in on early Stones rehearsals before vocally refuting The Stones and all the other British bands who attempted to play black American music, Dave being nothing if not a purist. Meanwhile, Godin wrote a letter to Norman Jopling of *The Record Mirror*, taking him to task for not reviewing a new Bo Diddley album, which led to other R&B fans contacting him via post. "I suppose it's like being gay," Godin said. "Everybody thinks they're the only gay person in the world until they realise there's more out there."

Founding the Tamla-Motown Appreciation Society, Godin promoted the label's 45s (released via EMI) with a true believer's fervour. Writing a regular column in *Record Mirror* made sure he had Norman Jopling's and Vicki Warham's (producer of *Ready Steady Go*) ears. Back in Detroit, Gordy paid attention and, in 1964, invited Godin to oversee Motown's European operation: EMI were indifferent to the Motown recordings they were now issuing on their Stateside labels and they were unaware of how to promote R&B. Godin insisted EMI start issuing the 45s on the Tamla-Motown label – so building brand identity – and took The Supremes' 'Where Did Our Love Go' (1964) to Radio Caroline, the pirate station embracing soul when the BBC declined to do so. The rest, as they say, is history.

After the disastrous 1965 'Tamla-Motown Revue' UK tour, Godin left the Tamla-Motown label to open Soul City on Deptford High Street, London SE8,

(Soul City 45) Courtesy of Pete Wingfield.

a record shop and label that he ran with fellow aficionados, David Nathan and Robert Blackmore. After 18 months, the reality of operating a specialist record shop in south-east London – no tube, poor rail links, few local mods – forced Soul City's shift to Covent Garden where it opened at 17 Monmouth Street, London WC2. There, as a shop and record label, Soul City excelled at making sure often overlooked yet excellent 45s and LPs were available.

Teenage soul fan Tony Rounce recalls: "I knew about Soul City from adverts in magazines, but didn't go there until I heard Radio 1 DJ Mike Raven play 'A Piece of Gold' by Bobby 'Blue' Bland on his show and say that it wasn't going to be available as a 45 in the UK, but that [co-owner)] Dave Godin might stock it in Soul City. Mike's show went out on a Saturday and Sunday evening then. On the Monday morning I bunked off school, went to Soul City and purchased a copy. I also bought two long deleted UK 45s, 'Cry Cry Cry' by Bobby Bland, and Garnett Mimms' 'I'll Take Good Care of You' on my first visit there. As I recall, they were £1 each – more than twice the price of a regular UK 45 at the time.

"Soul City was a long shop, always fairly busy and coolly kitted out, as much of a meeting place as anything else and I made some very good friends there. It only sold soul – no reggae or pop, and no British-based soul artists – so no Geno Washington and Jimmy James, for example. It did sell some blues, mostly contemporary artists. Dave was a fan of Chicago blues and of Howlin' Wolf in particular."

Pete Wingfield, soon to become one of the UK's foremost session keyboardists, also shopped at Soul City: "Godin was a very intense, rather camp individual. I remember him being into Wilhelm Reich. He issued 'We the People' by Allen Toussaint on Soul City. The record bag with art nouveau lettering – that's very Godin, he always did things in style. *Greazee Soul*, the Billy Preston LP from 1969, was also on Soul City. Both as a shop and record label Soul City very much focused on what we called then 'New Wave Soul Music', the kind of songs that Georgie Fame was covering."

The tag 'New Wave Soul Music' was quickly discarded but, while running Soul City, Godin came up with the titles for two distinct R&B genres: 'northern soul' (to describe up-tempo soul records free of any James Brown funk influences that visitors from the north of England were requesting) and 'deep soul' (to suggest epic emotional ballads). Soul City, both shop and label, closed in the early 1970s, Godin being more of a devotee than a businessman.

Godin continued to serve as a soul missionary and, in the 1990s, Ace Records (whose founders had shopped at Soul City) hired him to compile and annotate the four-volume *Dave Godin's Deep Soul Treasures* CD series. These magnificent compilations attracted much acclaim and, in them, Godin saw his life's work coming together as he battled cancer, gathering what he believed to be the most intense soul ballads ever recorded.

Northern Souls

If 1965's 'Tamla-Motown Revue' found the British public indifferent to what Gordy called "the sound of young America", the Detroit label need not have fretted too much for the future: the Revue's influence rippled across the UK as true believers spread the word. "Keep the faith" was Godin's slogan for the cognoscenti, and so they did with soul stealthily taking hold, especially across the north of England. In Castleford, Yorkshire, Iain Scott, later to manage Our Price shops then found the Triple Earth record label, found soul increasingly serving as *the* soundtrack to teenage life: "The shop in Castleford was small but still had listening facilities (headphones) and was run by an enthusiastic couple. The town and area were heavy industry, in particular coal mining. I think this demonstrates how strong the independent record shops were back then that in somewhere like Castleford you could buy really good non-chart records. I actually bought my first two African albums from a record stall in Castleford – they were Cameroonian albums, not particularly great, but amazing that they were for sale in a mining town! I wonder how they got there?

"Musically, it was before the northern soul explosion, but the seeds were most definitely being sown. My friends were equally divided between mods and rockers and so weekends were either going on the back of scooters to dances at the local

Mecca, or on the back of motorbikes to speed trials. The music I bought here, usually in the company of my friends, reflected that split but I particularly remember Aretha Franklin's 'The Thrill Is Gone' on Atlantic, and Taj Mahal's 'Further on Down the Road' on Epic. This latter at least was approved by my mod peers who rarely deigned to openly shop but traded among themselves and through a network I could only guess at. 'Heaven Must Have Sent You' by The Elgins was a big tune back then. Friends of mine were already dealing in rare 45s for high prices – this was through word of mouth or ads placed in small soul fanzines.

"Clothes and dancing were very important to us. This one guy, he wasn't very good looking or anything, but he was a fabulous dancer and that earned him respect. We would go to the Mecca ballrooms and dance to soul records all night. That said, I was never a good dancer and I remember one night I was dancing and closed my eyes and when I opened them the girl I had been dancing with had moved on!"

In Birmingham, R&B aficionados flocked to The Diskery. Northern soul DJ Carl Dene noted, "If you went into another shop and asked for The Impressions they would say, 'What are you talking about?', but Diskery would have all the stuff on Stateside, on Motown. It was a real goldmine for records."

Blackpool teenager Ian Levine, who went on to become a leading northern soul DJ and pioneered the bulk importation of US 45s, caught the rare soul bug via Gary Wilde, "the guy who claims he was the first ever rare record dealer". Levine says, "He had a cigarette kiosk in Blackpool town centre in Victoria Street. He sold cigarettes and rare records, and all the mods would congregate outside his kiosk."

DJ Ian Dewhirst grew up in Bradford and recalls a market stall called Bostock's that sold 20 singles for a pound ("all American imports with no centres in them"). In Wolverhampton, Max Millward opened his first record shop in 1963, selling all kinds of music while specialising in northern soul. In Mansfield, Syd Booth's – "a legendary record store", states Wigan Casino DJ Kev Roberts, "one of the biggest indies in the North" – employed Brian Selby and John Bratton. These two modish record obsessives supplied the hottest new releases for Roberts and other local youths who were unwittingly building what would soon become known as 'northern soul'.

Former miner Brian Selby left Syd Booth's to set up in nearby Nottingham, founding Selectadisc in 1966 as a market stall. Shifting from stall to shop, Selby became a major northern soul retailer – manufacturing bootleg 45s to meet growing demand – and Selectadisc flourished as Nottingham's foremost record shop.

Meanwhile, in Manchester, the Twisted Wheel Club served as genesis for the northern soul scene while The Spin Inn on Cross Street ensured that DJs and dancers had access to hot wax from Detroit and Memphis. The northern mods lacked the profile of their London counterparts – no Georgie Fame or Bank Holiday battles to boast about – but in their dedication to R&B they obeyed Godin's mantra and kept the faith.

Amphetamine Narcissists

In London in 1967, teenage mod Ian Hingle began working at the Fulham branch of the Musicland chain: "I started at the North End Road Musicland and it was tiny. I was 16. 'Ride Your Donkey' by The Tennors was massive. I learned to dance to 'Ride Your Donkey'. I loved soul music and we sold a lot of that. Motown and stuff like that. Maybe a hundred copies a week of a hit. Back then you didn't hear soul music on the radio so you had to hear it at parties – people would come in and say, 'I heard this tune at a party' and you would try and guess what song it was."

At the same time, the original mods were moving on: Guy Stevens would stay at Island but now worked closely with rock bands Mott The Hoople, Procul Harem and Free, while Jeff Dexter became resident DJ at hippie clubs The Middle Earth and The Round House. Stevens and Dexter's shift away from the music that soundtracked mod effectively mirrors the decline of mod – what had been initially a hip, exclusive London-based tribe saw its influence spread until the music and gear they so passionately championed became part of young

British life. Mecca ballrooms across the UK now played soul, while formerly exclusive fashions became available on every high street.

By the mid-1960s, The Who and Small Faces ranked among the UK's most popular rock bands and, as Franc Roddam's 1979 movie *Quadrophenia* gruellingly demonstrates, many new mods were amphetamine narcissists, brats with no sense of individuality in dress, music or thought. Noting this, the mod pioneers grew their hair, swapped suits for kaftans, amphetamines for acid, and R&B for psychedelic rock. Goings would soon get weird and, inevitably, it appeared that the weird liked nothing better than to go record shopping.

Chapter 8

Tomorrow Never Knows: Psych Shops Take Shape

Musicland, One Stop and Town Records offer exclusive American psychedelic imports. Harrods opens the Way In boutique. DJ Jeff Dexter survives a hippie pogrom at the Middle Earth club. A Clockwork Orange is filmed in The Chelsea Drugstore. Cameos from John Peel, Elton John, Stanley Kubrick and The Moody Blues.

Blame it on The Beatles: as soon as Paul McCartney admitted to taking LSD, every teenage pop fan wanted to get dosed, and 1967's fabled 'summer of love' came into being. By then, LSD-spiked sounds had illuminated many of rock and pop's most singular recordings, but the closest that most teens got to hallucinating was holding their breath while listening to Jimi Hendrix burble about being "ex-per-i-en-ced". The psychedelic idyll would be brief but, in spicing popular culture with mind-altering drugs and elements of Asian culture, it was extremely influential. Especially in the UK where pop music was regarded by many as little more than noisy music hall, a showbiz shtick to con kids out of their pocket money. Psychedelia added elements of arty esoterica and other-worldliness, thus ensuring everyone over 30 scratched their scalp and asked, *What the hell are they on about?*

"Palaces of Liberation and Enlightenment"

The more things changed, the more they in many ways stayed the same: psych rockers stuck to music industry convention in terms of the deals they cut; prices for product remained set; and fans trudged into WHSmith or the Co-Op to purchase *Freak Out* or *Sergeant Pepper's* (both 1967 UK releases). Still, there was something in the air, and spiky counterculture types felt that buying an LP by The Doors, The Mothers or Soft Machine from the 'squares' at HMV or Boots was a betrayal of the freak flag and all it flew for. Thus, alongside head shops and vegetarian cafés, a new breed of record shop began opening in the late 1960s: staffed by hirsute youths and loaded with West Coast import LPs, the psychedelic rock shop signalled a portal to a golden dawn.

Initially, the psych record shops followed the jazz and soul record shops by setting up in London's West End, encouraging a sense of elitism among habitué, and competing to bring in imports that no other record shop could offer. The UK may have been home to The Beatles, the Stones and Cream, but the American music industry, being far larger and, back then, quicker to realise the potential of psychedelic profits, released greater numbers of albums. Indeed, considering how inept the likes of Blue Cheer and The Fugs were, it appeared that any young White American male with a guitar and long hair got a record

Hendrix haunt: One Stop Records on South Molton Street. Photo by Eric Hayes.
Courtesy of International Times.

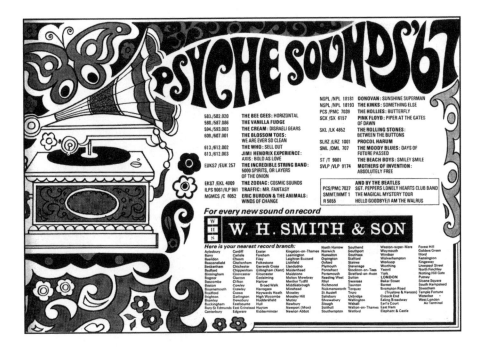

contract. Also, the US freak scene, with its access to huge amounts of dope and acid, existed on far wilder frontiers than the 'love-ins' that Chelsea's pop princes endorsed. The psychedelic record shops, blasting loud rock LPs full of fizzy guitar solos and obtuse lyrics, therefore acted as a matrix signalling the way into a new world, one so much brighter and groovier than the monochrome one we were forced to inhabit.

And things did start getting genuinely weird. Ian Hingle, formerly a teenage mod, remembers how strange he found the hippies when he was transferred from Musicland's London Fulham branch to the Portobello Road shop:

"Musicland in Portobello Road was very hip. I worked there one Christmas and there was this white geezer with dreadlocks who used to walk around with a block of ganja. No one had dreads back then. He used to walk in to say, 'Hello', and put this block of ganja on the counter! New Riders of the Purple Sage and Isaac Hayes' *Hot Buttered Soul* were the two big records in the shop when I worked there."

Chris Wellard's Jazz & Blues Record Shop in New Cross (see Chapter 3) attracted hordes of hippies after DJ John Peel let listeners know Wellard stocked exclusive imports. Wellard found his new clientele stinking of marijuana but, for the most part, very well-behaved. Wellard, always a man of the political left, then began stocking underground publications. "At that time there was the underground press, *Oz*, *Gandulph Garden*, etc., and we used to sell these magazines," he says. "On several occasions the Old Bill bought copies. God knows what they gleaned from them." Max Reinhardt, now BBC Radio 3's presenter of experimental music on 'Late Junction' but then a teenager in

Wembley, cautiously ventured into the new psych shops: "The thing about these record shops as a teenager was you would enter one and suddenly you were in this 'groovy' place. Full of light and sound and mystery. And, back then, your parents were excluded in so many ways. They were exciting places to visit. I rejoiced in the shops as palaces of liberation and culture and enlightenment!"

Psychedelic culture's potency certainly seduced many: Cliff White, an R&B enthusiast, and Steve Barrow, a ska-loving mod, separately embraced psychedelic rock with the help of jazz cigarettes circa 1967. White admits that he never even liked The Beatles until he began hallucinating! Yet the vast majority of Londoners – and those living across the rest of the UK – kept calm and carried on living a life that involved nothing stronger than pints of bitter and a packet of Woodbines. That The Beatles' psychedelic hymn, 'Strawberry Fields Forever' (1967), was denied the UK No. 1 chart position by Engelbert Humperdink indicates that things weren't changing quite as radically as some now suggest. Indeed, the soundtracks of *My Fair Lady* (1964) and *The Sound of Music* (1965) continued to outsell almost all pop and rock LPs.

The psych record shops, in their sense of 'them versus us', acted as meeting points for youths who wanted to engage with the nascent counterculture. Here the shock of the new – *sounds, ideas, movements, fashions, beliefs, politics, drugs* – could all be openly discussed with people who understood and shared what were, to outsiders, bizarre, subversive passions. And here the seeds of much of 1970s rock culture were sewn.

Musicland

How Musicland's owners, Lee Gopthal and Chris Blackwell, established the hippest record shop in Christendom when they were rubbing shoulders with Jamaican immigrants rather than the psychedelic aristocracy remains a mystery. Perhaps they just got lucky with the right staff. Or Gopthal might have surmised that the hippies now gathering in Ladbroke Grove, London, wanted shops catering to their musical tastes, just as the Jamaicans did. Mick Farren, the British counterculture Robespierre, first heard The MC5's *Kick Out the Jams* (1969) in Ladbroke Grove's Musicland, the LP's incendiary contents causing him to tremble in his biker boots.

Opening a Musicland in Soho's Berwick Street proved to be the right record shop at the right time. Initially run by Simon Stable aka Count Simon de la Bedoyere (who had previously worked at the Portobello Road Musicland), the Berwick Street Musicland prided itself on stocking imported American albums. Back then, US album releases often happened months in advance of UK releases or, in many cases, the album only ever received a US release. Jazz, blues and soul shops had long been reliant on US imports and, as a counterculture took shape in the USA, hippies and hipsters wanted to hear the sounds setting San Francisco and Los Angeles alight. Jeff Dexter, by now chief DJ at the Middle Earth club (43 King Street, Covent Garden, London WC2), became a regular customer, needing psychedelic tunes for enthusiastic ravers: "I started noticing the change towards what would be called 'hippie' in 1966, both in the clothes being worn and the music coming in from America. Obviously, once LSD arrived it had a huge influence. Musicland in Berwick Street was the best shop for West Coast imports so I started buying from them. The shop's managers were Ian Brown and John Gillespie. Gillespie went on to become a great sidekick of Seymour Stein [American record label executive and founder of Sire Records] – Seymour used to shop in Musicland all the time. That's where he got his info on what was hip. Middle Earth opened at the beginning of August 1967 and they had asked me to come and join them, but they couldn't pay my regular DJ fare. I did a couple of nights with John Peel there, but it wasn't until Tiles went under that I became a resident DJ. John was a very nice bloke. I met him when he'd just got off the pirate ship, *The Perfumed Garden* had come off air and he was about to start at Middle Earth. I really liked what he played, it was very different. Although, we didn't always agree on music: he once said to me 'Why do you play that awful Blue Beat music?' [laughs] He never could dance – I think his jumpers got in the way! But he was a very smart guy, very smart.

"At Middle Earth I would play blues and boogie and psychedelic pop and rock. But I'd still play lots of R&B because R&B is the best music for dancing to. By then lots of people were into idiot dancing. They were into free expression and, unfortunately, that invaded the dance floor.

The Middle Earth club was forced to move to The Roundhouse in Chalk Farm, London, after the King Street venue suffered a brutal attack: tabloid scare stories, aligned with middle England's condemnation of the long-haired dandies, fuelled a visceral hatred of hippies, and Covent Garden's porters came mob-handed one summer evening in July 1968. Dexter explains: "The porters attacked Middle Earth because the police had just removed two children from the club. They were the children of friends of ours and had come with their parents, but the police told the porters that we were crucifying children in the club in some mad orgy. So, all these market porters attacked the club. We tried to hold the doors shut but they smashed their way in ... forced us to take refuge in the box office. An axe came through the box office door while I had my back to it. It was terrifying. There was blood spilt but, luckily, no one was killed. We were on the phone to the police describing how the porters were destroying the club, trying to kill us, and it took them 20 minutes to arrive when the station was only a couple of minutes' walk away. By the time they got there the club was demolished and no one was around to be arrested. That was the end of Middle Earth in Covent Garden. After that we shifted to The Roundhouse. I was the DJ there for Implosion, which was sponsored by Musicland."

One Stop Records

Musicland may have ruled the roost in 1967, but fierce competition came when Mike Ashwell and Brian Gatland, two hip, young entrepreneurs, sensed a gap in the market. They set about filling this by opening branches of One Stop Records in South Molton Street in London's Mayfair, then a desirable residence for the new rock aristocracy who patronised the area's exclusive clubs and art galleries, and in Richmond, the leafy West London suburb with a musical connection due to it hosting the National Jazz and Blues Festival alongside a thriving live music scene focused on The Station Hotel, Eel Pie Island and The Bull's Head pubs.

One Stop Records shops were stocked with a strong selection of contemporary releases with the emphasis on rock, blues and jazz. However, what made the shops famous was Ashwell and Gatland's determination to get hold of American imports before any other retailer. This made them the pre-eminent shop for the hip rock fan: John Peel would often mention on his radio show how he sourced some of the records he was playing, giving shout-outs to Musicland and Chris Wellard's Jazz & Blues Record Shop. One Stop Records became Peel's favourite; he once detailed how he had travelled to London Airport with the store's manager to ensure that he got his hands on Captain Beefheart's *Strictly Personal* as soon as it came through customs.

Such praise meant that One Stop Records shops were achingly hip, and Ashwell would boast, "One Stop brought the record business from out behind the fridges." A great exaggeration, but his shops certainly made others like NEMS and HMV look very old-fashioned. Success saw the partners open a large branch in Dean Street, Soho, London W1, very close to Musicland, and a branch in Manchester's Gateway House. Chris Blackwell, founder of Island Records, invested in One Stop and made sure it catered to the hip rock and folk clientele that his label then focused upon.

Jon Newey, a music-obsessed Streatham teenager, moved on from shopping at Dobell's to One Stop Records and Musicland in 1967 as he followed his peers in embracing rock's radical new underground: "I'd buy *International Times* regularly and both Musicland and One Stop would take out little ads listing all the imports they had. I discovered One Stop Records in South Molton Street, close to Bond Street, in 1967. It was an absolute revelation, with all kinds of psychedelic imports, blues and jazz. At this time, very few psychedelic records had been released in the UK. I'd been to the 14-hour 'Technicolour Dream' in April 1967 at Alexandra Palace, which was one of the first major psychedelic happenings in the UK, a kind of gathering of the tribes, the British underground first coming together in all its hippie threads, and I was spellbound by this new music. Yet at the time it was very difficult to buy what we referred to as 'underground music'. You'd read about the Mothers, Velvet Underground, Grateful Dead, Jefferson

Airplane and Country Joe and the Fish in the underground paper *International Times* [IT] as well as the New York paper *Village Voice*, which I used to buy on Charing Cross Road at the Russian newsagents near Dobell's."

"I had spotted mention of The Velvet Underground in *IT* and their name alone intrigued me. One Stop had one copy left. I asked to hear it first in their listening booth before I bought it – imports were expensive, 32/6 compared to 22/6 for a British album – and the first tune I heard was 'Sunday Morning' which I thought sounded like The Mamas & The Papas, then 'Waiting for the Man' which was better but sounded like The Stones. I was about to say forget it when 'Venus in Furs' came on with its screeching electric violin and parent-baiting lyrics and then 'Run Run Run' and all that dissonant feedback came through the headphones and I thought, 'Yes! I'm having that!' So I was one of the first people in the UK to own the original US pressing of the 'Banana' album in mono.

"A week or so later I bought the Pink Floyd's *Piper at the Gates of Dawn*, which is still one of the most extraordinary albums ever made and, in summer 1967, sounded like a door into a mystical, new tomorrow, a million miles away from the grey straitjacket of everyday mid-1960s life. From here I ventured down to the UFO and Middle Earth clubs and got turned on to all this new music by John Peel and Jeff Dexter. Hearing this great new music, I wanted to get it before my friends. Back then it was really something to have the new releases by the best new bands before everyone else."

One Stop Records – named after the small US cash-and-carry wholesalers who supplied many an American mom and pop store – counted Jimi Hendrix as a customer, he then living in Mayfair, and the West End battle between the hippie record shops intensified with Musicland and One Stop sniping at one another, both in advertisements and across the counter. The West End battle between the hippie record shops intensified, with Musicland and One Stop Records sniping at one another, both in advertisements and across the counter. *International Times*, the counterculture bible, conducted a survey of London's West End record shops in 1969. They criticised One Stop Records for its expensive imports and concluded that Musicland offered the best selection and prices. Yet as the decades shifted, One Stop overtook Musicland as the West End record shop for rock's aristocracy. As Gopthal owned Musicland and his former business partner now controlled One Stop – the Gopthal/Blackwell partnership ended in 1971 – the competition might just have been personal. Blackwell turned out to be the superior record man, so it's no surprise that his chain won out. Not that the groovers who flocked to these shops knew such shenanigans were under way.

Psychedelic Shacks

The psychedelic shack was, so The Temptations informed the world, "where it's *at*". Inevitably, several quickly opened across London, and Dexter recalls, "Town Records on the King's Road at the bump before World's End. They had hot American imports and the owner of that shop is the same guy who put Marianne Faithful back in the studio for the *Broken English* album [in 1979].

Newey agrees, stating that Town Records was: "… a hip shop for imports and new music in the late 1960s. You'd walk in and the main part of the shop featured mainstream music and then you went downstairs and it was full of folk, blues and underground music. I bought Love's *Forever Changes* there the week it came out. The guy running the downstairs department had a little light show going with liquid slides projected on the walls – on a Saturday afternoon!"

Indica on Southampton Row, London – a bookshop specialising in Beat literature, abstract art, experimental film and avant-garde jazz records – was opened by writer Barry Miles (with finance via Paul McCartney), and Newey headed there: "I remember buying the Fugs there," he says, "and hearing Albert Ayler there for the first time. It didn't stock a lot of albums but what it had was pretty intriguing."

Oddly, the Apple Boutique (on Baker Street, London) sold clothes and hippie paraphernalia but never stocked records. The Magic Phonograph, a very small shop specialising in "underground sounds" (according to an *International Times* report), is remembered fondly by some. Even Harrods opened a 'psychedelic' boutique called Way In "for the groovy chick". Alongside a resident DJ and juice bar, Way In sold records and designer clothes and shoes. Painted a garish purple, Way In had London psych band Tomorrow play at the boutique's summer 1967 opening. While Way In might appear to exist as the antithesis of counterculture values, for a few years (at least) the boutique did very well, with pop royalty rubbing silk shoulders with aristocrats and jet-setters, all intent on sampling swinging London in the comfort to which they were accustomed.

Time Out's debut issue in 1968 listed Musicland's Berwick Street shop as London's No. 1 record retailer, and a year later *International Times*' October 1969 survey of London record shops felt the same. The *International Times*' survey focused largely on those selling psychedelic rock while disparaging Keith Prowse's shops ("more adept at providing tickets than selling records") and praising Dave Godin's Soul City. The writer determines Musicland as the best rock shop for *International Times* readers, noting it has 1500 imports, welcomes customers to listen to them, and supplies the following clubs: Implosion, Country Club, Freakeasy, Bag O' Nails and "the belated Middle Earth".

Beyond stocking the hippest sounds on earth, the psych shops made sure that the role of shop assistant became – at least in rock record stores – a highly desirable and venerated job. Where the jazz shops had often employed introverts who obsessed over catalogue numbers and recording session minutiae, the psych rock shop staff, young and fashionable, served as gatekeepers to the new releases from rock's gods, lending a glamour unmatched anywhere else in retail to stacking and racking vinyl. As minimum wage jobs went, this one attracted customer envy and admiration, rather than the contempt shop assistants too often received, as well as access to freebies/pilfering. One Stop's founders would shift from behind the counter to become record company insiders, and certain savvy staff would follow this path over the following decades. Yet, in 1969, the experience of serving up the counterculture's most prized artefacts was reward enough, and a soon to be superstar from Pinner, Reginald Dwight, has never stopped waxing lyrical over his time as a record clerk.

Elton John's True Adventures in Musicland and One Stop Records

Elton John is impossibly famous for many things. That said, the time he spent working behind the counter at Musicland's Berwick Street branch has possibly not attracted quite the attention his activities as a musician and entertainer have. This was in early 1970 and Elton, a devout record collector since childhood, immensely enjoyed the experience. In 1973 he told *Creem* magazine about his time at Musicland: "Just before I made it – about the time the *Elton John* album had been released – I was doing nothing. Two of my friends, who had an import record shop in London, gave me a job there for eight weeks. And I had a ball. If I wasn't doing what I do now, the best thing I could imagine would be to have a record store somewhere and just serve behind the counter. Records fascinate me. I could just watch a record going round and round for hours, that's what I used to do when I was a kid. I'd watch it go around; I couldn't believe it. And the label … any record that had a good label was an instant winner. That for me is magic. I mean, tapes are alright to take around with you, but there's no magic in watching a tape cassette."

In 2016, Elton spoke again of the experience on BBC Radio 6 Music's *The First Time*, noting: "In 1970 and '71 there was a record shop, Musicland, on Berwick Street, which imported records and some friends of mine worked there. And every Saturday, if I was off, I would go and work behind the counter and I absolutely loved it. I was just fascinated by what people bought – 78s, 45s, EPs, LPs, 8-tracks. As long as it's music I'm totally into it."

Elton remained a devotee of record shops even when he was the world's most popular rocker, regularly returning to his favourite London shops to seek out new releases. Once Musicland's Berwick Street shop went into decline, he followed his friends (shop managers Ian Brown and John Gillespie) to One Stop Records. Fifteen-year-old Danny Baker, having scored a job at One Stop in 1972, often found Elton dropping in to buy records, never encumbered by bodyguards, managers or other such trappings. Occasionally, Elton would help out behind the counter, leaving bemused shoppers with "You'll never believe who served me today" stories.

As well as Elton, Baker served Marc Bolan, Rod Stewart and Mick Jagger, while Gillespie kicked Queen out of the shop when Freddie and co. came flouncing in demanding their debut album be played. Once Brown and Gillespie moved on, One Stop Records stopped being special and became part of the Harlequin Records chain. Baker disliked his new bosses and only remained an employee long enough to fleece them of dozens of LPs, which he flogged in South London pubs.

Elton also moved on, but never stopped record shopping. During the late 1970s, he regularly double-parked his Bentley on the King's Road in London and popped into an Our Price shop where he would purchase every 45 in the Top 40. When based in the USA, he became so familiar at Tower Records' Sunset Strip store he would later claim that he was the "best customer in Tower's history". In the late 1990s, one of Elton's record shopping trips in London made headlines when he convinced Victoria Beckham to enter the Virgin Megastore on Oxford Street with him to buy new releases. 'Posh' found the experience a strange one – used as she was to being cocooned behind security guards and kept away from the public – while Elton got on with the important business of buying music.

When Elton was introduced to Prince Buster at a London awards ceremony in 2004, he yelped with joy and said, "I used to sell Prince Buster records when I worked in a record shop long before I was famous!"

The Chelsea Drugstore
Opening on the King's Road, London, in 1968, The Chelsea Drugstore was a three-floor chrome and neon complex styled on Le Drugstore on Boulevard St Germain in Paris, and stood as a symbol of a brave new world of psych

Alex in Melodica: the Chelsea Drug Store as featured in A Clockwork Orange.

and commerce. Open 16 hours a day, 7 days a week, The Chelsea Drugstore matched the boutique Granny Takes a Trip in being emblematic of the King's Road's achingly hip status. Mick Jagger, very much a dedicated follower of fashion, would eulogise the emporium on 'You Can't Always Get What You Want' when he sings of going to The Chelsea Drugstore to get a prescription filled. Many a stoned Stones fan must have wondered about what Mick and the Mr Jimmy he mentions meeting there were really scoring. And was Mr Jimmy actually Jimi Hendrix? Predictably I always wonder if Mick and Mr Jimmy/Jimi find time to get a vinyl prescription at The Chelsea Drugstore's record bar.

Paradoxically, I know both a little and a lot about The Chelsea Drugstore's record bar. A little, because this fluorescent vinyl cave has vanished from history, leaving no documentation about who established it, worked there, and so on. Jon Newey suggests it was not particularly memorable: "When it opened the stock was good, plenty of underground albums. But after that it was never so good again. The stock got less adventurous so I stuck with Musicland and One Stop." Certain Chelsea residents were appalled by The Chelsea Drugstore's dishevelled clientele and campaigned for it to be closed, which duly happened in May 1971.

A short existence, then, but a memorable one due to The Drugstore appearing as Melodica in Stanley Kubrick's *A Clockwork Orange* (1971), and this is why I also know a lot about it. Here, Malcolm McDowell wanders in, purchases an album of Beethoven's Ninth Symphony and, indulging in what then was possibly a regular social more for the hip young aristos who frequented The Drugstore, picks up two *devotchkas* (girls) for a little of what he memorably describes as "the old in-and-out".

This scene was shot in late 1970 and, while *A Clockwork Orange* is set in the near future, Kubrick chose to film The Chelsea Drugstore as it stood, only adding a Top 10 of pop stars in neon who come not from the charts but from author Anthony

127

Burgess's imagination (including Johnny Zhivago, Heaven Seventeen and The Sparks). Kubrick's dystopian vision is of a brutalist London, all vulgar emporiums and concrete cityscape. Surely, he seems to be hinting, no sentient being could shop *here*.

Kubrick's attention to detail ensures viewers get to see what The Drugstore stocked: Tim Buckley's *Lorca* is prominently displayed alongside albums by The Incredible String Band, Pink Floyd, Canned Heat, The Beatles, John Fahey, Neil Young, Johnny Winter and Rare Earth, all favourites of London's hippie elite. A poster of Mick Jagger in *Ned Kelly* is likely to have been the shop's nod towards Chelsea's very own Satanic majesty and Drugstore habitué – although it might be a Kubrick in-joke considering that Jagger was, initially, considered for the role of Alex before Stanley came on board. The soundtrack to *2001: A Space Odyssey* is surely Kubrick referencing himself (though that film's popularity with acid eaters means that said soundtrack could well have been stocked at The Drugstore).

The prominent cover of *Missa Luba*, a Congolese mass, is Kubrick acknowledging *If*, the film that launched McDowell to stardom, as music from the album appeared on *If*'s soundtrack. There's also the eponymous debut album by long forgotten London hard rockers Stray, and promo photos of the unforgotten Free. While the stock seems conventional, the setting is of interest: the record bar appears to snake around a circular passage, alongside a pharmacist and magazine retailer, Optical art decorates the central booth. The atmosphere is that of an air-conditioned nightmare, a bad trip. No wonder Kubrick, a master of alienation, felt that The Chelsea Drugstore fitted his cinematic vision better than any set he could create.

A Clockwork Orange provides the best visual detail available of what an achingly hip psych shop full of albums (45s or pop/easy listening albums are not visible in the film) looked like in the late 1960s and early 1970s. As Kubrick – whose films are laced with unease, cynicism and paranoia – never held any truck with the utopian fantasies psychedelic gurus spun, his bleak vision proved remarkably concise. When the 1970s began, hippie dreams would die and nihilism reign. In 2017, The Chelsea Drugstore's once striking glass and aluminium building is now a McDonald's restaurant. And so it goes.

Threshold Records: The Moody Blues' Suburban Psych Shops

Where The Beatles failed dismally as retailers, their Brummie contemporaries, The Moody Blues, succeeded. Critically derided and wildly unfashionable, The Moodys are among the most successful British rock groups and even today retain a loyal US audience. Naff as their concept albums and soft rock ballads might seem, the best Moody psych pop is a baroque reminder of days when mellotrons suggested altered states. Moreover, the Moodys remain the only band to have owned and operated a chain of British record shops: surely the old fellas deserve a Brit Award or a Mojo simply for this remarkable feat?

In 1969, following The Beatles' example of Apple Records, the Moodys set up their own record label, Threshold. While plans for Threshold to sign new talent didn't get far, the band did open Threshold record shops in Andover, Chichester, Cobham, Birmingham, Surrey and Swindon. Dosing the home counties with psych rock shops must have seemed a radical retail gesture, and the excitement generated at each store's official opening with the band appearing – all bouffant hair-dos, walrus moustaches and Carnaby Street togs – brought a splash of psych pop mania to the suburbs.

The 1970s found the Moodys ditching their engaging kookiness for Mantovani-style gush, while the Threshold shops also became increasingly opaque: Surrey and Swindon possibly not being the best place to sell Sly Stone and Silver Apples LPs. The Moodys' Cobham Threshold also served as headquarters for the band's fan club and it remained open until the early twenty-first century but, by then, both band and record shop existed to serve audiences more desirous of Ovaltine than euphoria.

If the Moodys made the only attempt to open a psych chain, it was largely because there was little interest in the new rock music beyond London. Admittedly, UK cities with large student populations found a handful of psychedelic record shops (and head shops) opening. When Beggars Banquet record shop and label founder Martin Mills was a student at Oxford University in the late 1960s, he remembers Sunshine Records opening and providing all the albums a young, long-haired lover of underground rock could want but, further north, record shops found little demand for Moby Grape and Electric Prunes LPs, with imported R&B 45s commanding far greater demand. Millers, the Cambridge musical instrument and records shop (see Chapter 1), may have been a formal emporium, but it's where the youths who became Pink Floyd did their learning, huddling in the listening booths to study the new Beatles 45, scratching down lyrics and chords as the shop assistant played it over and over. As Floyd's main man Syd Barrett was even placed second in a competition to dance the twist which was hosted by Millers, it might be fair to surmise that East Anglia's most noted music shop helped prepare the way for much freaky dancing to come.

"For some reason the mod and rocker tribes lasted longer up north than down south," says Iain Scott, who lived in a Yorkshire mining town before heading south. "In the late 1960s mod was still very big up there. There was no hippie activity – anyone who came out as a hippie left for London pretty quickly." Scott notes that his contemporaries primarily bought records they could dance to, not something a Jefferson Airplane LP encouraged. In the north of England people bought the new Beatles LPs but considered their hippie vogue as just another odd fashion from the smoke. In Liverpool the NEMS stores never allowed shop assistants to wear kaftans and love beads, instead remaining resolutely traditional.

Something that no one in UK record retail foresaw as the 1970s began was how Musicland and One Stop Records would soon be effortlessly outmanoeuvred by a gawky, upper-class teenager with little interest in music but with a burning desire to do business, *anyway anyhow*. At the dawn of 1971, he opened a new record shop above Shelley's Shoes on Oxford Street, London W1, appropriating the psych shops' spirit – reeking of incense and marijuana, serving free lentils, banning pop and easy listening – while aiming to make the hippie experience more student union than Chelsea pad. Virgin Records had landed and, almost overnight, nothing would be the same again.

Chapter 9

The Rock Shop Cometh: Virgin, Andy's and Beggars Take Over

By 1970 rock music ruled the charts and rock stars enjoyed iconic status. Virgin and Andy's follow suit by opening rock record shop chains. In Earl's Court Beggars Banquet offers a basement of quadrophonic LPs. Woolworths returns to dominate the pop 45 market. Richard Branson, Andy Gray and Martin Mills reflect on how they built empires. Cameos from Danny Baker, Peter Grant, Horace Panter, Gaye Advert and Gary Numan.

If the '60s had offered up heady optimism the '70s began with a bad hangover as the world's most popular band engaged in a bitter split. No matter, the music The Beatles had gifted the world grew at a remarkable rate: rock festivals drew hundreds of thousands, weekly newspapers (*NME, Melody Maker, Sounds, Record Mirror*) devoted to studying every rock star utterance enjoyed huge circulations and all the while rock albums shifted millions and millions of units. The Elvis era had been one where 45s far outsold LPs but The Beatles changed that, as they changed everything, and by 1970 the likes of Led Zeppelin and Rory Gallagher were refusing to issue singles. Dansette, the portable record player designed for British teenagers to stack their 45s, went into liquidation that year so ushering in the era of the rock album.

UK record shops were awash with money but, as the new decade began, none of them was the right fit for this vast new rock audience. One Stop and Musicland were too hip and too elitist, while the Harlequin chain was only a step above Woolies and Boots, not the kind of shops students wanted to be seen in. Three young English men recognised gaps in record retail and the potential for profit. As new money replaced old, this trio rolled out the rock record shop and all they touched turned to gold.

Virgin Records
Today, Richard Branson is more famous than the pop/rock stars whose careers he launched, a perma-tanned billionaire buccaneer who now wants to fly us to the moon.

Branson (born 1950) left a top public school aged 15 desperate to make his mark. Inspired by the energy of the nascent youth culture exploding around him, he founded *Student* magazine aged 17. *Student* got publicity – right from the start Richard wanted the media's attention – but struggled to sell copies and Branson, keen to find a way to generate income, seized upon selling discount rock LPs. In his autobiography, *Losing My Virginity* (1998), Branson notes: "One thing I knew from everyone who came in to chat or work for us was that they spent a good deal of money buying records. We had the record player on constantly and everyone rushed out to get the latest Rolling Stones, Bob Dylan, or Jefferson

VIRGIN RECORDS

Above: The 1970s dawn and so does our first shop. I had to do the live window displays personally.

Left: Pillows. Headphones. Music. Relaxed listening and free love in our first shop.

Hippie headquarters: Virgin Records, Notting Hill, early 1970s.

Airplane album the day it was released. There was tremendous excitement about music: it was political; it was anarchic; it summed up the young generation's dream of changing the world. And I also noticed that people who would never dream of spending as much as 40 shillings on a meal would not hesitate to spend 40 shillings buying the latest Dylan album. The more obscure the albums were, the more they cost and the more they were treasured."

Branson goes on to state that, although the British government had abolished the Retail Price Maintenance Agreement, none of the UK's shops were offering discounted records. *Student* magazine needed greater revenue streams so he set up a mail order service offering discount rock albums. The first advertisement ran in what would be the final issue of *Student* and it brought in more mail and money than anything else ever previously featured in the magazine. The kids wanted records – *cheap records!* – and Branson set about selling them. Guessing that students would buy records from Virgin at 35 shillings if WHSmith was selling them for 39 shillings, Virgin Mail Order began handing out leaflets on Oxford Street and outside concerts. In January 1971, a post office workers strike nearly ruined the start-up company and forced them to find a shop to sell stock from.

That year, Branson found an empty shop space above a Shelley's shoe store in Oxford Street and opened the first Virgin Records shop. Initially this was seen as a quick fix, yet from here Branson would launch a revolution in UK record retail. The Oxford Street Virgin shop was different from other British record shops: it had sofas and beanbags for customers to lounge on, headphones for listening to albums, copies of *NME* and *Melody Maker* for browsing, even free coffee to drink. Branson writes: "In 1971 music retail was dominated by WHSmith and John Menzies, both of which were dull and formal. The record departments were generally downstairs and they were staffed by people in drab brown or blue uniforms who appeared to have no interest in music. Customers chose their records from the shelves, bought them and left within ten minutes. The shops were unwelcoming: there was little sympathetic service and prices were high. Although rock music was very exciting, none of the feeling of excitement or even vague interest filtered through to the shops that sold the records ... None of our friends felt at home in record shops: they were just rather functional places where they had to go to buy their favourite records. We wanted the Virgin shop to be an extension of *Student*: a place where people could meet and listen to records together; somewhere where they weren't simply encouraged to dash in, buy the record and leave. We wanted to stay longer, chat to the staff, and really get into which records they were going to buy."

Danny Baker, then working nearby at One Stop Records on Dean Street, recalled in his autobiography the first Virgin as: "A tiny, fairly ramshackle space with threadbare carpet and covers of deeply underground LPs pinned to the walls as well as the one thing its rivals couldn't sell: illicit bootleg recordings of groups like Crosby, Stills and Nash, Led Zeppelin and Deep Purple. Hirsute old heads sat about under humungous headphones and the air was thick with cigarette smoke of dubious legality. This then was the newly opened Virgin Records; the scruffy runt of the early seventies Hip Vinyl Triangle."

The scruffy runt would quickly outperform its chic competitors and Branson, who never pretended to possess any musical knowledge, surrounded himself with people who did. His youthful associates advised him to concentrate on rock albums and to avoid 45s (pop/glam/soul/reggae being treated with contempt by the youths who purchased prog/metal) and easy listening ("the Andy Williams rule"). While this attitude reeks of rock snobbery, it proved sound advice: in 1970 Woolworths, having wised up to the huge number of records now being sold across the UK, had re-entered the record trade with a vengeance, stocking Top 30 singles, compilation LPs, ex-chart LPs (at mid-price) and nine different budget LP label lines: Hallmark, Camden, Contour, Pickwick, Marble Arch, Warwick, K-Tel, Music for Pleasure (MFP) and Classics for Pleasure (CFP). Woolies quickly became the UK's largest seller of Top 30 singles while also dominating the easy listening/budget LP market. Virgin instead focused on battling it out with the rapidly expanding HMV chain for dominance of the full price album market.

Branson, loving the hustle and flow of the music industry, determined to emulate Woolies by undercutting the competition. Taking albums out of the UK meant there was no sales tax to pay so Branson began stocking his van with brand-new albums, grabbing a ferry to France, then returning, van still loaded, and selling said LPs cheap, cheap, cheap! Word got around and youths flocked to the Oxford Street shop. As did Customs and Excise, who picked up on the scam and threatened to jail the 21-year-old entrepreneur. He got off with a fine of £60,000 – his mother remortgaged her house to pay it. Branson's business partner Nik Powell announced that opening more Virgin stores would generate the income needed to cover legal expenses and ensure they stayed in business. A second Virgin shop opened in Liverpool in late 1971. This proved so popular with Scouse youth – they gathered in large numbers, splayed on bean bags listening to loud prog rock, treating the shop as a youth club cum party central – that Branson had to hire a bouncer to make sure it functioned as a record shop.

Powell and Branson determined to open a Virgin Records every month from December 1971 onwards. By Christmas 1972, they had 14 record shops: several in London – a shop at 130 Notting Hill Gate, then counterculture central, quickly overtook Oxford Street as *the* Virgin hang-out – and one in every big city across the country. The British record industry had never seen anything like this rapid expansion. That in 1971, beyond a selection of specialist record shops, no major rock music retailer existed in the UK reflects how hidebound the British music industry remained almost a decade after The Beatles first blew things apart. HMV continued its expansion but the EMI-owned chain was a stoic beast, failing to realise the potential of a nationwide chain that catered to youth. Virgin's success woke HMV up, but their stores lacked atmosphere and Richard Branson, possessing the luck of the devil, mined a vast gap in British retail.

Luck and good business practice: Branson delegated wisely. When his South African cousin, Simon Draper, arrived in town possessing a fervour for prog rock, Branson hired him as senior buyer, noting: "Simon's taste in music quickly became the single most critical element of the Virgin ethos. A record shop is not

Virgin Records and Tapes
Marble Arch
Up to 60% off any album

just a record shop: it is an arbiter of taste. I had no idea what music to promote, but Simon was full of wonderful plans to bring in unknown foreign albums unavailable elsewhere. There was a thin dividing line between what was 'hip' and what wasn't, and Simon made Virgin the 'hippest' place to be."

Branson fails to mention it in his autobiography, but Virgin shops initially prided themselves on stocking large amounts of bootleg albums. This ensured Led Zeppelin's thuggish manager Peter Grant would regularly charge into Virgin shops and confiscate all the boots. Legend has a clerk failing to recognise Grant so trying to stop him: the former wrestler reacted by breaking the youth's arm.

Jon Newey, already an acolyte of Dobell's, Musicland and One Stop, heard about a new record shop above a shoe store and went to investigate: "I recognised that Virgin were trying to grab the market that Musicland and One Stop had. Imports were still the main draw for those in the know. All they sold was hip stuff. Beanbags and cushions on floor and loads of headphones. They were very cool about playing lots of records for you there. Stay as long as you want, no bother. And they employed gorgeous hippie girls behind the counters. That's one of the things that has been forgotten about hip record shops – they were gathering points for turned on people so you not only met friends and like-minded people there but you also met lots of girls too. I got chatted up by this girl in Virgin's first shop and went back to her house for a joint and the rest! That was the era! Everyone had a groovy time! When a great new album came out and someone got it you would go around to their place, skin up and turn on to the new sounds."

Outside London, Virgin's impact was huge: in 1972 many music fans still relied on WHSmith, Menzies, Woolworths and Boots – or shops that kept records in the basement while white goods occupied the ground floor – thus Virgin's arrival provided a delicious sense of the circus coming to town, deciding to stay, and letting the clowns run things. New Virgin openings would often find rock bands (inevitably those signed to Virgin's record label, founded in 1972) playing on a makeshift stage while bowls of hot lentils were handed out and incense filled the air. Virgin opened in Glasgow in 1973 and a female employee recalled her job interview involved one question: "Do you smoke?"

Simon Robinson, Sheffield music historian, recalls: "Virgin opened a Sheffield store in 1973 and, in some ways, that was that for Sheffield record shops – us teenagers didn't want to go anywhere else. Admittedly, it felt a bit intimidating if you didn't know all about the music they stocked. They had kraut rock and prog rock and artists on the Virgin label, the kind of non-Top 40 new rock music that the other shops weren't really stocking. When they first opened the Sheffield Virgin store, they put on a free concert on one of the city's bomb sites. Gong played and some other Virgin bands. This was at The Moor on the edge of the city centre where rates were cheap. Then they promoted concerts. One featured Faust and was three bands for 35p.

"When Virgin started, they were this great alternative chain of shops but, within five or six years, they had become much more anonymous. But initially, well, Virgin were the best. They had Rags, a clothing department, and aircraft seats where you could sit and listen to the entire side of an album. Unlike other shops, Virgin didn't care that you wanted to bliss out and listen to Pink Floyd. The Sheffield branch also had a wall where musicians could put up advertisements – you know, 'guitarist wanted'. I'm pretty sure it was the Virgin shop where The Human League and Cabaret Voltaire found their members. Virgin was *the* big record store in Sheffield and pretty much had the city sewn up."

Horace Panter, bassist in The Specials, remembers Coventry's Virgin Records playing a role in his band's origins: "Sometime in the mid '70s a branch of Virgin Records opened in Coventry at the top of the City Arcade. I frequented it frequently. The people who worked there seemed to do so under a great deal of duress as their attitude was one of either total indifference or outright animosity. Two members of what would become The Specials – original singer Tim Strickland and eventual drummer John Bradbury – worked there. Upstairs from Virgin Records was a place that only seemed to be open at weekends and sold highly sought-after and obscure northern soul records. The place was called The Soul Hole and was staffed by a local DJ and sometime record plugger Pete Waterman."

In contrast to the psych rock shops that had ruled Soho in the late 1960s, Virgin's smoky lodges appeared largely free of both elitism – like a student disco, all were welcomed – and sexism. These qualities attracted hordes of young female rock fans who enjoyed the boho ambience and relaxed atmosphere. Here, no one demanded you know the name of the Mothers of Invention keyboardist and then sneered when you guessed, "Umm ... Keith Emerson?"

Gaye Black, later to gain fame as the bassist in punk band The Adverts, recalls the first time she ever set foot in Virgin as a pleasurable shock: "I grew up in Bideford in the West Country and the local record shop, Nichols, was very old-fashioned with glass listening booths. I'd go in there all excited and ask 'Can I listen to this?' When I was 13 I got to visit London so went to the Virgin store on Oxford Street and was hugely impressed. They had free coffee and bar stools to sit on and headphones to listen on and there was a chap in a Dracula cloak. I spent all the food money I had been given there on records."

Rita Ray, who ruled the charts as a vocalist in Darts, was sent from Ghana to convent school in Brighton in 1972. There she allowed the local Virgin store to wilfully corrupt her: "I was only used to African or black American music, so going into this crazy shop full of loud hippie music was unlike anything I'd ever experienced before. It was a revelation and got me thinking about music and life in different ways. I started listening to The Doors and Jethro Tull, and changed in ways my parents and teachers didn't appreciate."

John Williams, biographer of Shirley Bassey, was at boarding school in Bristol in the 1970s. He remembers the school masters viewing the city's Virgin shop as a den of iniquity, "and any pupil caught with drugs would claim 'I bought them at Virgin!'"

Virgin was attuned to rock's fashions and certain Virgin shops became gathering points for all the kids excited by what they had read about punk. Jeff Barrett, owner of the Heavenly record label, grew up in Beeston and notes: "Punk really hit Nottingham, at least as far as making an impact on the record shops. The Virgin record shop on King Street was the first place to start selling punk. They initially had a little cardboard box on the counter with 'Punk' written on it. Each week the box got bigger as there were more punk records released. I'd go in there as a 15-year-old and get to know like-minded people. People you had seen at gigs. Nodding acquaintances became friends. For me record shops were places you could gain important information like 'Where did you get your shoes?' I made mates, learned style, in them. That's where my fascination and love for record shops came from. The local Virgin store got put on trial for having the posters for *Never Mind the Bollocks* in the window so it was all over the news. HMV was mainstream while Virgin had the whiff of the counterculture."

Brian O'Neill arrived in London from Cardiff in 1977 aged 22 and immediately got a job in Virgin's then flagship shop at Marble Arch: "Like everyone else applying to work at Virgin I had to do the 20 Questions test and, being a music fanatic, I aced it. It was a very young staff, lots of energy and camaraderie. It paid less than HMV but we didn't mind as we loved working there. It was very exciting to be working for Virgin in London in 1977 – you felt you were riding the energy wave of punk.

"When *Never Mind the Bollocks* came in – and I think our initial delivery was something like 800 copies – I had to shrink wrap every bloody one of them. So, I've just had my break and I come back to work and there's this bearded bloke I'd never seen before standing there and he asks me 'Where are The Sex Pistols albums?' and I pointed and said, 'All around you!' Then I realised it was Richard Branson. I must say, he was very gracious and friendly to all of us who worked at Virgin. He didn't try and remember all our names but he treated us all equally. He was just 'Richard' to us, no airs or graces. I know people now love to slag him off but I'll always defend him for the way he ran the shops and the label back then and the way he treated everyone who worked for him."

Virgin effortlessly rode changes in public taste: its origins may have been selling prog to suburban hippies but Virgin's shops and record label immediately latched on to punk and new wave. Then, as Thatcherism took hold in the UK, Virgin morphed again, the opening of Virgin Megastores across the globe earning Branson vast sums. No more lentils, no more bootlegs, no more lazing around on beanbags sipping free coffee while smoking cigarettes that smelt stronger than the incense. And, thankfully, no more bloody incense. Virgin Megastores (covered in detail in Chapter 18) meant mega-business.

Andy's Records

From reselling used jukebox 45s on Felixstowe Pier to running the third largest record shop chain in the UK, the rise of Andy Gray gave Suffolk a rags-to-riches story that, at one point, looked set to match Richard Branson's. Gray, a blonde Viking of a man, pioneered the Andy's Records chain, consciously avoiding London and other large metropolitan areas, instead focusing on East Anglia and the Midlands. Andy's Records offered low prices, imports and a vast range of albums to choose from and, by 1994, Gray had made it onto the *Sunday Times Rich List* and drove a Rolls Royce. For a decade, Andy's Records was the UK's largest independent music retailer and won *Music Week*'s prestigious Independent Retailer award every year from 1993–8. Gray says: "I grew up in Felixstowe and started buying records in 1957 or '58. Lots of my friends played in bands and all the bands working the UK at the time would come out and play in Bury St Edmunds. Geno Washington, Cliff Bennett, Jimmy James were regulars and I would set up a record stall at the back of the hall on a Saturday night. Quite a few played on the pier in Felixstowe, even the Stones and The Who. Back then, music was the popular culture and every village had a hall so across the country you would have a gig on everywhere every Saturday night. There was a guy who had a record stall on the Felixstowe pier pavilion and I'd buy ex-jukebox singles from him. He used to say, 'Do us a favour, Andy, buy that lot from us for a shilling.' I used to resell them out of the go-kart hut at Felixstowe seafront over the summer.

"I used to drive to Romford to go to a clothes shop and across from it was a record stall called Clive's Records. I used to advertise in the *Ipswich Evening Star*

ANDY'S RECORDS

84 BRIDGE ST.
PETERBOROUGH
TELEPHONE 55252

67 ST. JOHN'S ST.
BURY ST. EDMUNDS
TELEPHONE 67502

56 MILL ROAD
CAMBRIDGE
TELEPHONE 61038

95 HIGH STREET
HAVERHILL
TELEPHONE 61140

73 REGENT ST.
CAMBRIDGE
TELEPHONE 66544

CAMBRIDGE
MARKET
MON.—SAT.

94 HIGH STREET
BEDFORD

– "Records wanted" – and I'd go around and put them on the stall. I left school in June '68 and worked on a building site for three months, still selling records at the dance hall in the weekend. I started up my record stall at Bury St Edmunds market in January 1969. The stall was a wallpaper table, a cover and boxes of records. I quickly realised that Cambridge was the place to go because of the students. At one point I was driving from Felixstowe to Cambridge every day – and this was before the motorway was built! I moved to Cambridge in 1970 and did the stall Monday to Friday and then back to Bury to do the Saturday market. Across the summer months I would drive to Felixstowe and run a stall on the pier in the evenings. It was busy! I did this for three years and while doing it I got to know an EMI area manager and got to be the first market stall with a record label account. This made it easier as I had product delivered straight to the Cambridge stall. Before that I used to have to place my orders using the phone box by the market.

"It was a big stall. I had a Mercedes truck with Andy's Records painted on the side of it. I would be lifting three or four tons of records on and off that truck every day. Vinyl is heavy so it made me strong! I ended up with three or four employees on that stall. Winter's a hard time to be working on a market stall so that's why I set up Andy's as a shop in Cambridge. I got Alan 'Fluff' Freeman to open the shop and he spent two hours signing things then, when we went to an Italian restaurant, got notoriously drunk and had the hots for one of the waiters!

The singer Terry Reid was living just outside Cambridge at the time and he'd come round and light up a huge joint and I'd go, 'Terry, you can't do that here!'

"I sold LPs and 45s. I used to fly over to Holland every month to a shop that did wholesale there. They had stuff that wasn't yet released and American imports. It was a great place for stock. I opened Andy's in Bury in 1976, Haverhill also in '76, Ipswich in '79. I didn't analyse it. There was demand for records so I went out to satisfy that demand. Back then records sold themselves. You didn't have VHS or mobile phones. Even football was on a much smaller scale. Nowadays you have so much to choose from.

"Back then you had electrical shops and Boots, Woolworths, WHSmiths as the main outlets for records in Suffolk and East Anglia. This was before the supermarkets got into selling records. And I could run rings around Woolies and Smiths because they were so slow in promoting the big new albums. I'd know the exact date a big album was coming out, so I'd drive up to Peterborough, get stock and have it on the market stall by 8 a.m. Then I started to buy albums from Portugal: the Portuguese were getting around copyright law so I could sell new albums for £2.99 when everyone else had them for £4.50. I also used to stock bootlegs. I'd buy them off a guy called Jeffrey Collins – he had a shop in Chancery Lane. Peter Grant, the Led Zep manager, once went in there with a big cane and smashed the shop up. And there was a guy called Mr Ali who used to buy deletions from record companies. He used to carry a big bag full of money with him. Paul Levinson sold all kinds of records from a lock-up close to Liverpool Street. The first time I visited he said, 'You hungry, boy?' 'Starving.' 'Good. We don't know much about music but we know a good salt-beef sandwich!' Fred Moore was a good guy. He had a chain of shops, Moore's, and dealt in cut-out [returned unsold from shops with cut-out corners] albums. SPNS was a deletions place in Stratford that I was using. Also Paul Feldman and Warren Goldberg ran Simon's Records – a wholesale import business – in Barkingside. There were lots of characters in the record business. They're all gone now."

Andy's Records had cheap stock but, more importantly, it had deep stock: as well as the Top 40 it had all kinds of weird and wonderful titles. Geoff Travis, a student at Cambridge University in the early 1970s, recalls Andy's Records as his favourite record shop of that era, and an inspiration for his own Rough Trade shops. Later that decade, Joe Cushley, the actor and promoter, found Andy's a revelation: "My first Aladdin's cave in terms of vinyl was David's Bookshop in Letchworth Garden City. It's still going strong. The über-cool hippies who worked in the aromatic back room which housed the records and tapes were the first to infect me with collectivitis. But my real music guru around then was a kitchen porter at the school. He pointed me towards Andy's Records in Cambridge. I had encountered the market stall on an earlier visit to the town, and thought it was pretty damn impressive, but it didn't prepare me for the shop. The staff showed off their pitch-perfect musical aesthetics by playing unheard of gem after unheard of gem. They were like elves to John Peel's Santa Claus. I spent hours flicking through the racks, especially in the basement – frequently popping up to ask – 'What's this? What's this?' And the elves were always pretty kind to the inquisitive, spotty teenager with a penchant for primitive blues, art rock, blazing rockabilly, esoteric punk and even a spot of be-bop."

Says Gray of starting the Andy's Records chain: "I used to go looking for places to open. I still had the market stall in Cambridge. I used to advertise on East Anglia TV. It was very basic. First it was just a picture of the stall. Then I started doing deals with record companies to promote certain albums. I kept opening shops because the demand was there. When *Saturday Night Fever* and *Grease* came out, the albums would just fly out of the shops. Vinyl was at its peak then and we sold tons of cassettes. *Thriller* was huge! People forget these days how popular cassettes were back then. Daniel O'Donnell and these six-pack dance cassettes. Rave music, the kids would buy and buy them. Then I began selling videos. At first they were incredibly expensive but once the price went down people would buy their favourite films on VHS. All those *Top Gun* videos that are now landfill. We also started selling T-shirts.

"Initially, there weren't that many titles available on CD. They seemed a bit of an expensive novelty – you would have this one special rack of CDs in each shop. Then, once it started to roll, more and more space got devoted to them. The record labels pushed them and people started buying them – even though they were more expensive than LPs. Soon half of the space in each of our stores was given over to CDs. That was an amazing time, everyone making great money, and by 1992 I had 15 to 20 Andy's Records. The Oasis albums just sold and sold – when a hit album like that came out all the shops did well. The early '90s were the peak years. I kept on expanding and by 1999 I had 40 shops."

And by the end of 2003 he had none. The British public found cheaper, easier ways to buy their chart CDs and so consigned Andy's Records to the graveyard of British retail. The decline of the chains is dealt with in Chapter 18, but Gray remains a happy man who reflects on his rise and fall in the music industry with great affection.

"It was good fun while it lasted. I thoroughly enjoyed it. Hard work. But I had some luck. My first day on the stall at Cambridge Market some old guy came up to me and said, 'You won't do any good here'." Gray then whoops with laughter.

Beggars Banquet

Ever since Levy's of Whitechapel set up their Levyphone record label in the 1920s, many a British record shop has attempted to do something similar. You can imagine the thinking behind such projects: "We know what the public wants so let's start a label!" In most cases, this never got much beyond hoisting boxes of unsold records around the stockroom. But the mid-1970s saw a literal boom in shops-to-labels, with Virgin, Rough Trade and Beggars Banquet all enjoying spectacular success.

The Beggars group – as it is now known – is still owned by Martin Mills, who co-founded it in the basement of his Fulham record shop in 1977. While Mills no longer owns the small chain of Beggars Banquet record shops that marked his

entry into the music industry, he has never wavered in his command of the Beggars group. This now includes a network of record labels with none more prominent than XL, launch pad for The Prodigy, Adele and other huge British success stories. Mills has been a major player in the British music industry ever since Beggars first scored an out-of-left-field success with Gary Numan's android rock in 1979, yet this tall, gently spoken mogul remains free of the boorish behaviour and corporate greed often associated with record label major domos. He's also barefoot when we meet; it's not often I interview a CEO who is genuinely footloose!

The remarkable success of the Beggars group of record labels is beyond the realms of this book. Instead, our conversation focuses on the Beggars Banquet record shops. Mill says: "I grew up in Oxfordshire and the first record I bought when I was 10 was an album of sea shanties. [Mills chuckles at the memory] But I quickly moved on to The Shadows. In Oxford there was Russell Acotts, a department store with a record bar. It had a decent selection of music available and they had listening rooms – not booths, rooms! – where you could go and listen to an album. It was all very civilised. I got a lot of great albums there – my first Van Morrison and lots of others. I also went to university in Oxford and, while I was studying, a record shop that was more oriented to psychedelia opened called Sunshine. It catered to the new tastes of students. I got The Incredible String Band and other albums I loved there.

"I'd read magazines like *Zig Zag* and the *New Musical Express*. There was pirate radio – Radio Caroline, Radio London. And just going into record stores and picking out albums that looked to be of interest. I always trusted Island as a label so pretty much anything they released was of interest."

Mills graduated from Oxford but – like his near contemporary at Cambridge, Geoff Travis – entered the world of work with little idea of what he wanted to do (beyond listening to music): "I came up to London and tried very hard to be unemployed. I went to the Labour Exchange one day and they asked me if I was a Catholic. 'No, I'm not.' 'Well, we have a job for you then – reporting on the reform of the abortion law.' So I did that for a while and then I wanted to do something in the commercial marketplace so I got a job in Record & Tape Exchange in Goldhawk Road. It was a fascinating enterprise. It had incredible supply and demand. … I lasted a year or so. It was fantastic money – I worked four days a week and you could earn £20 a day, which was a lot back then."

Mills then set up a mobile disco and worked weddings and parties, fêtes and fairs, earning a wage while working out how he might enter the music industry. He quickly teamed up with Nick Austin's mobile disco, then calling itself Beggars Banquet, and together they DJ-ed across Greater London. Back then, he emphasises, there was no cult of the DJ and you were simply expected to play tunes that people knew and liked. Tiring of the circuit the duo then opened a record shop in Earl's Court at 8 Hogarth Road, London SW5, calling it Beggars Banquet simply because they couldn't think of a better name. His experience at Record & Tape Exchange meant Mills understood both the value of second-hand albums along with what punters most often came looking for, and this informed the Earl's Court shop: "Nick and I put our DJ stock into the shop as we weren't going to be a mobile disco anymore. Our idea always was to sell new and second-hand side by side. So, you would have, say, the new David Bowie album next to a second-hand copy – the customer could choose which one they wanted to buy. It worked really well straight away.

"Earl's Court back then was moving from being very Australian to very Middle Eastern. We'd stay open from 11 a.m. to 9.30 p.m. as we had all kinds of people dropping by, not just the daytime shopping crowd. Earl's Court was full of cheap hotels back then and so you had backpackers and Arabs and the local music fans. We'd have funny requests: several times Middle Eastern men would come in with a blank cassette and ask us to tape an album for them. That was obviously how it worked back home.

"In those days, there were at least three record shops just in Earl's Court. We didn't sell singles at all, just albums, and we started out with a lot of funk and soul – Barry White was very popular! – as well as the West Coast sounds: Jackson Browne, Warren Zevon, artists like that. And, for a while, we had a Quadrophonic record centre in the basement. We didn't sell quadrophonic stereo systems, no, we sold quadrophonic albums. We got a lot of mail order business as there were very few places selling quadrophonic albums. It was a strange time – a bit like what happened when you had VHS versus Beta – as you had these competing stereo systems that were completely incompatible. Quadrophonic sound was great but the system lost out, it had all kinds of problems, but we did well out of it. Back then mail order was important if you stocked a wide variety of records as most towns had a record shop of some sort – often a shop that sold records alongside lots of other things – but we had second-hand stock and American imports and other things that music fans outside of London wanted but might not have had access to locally. So, we advertised in the music papers and got lots of orders".

The success of the Earl's Court shop encouraged the duo to expand, opening a second store on North End Road in Fulham. Mills says, "We thought it would be a happening shop as it had a street market and lots of foot traffic but it never really worked well. Always struggled, that shop, but the good thing about it is it had a room below it that we turned into a rehearsal space and that's where we later worked with our first bands."

The Fulham shop's struggles didn't stop the partners from opening more Beggars Banquet records shops across south-west London: Ealing ("Always did well"), Richmond ("Did okay"), Putney ("Never did well"), Kingston ("The last one and it always did great"). Mills emphasises that, as well as the Earl's Court branch, the Ealing and Kingston shops were the star performers yet, with five shops, he and Austin felt they had taken the Beggars Banquet chain as far as they wished to: "We never really thought about following Virgin's lead and expanding across the UK. Economies of scale come into play and we knew south-west London so it suited us to stay local."

Back in the 1970s, Mills comments, running an independent record shop meant you were a nerve centre of sorts for music lovers among the local community: fans would enquire when their favourite artist's new release might be; DJs came seeking out rare imports (Beggars were noted for their excellent jazz-funk and West Coast singer-songwriter LPs); bands would hand out flyers; people would ask for help in ordering a hard-to-find album; school boys would gather to leer at Roxy Music album covers; people would request whatever album was being talked up in the press and much more.

"I enjoyed working behind the counter," says Mills. "I liked seeing what people wanted, hearing what they were interested in. I never had that experience of loathing your customers that some record shop staff do."

Mills admits to being surprised when punk detonated in late 1976 – "I hadn't seen it coming" – but recognised its importance immediately and the Beggars shops started stocking punk 45s: "Record shops changed overnight – in a way – as the musical climate changed. People went from wanting prog and metal albums to wanting punk and new wave. It wasn't so much the customers changed as their tastes did and the shops reflected that. It was incredible to watch – some chap who had bought the Grateful Dead one day was buying the Damned the next! [Laughs] But, at the same time, we stocked music from across the board. We were selling all the big artists – Fleetwood Mac, The Bee Gees, all those acts. Unlike Rough Trade, which followed a very unique trajectory, we ran the shops as broadly as possible. We had all the new punk records, we made sure of that, but at the same time if someone came in and wanted whoever was No. 1 in the album charts we were sure to also have that.

"In those days, you were either a singles shop or an albums shop and if you were an albums shop you ensured you had a wide range of stock. These days only HMV do that and the independent shops are far more specialised. Most won't stock the chart albums because the customers who use them don't want that type of music. But, back then, you made sure you had pretty much everything – and people were buying a lot of records! We'd have the customers come in and say, 'Have you got the record that goes' and start humming! [Laughs] And if we could work out what it was they wanted we'd sell it to them!"

Mills smiles at the memory, still delighted by the pleasure of making a sale, and adds, "There were so many record shops back then! In Kingston alone you had Tower, Our Price, Virgin, HMV, another independent and our shop – six or seven record shops all in one area! There was a culture of buying music then and all kinds of record shops could survive."

Punk, initially, didn't make for large sales: sallow youths may have wanted The Ramones and Stooges LPs and the latest 45s, but there weren't that many releases, while artists like David Soul and Leo Sayer were shifting vast quantities of vinyl. Mills, never having lost his taste for what had once been called 'underground', correctly guessed that the new rock sound would win through. When a local punk band called The Lurkers started rehearsing in the basement of the Fulham Beggars, he paid attention: "The Fulham shop manager discovered The Lurkers. They asked him to manage them. We tried to help him get them a deal but, by then, every major label had signed one punk band and no one was interested. So, we decided to put the record out ourselves. Back then it was a pretty adventurous thing to do – there was no instruction manual, you just had to do it and learn as you went along. We got a distribution deal with this very old-fashioned distributor and he got the record out and it sold well. We then got a bigger distributor and the second Lurkers single went Top 30 and we were up and running. The thing back then was there were so few punk records coming out that everyone bought everything, people just swallowed it up. When we started the label it was just to release one Lurkers single. When that sold okay we thought, 'Well, we can release another one'. Then we decided to release their album and once that sold well we thought we might as well sign another band. There was no great plan. We made it up as we went along, put one foot in front of another."

Mills initially ran the Beggars Banquet label out of the Earl's Court shop. However, it was, he notes, the Ealing Broadway shop that provided the label with much of its talent: "Ealing seemed to be the shop where we found most of our first bands. Gary Numan's bass player walked into the shop and handed a demo tape over the counter. A lot of our early bands passed demo tapes over the counter at Ealing. It seemed that a lot of bands were happening in Ealing and they were using the shop. Once they heard there was a label attached to the shop they came in and gave demos. Once the label got up and running I guess we turned our interest away from the shops so we started offloading them. Fulham and Putney we needed to get rid of because they weren't viable. Kingston was the last shop we held on to because it always did well and, in the end, we gave that to the management. And it's still doing brilliantly today [as Banquet Records, 52 Eden Street, Kingston Upon Thames, Surrey KT1].

"We'd probably closed the shops – other than Kingston – by the early '80s. We held on to Kingston until the end of the '80s, maybe even the '90s. But by then I was so busy with the label that I was not paying any attention to the shops. I should add that, for a long time, once the label was happening I would still work behind the counter of one of the shops on a Saturday as I found it a really good way of keeping in touch with what was happening in music. You got to experience what the public wanted, what they were looking for. I enjoyed it too. For years and years I did this. We certainly put out records on Beggars that were informed by what was popular in the shops. And we even did the occasional sidestep of putting out something that reflected our past – for instance, the Arthur Lee album we put out."

Mills had carefully read the mood of a new rock audience who desired a dark, moody, post-punk music – Gary Numan became the biggest selling UK artist in 1979–80 – and both Beggars and its first offshoot label, 4AD, signed bands (Bauhaus, The Cult, The Cocteau Twins, The Charlatans, The Pixies, The Throwing Muses) that sold strongly. 4AD was founded by Ivo Watts-Russell and Peter Kent, two Beggars shop workers. Mills says: "Ivo and Peter were good shop managers. Ivo had got pretty pissed off with being a shop manager and gone off to America for six months. When he returned we put him in control of all the shops and that only made him even more pissed off. [Laughs] So we let him set up 4AD. And he really found his mettle."

4AD discovered many of the biggest bands for the Beggars roster across the 1990s and Mills continued to cut similar deals with other fledgling record labels, so bringing Cornershop, The Prodigy and Adele to the Beggars group. Never having lost his taste for record shops, in 2007 Mills went into partnership with Rough Trade record shop, bankrolling and overseeing their expansion into Rough Trade East (London), Rough Trade Brooklyn and Rough Trade Nottingham. He says: "I think record shops are thriving again now. They appeal to locality and specialisation and all those things that people are getting interested in again. The vinyl revival has, of course, helped – people like to buy something tactile and beautiful that they can put on their shelves and all their friends can see. It's the same with the interest in bicycles. I think if you open an independent record shop today and specialise in an area that your community responds to then you can do very well. It is a very healthy time to be running independent record shops. Every independent record shop I speak to is doing well."

Having said that, Mills, the barefoot – and possibly nicest – business mogul going, returns to overseeing his Beggars empire, his mind surely musing on an Earl's Court basement full of quadrophonic LPs.

Chapter 10

Camden Cowboys: Rock On's Incendiary 45s

By looking back while moving forward, a tiny Ladbroke Grove record stall inspires the future sound of London. Cameos from Phil Lynott, Charlie Gillett, Lenny Kaye, Malcolm McLaren and The Sex Pistols, Joe Strummer and The Clash, Lemmy and Motorhead, and Shane McGowan. Also noted: how Deep Throat enabled the spiriting of several thousand 45s out of Portugal.

As Virgin and Andy's Records got busy launching record shops across Britain, a tiny record stall run by a big Irish man opened without fanfare. Rock On – as the stall was called – initially occupied a 2.4 metres by 2.4 metres space in Ladbroke Grove, London, and it was here that the blueprint for much of the best rock music of the 1970s took shape. The records stocked by Rock On seemed almost alive, the elements conversing among themselves with an occult vitality, conjuring up an incendiary London sound that would go on to shake the city.

Rock On
Ladbroke Grove
In 1971, Ladbroke Grove in London had a reputation as a place of paupers, with Gypsies, West Indians, hippies and the poorest English living side by side in slum housing that landlords (like the notorious Peter Rachman) neglected and exploited. Forlornly stranded between the wealth of Holland Park and bustling Bayswater, the neighbourhood's polyglot populace supported all kinds of musical activity. Alan Johnson's autobiography, *This Boy*, Sam Selvon's novels, Charlie Phillips's photographs and even the glimpse that Nicolas Roeg's film *Performance* offers of Powis Square, hint at the world in which Rock On set up. A man on a mission, Ted Carroll instinctively knew the Grove suited his vision: "I was first attracted to Golborne Road as it had street stalls at weekends and was a continuation of Portobello Road market. I started going there with friends after moving to Belsize Park early in 1971. We would start at the Notting Hill end of Portobello and keep going until the stalls stopped, just before the big iron railway bridge on Golborne Road, near Trellick Tower. The local population was predominantly black along with a few older bohemian types, some poor white families and lots of hippies living in squats. Everyone appeared to get on well on a 'live and let live' basis.

"We soon discovered the Record Exchange shop on Golborne Road. It was basically an overflow outlet for the better known main Record Exchange shop in Shepherd's Bush. All the old and less desirable stock was shunted on to the Golborne Road branch. At this time, stereo LPs were still quite new and mono albums were considered 'old hat'. Consequently, most of the stock at the Golborne shop was old mono albums and this suited me fine. At this time, the rest of the

ROCK ON

(Established 1972)

3 KENTISH TOWN ROAD, CAMDEN TOWN, LONDON NW1

O P E N   7   D A Y S   A   W E E K

shops on Golborne were just local businesses and it was fairly quiet during the week but came alive on Friday and Saturday when the street market set up. At weekends the market attracted thousands of people and the Golborne section was especially popular as apart from fruit and veg it was mostly 'tat' – old house clearance stuff – where you could almost always get real bargains. Everyone shopped there – not just locals – lots of musicians and fashion designers and writers. In the late '60s and early '70s Golborne was definitely as hip as you could get.

"In July 1971 I noticed a sign in the window of an empty shop at 93 Golborne Road advertising an indoor market due to open in a month's time. It struck me as the perfect place to open a record stall at weekends to sell a rapidly growing stock of 45s and 78s. Rock On opened on around 16th August 1971, in a tiny stall opposite a tiny Wonder Workshop stall, right at the back of the flea market."

Music had always dominated Carroll's life and, as a teenager in 1950s and 1960s Dublin he played in local bands. Yet his true passion was for records, specifically American rock 'n' roll and R&B. He says, "I've been serious about collecting records since buying my first 78 of 'Tutti Frutti' by Little Richard after hearing it on AFN radio broadcasts out of Stuttgart in the mid-1950s." By 1970, Carroll had stopped performing and graduated to tour managing Irish rockers Skid Row. Touring the USA in 1970 with Skid Row, Carroll discovered Big John's Oldies But Goodies Land, a Boston shop focused on selling doo-wop, rockabilly and soul 45s. *Ka-ching!*

While Big John's inspired Big Ted to set up a similar shop, Carroll emphasises that he'd been selling records via mail order prior to opening Rock On. In the late 1960s, while working as a bus driver in Bournemouth, he scoured that city's junk shops for old 45s and 78s ("People would get rid of great collections for nothing back then"). He also mentions Bargain Wallpapers, a chain that somehow stocked American cut-out R&B LPs for 6/8d (33p or 3 for £1):

"Richard Berry, Young Jessie, Etta James and Johnny 'Guitar' Watson, James Carr and the ultra-classic Van Dykes' Mala LP *No Man Is an Island*; I used to buy up and sell them via ads in Record Mart; even Tesco would have used records for sale by the check-out counters."

Before Carroll opened Rock On, he began co-managing a promising London-based Irish band. They were called Thin Lizzy, and an Irish tour led Carroll to discover a Dublin distributor with an attic full of 45s on the London label: these included mint pressings of Bo Diddley, The Ronettes, Ike & Tina Turner, and other such gems. Carroll bought 1850 singles for £65 and these provided much of the initial stock for Rock On when it first opened. Rock On occupied a tiny space in the Portobello Road market, but Carroll blasted his stock through a formidable pair of speakers to attract passing trade. At the start of the 1970s, rock music grew increasingly profligate – heavy rock, prog rock and art rock all allowed for much grandstanding and yet lacked the raw essence that had made the music so compelling – and reissues of 1950s and 1960s era rock and R&B were rare. Carroll's stall provided a solution to both these quandaries and, within a matter of weeks, word had got out about the quality and rarity of Rock On's stock: Carroll would arrive on Saturday mornings to find a queue gathering.

ROCK ON

THE INTERIOR OF
OUR SHOP AT CAMDEN
TOWN,ALWAYS CRAMMED
WITH ROCKIN' GOODIES

EXPERT AND FRIENDLY
STAFF ALWAYS AT
YOUR SERVICE

3 KENTISH TOWN ROAD,LONDON NW1.(next to Camden Town Tube)Tuesday to
Saturday.10.30 to 7.00 pm....also...1.2.3 SOHO MARKET, NEWPORT PLACE
LONDON WC2. (Leicester Square tube). Monday to Saturday.11.00 to 7.00
....AND...93. GOLBORNE ROAD, PORTOBELLO MARKET,W.10. Saturday.9.30-5.30.

2

Among the many people who flocked to Rock On were a young Joe Strummer ("He bought 'Brand New Cadillac' and 'Junco Partner' amongst others"); Jimmy Page ("Looking to fill gaps in his collection of Sun Records 45s"); Lemmy ("A good fella"); Malcolm McLaren ("With Steve Jones and Paul Cook in tow, looking for songs the band they were forming could cover"); and Carroll's charge, Phil Lynott. Thin Lizzy's leader was so impressed by Rock On that he wrote 'The Rocker' ("I get my records at the Rock On stall / sweet rock and roll / Teddy boy, he's got them all"), which is, I think, the first song ever written about a record stall or shop. Carroll smiles when I mention this Lizzy tune. "It was a great compliment for Phil to write that about me. He was a lovely chap. He'd come along to Rock On and hang out. Phil loved listening to the records."

Soho Market

Success ensured that Carroll decided to open a second Rock On stall in Soho market in August 1974. He hired Roger Armstrong, a Belfast native, to run it. Sharing similar musical passions – both men loved raw, elemental music and had no taste for the era's ruling rock behemoths – Carroll and Armstrong became the Butch and Sundance of record traders, building Rock On into Europe's foremost oldies vendor. Today, Armstrong's primary recollection of his Soho market stall is, "how bloody cold it could be in winter. You were open to the elements, standing all day, freezing! Jesus, I don't miss that at all!" Armstrong laughs then adds: "I think the thing with the Soho market Rock On stall is that it was open all week and right in the middle of the West End. It got collectors and musicians coming in and then just the passing trade who heard music playing and dropped in to have a look. Ted placed ads in *The Gleaner* – we were still doing mail order – and one day three sharply dressed West Indian guys came into the shop and asked, 'Hey man, you have the Shirley & Lee album?' They'd seen the ad in *The Gleaner* and come all the way from Birmingham to buy it!"

Among the regular customers at the Soho stall were radio presenters John Peel and Charlie Gillett. "The BBC was close by and someone tipped Peel off about our stock of Cajun 45s, so he came down and quickly became a really good customer," says Armstrong. Gillett (1942–2010) had influenced Carroll's 1970 US purchases through his *Sound of the City* book and Rock On, recognising Gillett as a kindred spirit, always attempted to stock the records he played on his *Honky Tonk* radio show.

With business booming, Carroll resigned from managing Thin Lizzy in 1975, choosing to focus on hunting out old records for Rock On's stalls. He already excelled here, having purchased 20,000 rare US 45s from Ace Records in Jackson, Mississippi, in 1973 and, not long after, a huge haul of extremely rare 78s from a Dublin shop. But it was the realisation that there were British warehouses stocked with old American records that shaped Rock On's future. Carroll says: "I'd found that there were people over here importing cut-out records from America. There was one guy who bought in huge numbers of albums including a lot of Stax product. He had hundreds of copies of Big Star's first two albums and I went and bought them all up. No one knew about them at the time – unless you had been paying very close attention – but I guessed they would sell well. And they did.

"And up in Luton there was F. L. Moore's. He imported ex-jukebox singles from America in massive numbers. Maybe 100,000 records a shipment. He had three or four shops around and had cottoned on to the northern soul thing taking off so was looking for those types of records. I'd go through all these 45s and pull out all kinds of things. We quickly got a reputation for not being a specialist dealer like Moondog in East Ham that only dealt in 1950s era records. We loved to play new arrivals to our customers and make them passionate about the music too.

"I also sold Chris Barber's magnificent collection of vintage 78s. All these mint American jazz and blues 78s! Chris had imported a huge stash of blues and jazz, R&B and gospel 78s from America at some time in the early 1970s. We did a deal and I sold 78s for Chris on a sale-or-return basis. I also bought 10,000 ex-jukebox R&B and soul 45s outright from him at around the same time."

Camden Town

Having access to these gold mines of vintage vinyl and shellac, Carroll determined that he should open a shop. Entering into a partnership with customer Barry Appleby, Carroll rented 3 Kentish Town Road, London NW1 (right next to Camden Town tube station). The Rock On shop opened in late 1975 with a party attended by every London music head of note. Visiting US band The Flamin' Groovies all turned up and a very merry time was had.

Camden had long been home to a large Irish community and, apart from The Roundhouse being used as a venue for hippie happenings and concerts in the late 1960s, it had little rock pedigree. It was appropriate then that Carroll would link Camden's Irish and rock communities with Rock On. In 1975, the Irish ballrooms were still standing although many had closed as a younger generation no longer fancied dancing to show bands. The Carousel (formerly The Buffalo) at 184 Camden High Street, right behind Rock On, had been one of the premier London show band ballrooms since the 1940s and, in 1978, reopened as a rock venue called the Electric Ballroom (booking punk, new wave, 2 Tone). Just down the High Street, by Mornington Crescent tube station, the Camden Hippodrome reopened in 1977 as the Music Machine (quickly becoming a major rock venue), while Dingwalls on Camden Lock employed an eclectic booking policy. Carroll remembers: "At the time, Camden was pretty downtrodden. Rents were low – we got the entire building, basement, shop and two apartments above the shop for £2500 rent a year. I lived in one of the apartments and operated Ace and Chiswick from another. Camden, like Soho and Ladbroke Grove, was the right place for a specialist vinyl record shop. Things were happening there, lots of pubs and bands and the market, but it wasn't commercialised in the way it would later become."

Carroll, Armstrong and Trevor Churchill (a music industry veteran) set up the label Chiswick Records in 1975. Launched to capture the raw rock energies that were starting to be heard in London pubs, Chiswick's debuted with The Count Bishops' *Speedball* EP, a record so abrasive it made Dr Feelgood sound tame. Much praise and strong sales indicated that the trio were onto something, and Chiswick followed with a reissue of Vince Taylor's 1959 single 'Brand New Cadillac', the record Carroll had more demand for than any other. This sold so strongly that it nearly cracked the Top 40 – not bad for a fledgling record label run from a market stall.

Rock On's reputation established itself internationally and Lenny Kaye, guitarist in Patti Smith's group, spread the word about "the best oldies stall anywhere" after he first visited Rock On in 1973 and found 'Crazy Like a Fox' by Link Cromwell in the punk box for 40p. Carroll says: "Lenny asked me why it was in the punk box, and I told him that I thought the rather Dylanesque record sounded 'kinda punky'. He grinned and admitted that it was the first 45 he ever released (aged 15 in 1965) and had been looking for a copy for years!"

"I loved Rock On", Kaye says. "I'd worked at Village Oldies in New York so wasn't that interested in finding old American records. Instead, I wanted offbeat British 45s and Jamaican ska and reggae records. And Rock On always held something of interest." Kaye championed Rock On to his CBGB cohorts and Armstrong arrived one morning to find four bedraggled looking figures in leather jackets hovering outside: The Ramones, having played their first ever London show the previous night, were now wanting to buy old records. "Joey was very impressed that UK Sweet 45s had different B-sides to the US ones," Armstrong recalls.

Rock On played a major role in shaping punk's sound, supplying records to all the major players "except John Lydon", says Carroll. "I don't recall him ever dropping by." Still, Lydon did study Rock On 45s because Carroll supplied Malcolm McLaren with 45s both for his jukebox and to sell in the Let It Rock shop. Carroll would, at McLaren's request, then work as DJ at early Pistols gigs:

"I was DJ at their first gig at the Nashville Rooms – the one where Rotten and co. made headlines by jumping off the stage in the middle of a tune to join in a fracas with some of the audience. I was billed as the Rock On disco and warmed up the audience for the band. I also DJ-ed at a few more of their early gigs."

Rock On helped fuel punk's seismic tremors and, on 16 October 1976, The Jam drove down from Woking, plugged into the Soho market stall's light socket and performed on the pavement outside. "I already knew Paul as this moddy-looking teenager who would drop by the stall", says Armstrong, "so when he turned up with his dad and wanted to play I was happy to help out."

Strummer and Lemmy

Also in 1976, Armstrong produced The 101ers 'Keys to Your Heart' 45, recalling, "Joe had this ferocious energy, he really could project like very few people. The first time I saw him with The 101ers' they were playing a student union, no stage, just a few people watching, and he came across like he was playing Wembley Stadium. He had remarkable presence." Strummer then left The 101ers just before the 45 came out. Armstrong continues: "We were a bit annoyed with

Joe that he split up The 101ers before we even got to put their record out but we were still family, we wished him well. He and Mick were originally calling themselves The Heartdrops and that was what went on the press release for The 101ers' single – 'Joe is leading a new band called The Heartdrops'. He came in one day to the stall and said, 'We've got a new name – The Outsiders!' We were just pricing up a bunch of American import LPs and I dug through them and pulled out an album by an American band called The Outsiders and said, 'Sorry guys, name's already taken!' We got to know Bernie Rhodes and he invited me to the very first Clash gig and I thought they were great right there.

"When punk came along, a lot of old rockers hated it, but not Ted and me. To us it sounded like the chance to have a second childhood. We were selling Dolls and Stooges and Flamin' Groovies when no one else was so we knew all the musicians. I saw the Count Bishops and 101ers as a bridge between the Feelgoods and punk. We were bringing in all kinds of remarkable music, stuff that influenced the next generation. In Rock On you didn't have to dig through two tons of crap to find a good record. And with Chiswick we were the first of the independent labels of that generation. We got going and then Stiff followed us. I wanted to sign The Damned but Stiff stole them away!"

Carroll financed (and released) Motorhead's eponymous debut album in 1977, the friendship forged with Lemmy over the Ladbroke Grove stall inspiring him to take a chance on the snaggle-toothed rocker's metallic trio when no other label dared touch them. Carroll notes: "I first met Lemmy at the Golborne Road Rock On and found him a very interesting and musically knowledgeable young man. He was deeply interested in '50s rock 'n' roll, as well as the great but obscure British beat groups of the '60s. He used to buy classic 45s by virtually unknown groups at the stall, despite never having much spending money in the early Hawkwind days. Shortly after Hawkwind got their US deal with Atlantic, Lemmy appeared one day at the stall with a cheque book and splashed out on some primo 7 UK beat goodies. Following his dismissal by Hawkwind, Lemmy was obliged to cash in his cache of rockin' 7 vinyl. Soon after this, he dropped by the stall one Saturday afternoon to introduce Larry and Lucas from his new band Motorhead. All three were identically clad in black leather motorcycle jackets, black jeans held up by those tough looking cartridge-shell belts. This eventually led to Chiswick Records getting the opportunity to record and release the first single and LP by Motorhead – a true honour!"

Chiswick Records grew rapidly into one of the UK's foremost independent labels, while the stalls and shop did boffo business. Armstrong says: "By late 1976 I was out of Soho. Two guys, Stan and Phil, took it over and eventually bought the stall with half the stock off Ted. When the market got demolished they shifted to Hanway Street and set up as Rocks Off. They also set up a record label, Soho Records, and released The Nips singles. They opened another shop in London Bridge but overstretched as they closed not too long after. Stan went on to produce the first Pogues album. Shane McGowan was always hanging around Rock On. He never officially worked there but he was often behind the

Buried treasure: crate digging in Camden Town.

counter playing records and such. Some musicians are only really interested in their own music but Shane loved a great range of music."

Ace Records

In 1978, while negotiating to license 1950s era R&B recordings from Ace Records in Mississippi, Carroll decided to also license the label name (Ace having been dormant for many years) for his reissue label. A beautiful future curating old American music began. The year 1978 also saw Vicki Fox working in Rock On, Camden: "Early in 1975 I got to know Ted as I'm from Southend and knew the Feelgoods and Lew Lewis and other local musicians, all of whom made use of Rock On. I began helping out at the Rock On Golborne Road stall then got the job at Camden. Rock On was packed all the time, punk was happening and we stocked the kind of records that punk fans wanted, and we were very near Dingwalls dance hall on the Camden Lock so bands would drop in after soundcheck or if they were visiting London. Norman Jay and the rare groove DJs would regularly come in to buy soul singles. As would old Jamaican guys who loved New Orleans R&B.

"We tended to live our lives in Camden back then. If we weren't working in the shop, we were in local pubs or going to gigs at Dingwalls as we always got in free. I was female in a very male environment and, back then, not that many women came into record shops. Well, not the specialist ones like Rock On. I don't know why that is as women love music just as much as men. I guess collecting old records is more of a boys' thing. I wonder if it's changed? Back then there weren't many female bands or female DJs while now there are loads. I got a tattoo on my arm when I was working at Rock On and people would curse and spit at me on the street because of it!"

Running three of London's foremost record temples and a brilliantly idiosyncratic record label didn't stop Carroll from continuing to behave akin to Indiana Jones, seeking out treasure chests of 'lost' records across the globe. In 1976, he purchased 10,000 mint UK 45s from a forlorn Gibraltar record shop. Then, in 1978, he took thousands of rare and unique picture sleeve 45s out of Portugal in the trunk of a 1952 Cadillac DeVille: "I bought the Cadillac for £250 in Lisbon. I had access to unlimited Portuguese currency through the auspices of Jimmy Vaughan, a friend in the movie business who held the European rights to *Deep Throat*. This film was doing sell-out business at two small art house cinemas in Lisbon due to the loosening of censorship restrictions following the 'Carnation Revolution' in Portugal. Prior to this, Portugal being a deeply Catholic country, no filth had been shown in its cinemas. At the time, there were very strict currency exchange control restrictions in force in Portugal and it was virtually impossible to get money out of the country, so I bought several thousand fabulous picture sleeve singles and EPs from various record shops in Lisbon and Oporto (Beatles, Stones, Small Faces, Dylan – all in picture sleeves different from the UK releases). These were loaded into the boot of the Caddy, together with a few dozen bottles of fine Portuguese wine and a couple of hundred tins of Portuguese sardines. All the vinyl, wine, sardines, etc. were purchased with *Deep Throat* cash obtained from the owner of the two cinemas in Lisbon.

"When I arrived in Southampton on board the Caronia, a luxury passenger cruise ship just ending a round-the-World trip, I was met with the deepest suspicion by HM Customs and Excise, who decided that the vinyl, sardines and vintage Cadillac *must* be a front for some smuggling scam. They searched inside the door panels, under the dashboard, under carpets looking for drugs. In the end, finding nothing untoward, they settled for relieving me of £280 in import taxes and VAT and allowed me to proceed back to Camden Town."

Rock On attracted all kinds of new musical energies to Camden and as venues opened so did record shops. Appleby left Rock On in 1978 to set up his own Camden oldies record shop, Sea of Tunes, in Buck Street. Nick Hornby referenced this shop (without naming it) in the book *High Fidelity* (1995) when Rob Fleming mentions his admiration for a Camden record shop that has the logos of seminal US record labels painted on the wall. Fleming goes as far as saying that he wants to hire the bloke who painted the logos to do the same in his flat. The name of said artist? Take a bow, Ms Vicki Fox.

In 1979, Carroll closed the stalls, focusing on running the Camden shop and his record labels. By then Rock On existed as *the* oracle for anyone interested in elemental music: American rockers The Cramps and the Stray Cats headed straight from Heathrow there, while the likes of Bob Dylan and Doug Sahm would drop in when in town. Local lads Madness were regulars and Rock On features prominently in their 1981 film *Take It or Leave It*. More than any other record shop, Rock On understood the visceral qualities that underpinned the best rock, pop and soul. Any music lover who responded to the throb in primal music – whether a superstar or an office clerk – headed to the Camden shop.

Through both the shop and the Ace Records label, Carroll was able to focus interest in such diverse, forgotten formats as rockabilly, Southern soul and 1960s US garage rock. With Rock On serving as *the* London music temple, Camden Town prospered, the market burgeoning while all manner of preening youth gathered to shop and pose. Ironically, by raising Camden's profile Rock On would price itself out of the neighbourhood: by the late 1990s, with Camden now a tourist hotspot and home to Brit-poppers, Carroll was informed that the annual rent would rise to £36,000. He considered how the vintage vinyl he took pride in stocking in Rock On was now far harder to source, and how, by refusing to stock CDs during a decade that saw sales accelerate, Rock On had missed out on the big music industry boom. Finally, Carroll considered whether he wanted to continue dealing with the assorted headaches that come with running a record shop.

"While Rock On lasted Camden served as the perfect place," Carroll says, "but it was time to move on." And so they did. Ace Records relocated to an industrial park in Harlesden and, in 2008, issued *Rock On*, a fine compilation album gathering tunes Carroll and Armstrong once sold on their stalls. They have also issued two *Honky Tonk* albums (2009 and 2014) celebrating the music Charlie Gillett championed (as well as keeping Gillett's seminal swamp pop compilation album, *Another Saturday Night*, in print). Fox says: "The closing of Rock On Camden was inevitable, with Camden being killed by its own popularity. You look at Camden now and almost all the interesting shops in and around the market

Spill the wine: Ted Carroll toasts his shop's success. All Rock On images courtesy of Ace Records.

have closed. It's just T-shirts and fast food. It used to be full of crafts and vintage clothing and hippie food and bootlegs, a completely different vibe."

From Ladbroke Grove to Soho to Camden Town, Rock On both nourished and channelled London's raw energies. In doing so, it played a part in shaping pub rock, punk and thrash metal while framing the revival of interest in niche American music: veteran rockabilly singers Wanda Jackson and Sonny Fisher experienced major career lifts after Ace Records reissued their 1950s era recordings. The friendship of Carroll and Armstrong continues at Ace Records; Butch and Sundance remaining determined to enrich the lives of music lovers.

Many more record shops followed Rock On's lead; at one point, there were some 20 shops and market stalls operating in close vicinity, Camden Market serving as the UK's grand bazaar for music, vintage gear and tourist tat. Closest in spirit to Carroll's vision was Compendium Books, a superb venture that stocked a great selection of music-themed books, magazines and fanzines along with bootleg albums and obscure tapes from maverick and outsider musicians. Compendium closed not long after Rock On, leaving Camden High Street – and much of London's used record trade – to be dominated by a West London chain: Record & Tape Exchange.

Chapter 11

Steptoe and Shop: Second-Hand Record Psychosis

Recycling records becomes big business and used record shops open across the UK: Record & Tape Exchange, Beanos, Cheapo, Cheapo, Reckless, Plastic Passion, Reddington's Rare Records, Cob Records, Violet May. Cameos from Bobby Gillespie, Shane McGowan, Epic Soundtracks, Bim Sherman, Elvis Costello, Paul Kossoff, Chrissie Hynde, Oasis, Richard Hawley and Cornershop. Also noted: beware men who buy and sell used records.

Stinky, surly and quite possibly psychotic: such were the traits found in many a used record vendor. The Albert Steptoe-style misanthropes who often ran such outlets made shopping a challenge, but for many, crate digging often proved the only way to increase a record collection. Prior to the internet making 'everything ever recorded' available, treasure hunts through grimy used record shops in search of particular records were commonplace, and the following caves were home to many a Gollum.

Record & Tape Exchange

Record & Tape Exchange (R&TE) appeared, at one point in the 1990s, to be spreading its grimy tentacles from West London across the city and further afield. Not only did the chain seem to operate most of the shops along Notting Hill High Street, it could be found in Shepherd's Bush, Camden, Greenwich and Soho, Birmingham and Manchester. By then the record shops were called Music & Video Exchange, but nothing else had changed: scuzzy shops, churlish staff, ridiculous prices offered for your goods, outrageous prices posted once goods went on sale. The chain employs a system known as the 'Dutch auction' (items are marked down £1 after every week they have sat on the shelf) and I have, occasionally, found bargains. 'Occasionally' being the operative word.

This century has seen R&TE slowly retreat towards its Notting Hill base: the original Shepherd's Bush shop at Goldhawk Road was the first to go. Then the Manchester shop. The Camden branch, which opened in 1982 and, in the heyday of Britpop must have been a goldmine, closed in 2012. The Soho and Birmingham shops both went in 2015. The Notting Hill stores are now far fewer although several vintage clothing/accessories remain and the chain's death star – Music & Video Exchange, 30 Notting Hill Gate, London W11 – offers three floors stuffed with vinyl and CDs.

Considering R&TE's first second-hand shop opened nearly 50 years ago and, across the decades, the chain has employed several hundred workers and sold millions of used records, it is puzzling that the business has little documented history. There is no Wikipedia entry. No magazine profiles. No celebratory

RECORD, TAPE & VIDEO EXCHANGE

38 NOTTING HILL GATE
LONDON WII
01-243 8573

28 PEMBRIDGE ROAD
NOTTING HILL GATE WII
01-221 1444

123 NOTTING HILL GATE
LONDON WII
01-221 1075

90 GOLDHAWK ROAD,
SHEPHERDS BUSH W12
01-749 2930

229a CAMDEN HIGH STREET
LONDON NW1
01-267 1898

ALL RECORDS, TAPES & VIDEOS BOUGHT, SOLD & EXCHANGED

blogs. No cult following. No love. This being how Brian Abrams likes things.

Abrams is the opposite of Richard Branson or Geoff Travis, men who embraced being the face of their record shops. Instead, Abrams stays in the shadows, doesn't give interviews, and is only interested in business. Which he is very successful at and, if he owns any of the chain's Notting Hill properties, worth many millions. Among the countless minions who have toiled at R&TE were Martin Mills (later to found Beggars Banquet) and, decades later, a gormless Kiwi rapper called Zane Lowe. Lowe held down a job in the Notting Hill shop before going on to earn a fortune on MTV, XFM, Radio 1 and Apple Music.

I asked Mills about his experience at the London Goldhawk Road shop in 1972, and he recalled its owner thus: "It was a fascinating enterprise. It had incredible supply and demand. Brian Abrams was quite an interesting character: at one point he was only hiring shop assistants who had degrees in primal therapy. And he fired someone while I was there for not having a second hand on their watch. He had these timing tests for pricing second-hand records. I lasted a year or so."

Gary Jeff, who worked for Abrams 15 years after Mills, recalls of his time behind the counter: "I went along, not expecting to get offered a job, and Brian Abrams met me on the street outside the Shepherd's Bush branch and interviewed me standing on the pavement. His main line of questioning revolved around The Byrds. He was pretty strange but, luckily, he seemed to like the look of me; apparently if he didn't he asked what you knew about Poco! I passed The Byrds test and got invited back for an interview with the shop manager who turned out to be a normal bloke. I got offered the job and started at the branch in Goldhawk Road. It was the oldest of the shops and a pretty strange place. Brian's dad lived upstairs. He was an elderly Polish gentleman and not in the greatest health. Sometime we would find him wandering about the shop in his pyjamas looking quite disoriented.

"Back then a lot of people were re-buying their album collections on CD, so dumping vinyl collections on Record & Tape. We got great collections in, often very cheap. That's what led Brian to open so many stores across London – he just had so much stock. After 18 months I moved to the Camden store, where lots of rock musicians hung out. Bobby Gillespie and his mates would often be in. Epic Soundtracks worked there and, as he was in These Immortal Souls, the band's guitarist, Roland S. Howard, would often drop in looking very strung out. Epic had a taste of success with Swell Maps but here he was working in a second-hand record shop. And there were loads of wannabe rock stars coming in, guys who were in bands that maybe had got a bit of attention from the *NME*.

"My most memorable famous customer came in around 7.45 one night. I was getting ready to close up and saw this tramp pulling out lots of LP sleeves and looking at them. I think, 'What's this guy up to? Should I tell him to leave?' Then he comes up to the counter with all these LP sleeves – mainly classic rock stuff, Stones, Springsteen, Dylan – and says, 'I'd like to buy these.' As soon as he opened his mouth I realised who it was – those teeth! So I say, 'Okay Shane, I'll get the albums for you to check.' He's pissed but as I put the LPs on the counter he said, 'Make sure I've not got any doubles in there' so he was aware that he

ALL CHANGE JAZZ RECORDS

20 BAKER STREET, LONDON W.1. 01-487-5027

Nearest Tubes: Baker Street—Marble Arch

Thousands of secondhand jazz LPs always in stock. Plus a wide range of U.K., European and USA deletions at cheap prices. Best prices for your unwanted LPs—any quantity. Cash or part-exchange against secondhand or new LPs.

CHRISTMAS BARGAINS

1. Zoot Sims — Zootcase — PR 24061 — 3.15
2. Wardell Gray — Central Avenue — PR 24062 — 3.15
3. Miles Davis — Green Haze — PR 24064 — 3.15
4. Donald Byrd — House of Byrd — PR 24066 — 3.15
5. Zoot Sims — Soprano Sax — Pablo 2310 770 — 2.75
6. Basie and Zoot — Pablo 2310 745 — 2.75
7. Zoot Sims and the Gershwin Bros. — Pablo 2310 744 — 2.75
8. Dizzy Gillespie y Machito — Pablo 2310 771
9. Count Basie — I told you so — Pablo 2310 767
10. Peterson/Pass — Porgy and Bess — 2310 779
11. Ellington and Ray Brown — This one's for Blanton — Pablo 2335 728 — 3.05
12. Ray Bryant — Alone at Montreux — Atlantic Import 1626 — 3.00
13. Paul Desmond Quartet — double LP — A&M — 3.40
14. Jim Hall — Commitment — A&M Horizon — 3.05
15. Sonny Fortune — Waves of Dreams — A&M — 3.05
16. Charlie Haden — Duets — A&M — 3.05
17. Randy Weston — African Cookbook — Atlantic Import — 3.00
18. Joe Venuti/Zoot Sims — Vogue double 523 — 2.75
19. Duke Ellington — Carnegie Hall — DJM double LP — 2.55
20. Ray Noble plays Ray Noble — World Records SH 198 — 1.70

Postage/packing—1-3 LPs—50p/4-9 LPs—75p/10 and over—£1.00. Please send cheque/P.O. payable to All Change Records. For complete list of Bluenote LPs or for bi-monthly lists of deletions, secondhand and special offers please send stamped addressed envelope.

EXPORT/ WHOLESALE SECONDHAND/NEW LP ENQUIRIES WELCOMED.

might not be very capable but didn't want to waste money. I go through the LPs and check condition and they're all in good nick. No doubles. I tell him this and he's happy, asks how much. It's a lot of LPs and comes to around £300. He pulls out this wallet that is just stuffed with £50 notes and pays. I put all the LPs into one big bag and pass it to him and it almost pulls him to the floor when he tries to pick it up. I repack the LPs into two separate bags and this provides some balance so he staggers out with all these LPs. Later, when we've shut up shop, I go to The Good Mixer for a pint and who's there drinking? Shane McGowan.

He was already pissed when I served him so God knows what he will be like at the end of the night. I wondered, 'Will he remember to take all those LPs home with him? Or is he going to leave them somewhere?'

By the '90s there seemed to be a lot of people coming in with brand-new albums to sell. Some were journalists and some were people who worked for distributors and had found a way of smuggling stock out of the warehouse. There was a lot of theft from Rough Trade's warehouse that came into the shops. Some of the guys working there were Hackney squatters and they were intent on doing all kinds of dodgy deals. No surprise Rough Trade collapsed not long after. Brian's wife started running the Camden shop. I found her impossible to work for and so, when I asked for leave as my band God were going on tour, I was fired."

Petra Paignton stumbled into the Notting Hill R&TE after a pub session in 1990, announcing that she wanted to apply for the job advertised in the window. Abrams tested her on The Byrds ("Which I annoyed him by failing!"), then said she could start the following morning. Paignton says: "For some reason Brian liked me, and whenever I got into trouble – and I got busted a couple of times – he would promote me and give me a pay rise! I ended up being his personal assistant! He was a complex man, obviously wealthy yet he dressed like a tramp. He was very relaxed about time as long as we made up our 40 hours a week. The shops were packed with musicians, both working there and coming in. Bim Sherman, a lovely man, used to often drop by and we'd have a smoke out back. Elvis Costello, another lovely man, used to come into the classical music shop and he always made interesting purchases. And Killing Joke lived above the Portobello Road shop. I'd see them occasionally emerge looking like junkie vampires. As a work environment, I found myself easily distracted by the substances going around I ended up fleeing to Israel to try and escape my problems. But they weren't R&TE's fault; it was a brilliant place to work. The oddness of those shops is, I think, something to be celebrated. There's certainly not many other retail chains that tolerate the kind of staff Brian did."

Indeed, for keeping London high streets scuzzy and loaded with old records, we should doff our caps to Abram and his empire. Intriguingly, during the 1970s it wasn't Record & Tape Exchange but another chain that dominated London's second-hand record trade.

All Change Records

Geoff Francis opened All Change Records on Golborne Road, London W10, in 1973. Renting an empty shop from Portobello Market for £12 a week, he began with used albums worth £125. Immediately partnering with Graham Griffith, a jazz fan with a year's experience managing the Goldhawk Road branch of R&TE, All Change proved an instant success. In the early 1970s, Ladbroke Grove was home to many musicians and Griffith remembers a strung-out Paul Kossoff turning up with his record collection for sale: "I had to refuse all of them because they were in such bad condition."

Next, All Change opened a branch at 231 Baker Street, London. "Sherlock Holmes was supposed to have lived at 221B so we always had lots of tourists

Soho's Bedlam: Cheapo, Cheapo Records. Photo Garth Cartwright

dropping by," recalls Griffith. Francis remembers the shop being "painted groovy green and post box red and like a living room". Much of their stock was new. Griffith says: "We bought a lot of deletions and from DJs, journalists and record company employees. Actually, our main supplier was the head of PR at Warner's and he would get all these boxes of records from the US and I'd drive around to his house and collect them. They were all brand-new albums he had ordered purely for the purpose of reselling so as to fund his rather extravagant lifestyle. It got to the point where I could say, 'We'd like stock of the new Led Zeppelin album,' and a few weeks later he would have boxes of them for us."

Such albums were sold at lower prices than the high-street record shops, making All Change very successful.

Opening another shop at 21 Baker Street, the partners established a jazz basement – run by free jazz drummer John Stevens – and mail order. All Change was doing so well that the shop's accountant encouraged the duo to set up a chain of stores. They opened an All Change in London's Hanway Street, behind the first Virgin record shop, and made its focus reggae and soul. Here they installed Steve Barrow and, in 1975, sold him the shop. Retitled Daddy Kool, this shop brought the freshest Jamaican dubs to the West End. Meanwhile, the

Golborne Road All Change was passed to employee and college friend, Jon Clare, who reopened it as Honest Jon's. Later shifting 200 metres to Portobello Road, Honest Jon's remains an exceptional shop.

All Change then took over a failing Streatham record shop and opened a branch on Tottenham Court Road. By now, the partners were beginning to disagree, with Francis wanting to open ever more shops. Inevitably, they parted and Griffith founded Mole Jazz, London's last great jazz record store (see Chapter 12), while Francis oversaw eight different All Change shops. He opened one in the old Dolphinarium on Oxford Street and another in a 232-square-metre store at 136 Marylebone Road, London NW1. All Change had accounts with all the major record labels and offered new and used albums; it was a major player in London record retail. "I opened too many shops," says Francis, "and, once Graham had gone, the magic went. It just became a business and we never started out thinking we were doing this for business reasons. It was about the music." In 1979, Francis closed the shops and went travelling. "It was," he says, "time for me to move on."

Cheapo, Cheapo Records

As much a madhouse as a record shop, Cheapo, Cheapo Records (CCR) never attempted to set up a chain or 'move on'. Based in Rupert Street, London W1 (at the bottom of Berwick Street), CCR existed from 1972 to 2009, never failing across those decades to match its name. Its central London location and all day, every day opening meant many music industry and media types rinsed stock through it, while bargain hunters jostled one another as they dug for gold in narrow aisles. More notable than the stock was Phil Cording, CCR's proprietor, who possessed a spectral presence and acerbic personality that lent a Dickensian touch to proceedings.

Packed from floor to ceiling with stock, by the time I landed in London in 1991 the front section featured used videos. The back of the shop had all manner of tired LPs in bins and rock CDs locked in racks. The basement stocked blues, jazz, country, world and soul. Stalls outside once sold 45s, but by the 1990s were dedicated to rinsing junk CDs; although any time spent here meant you risked being approached by Soho sex workers who would proposition customers as they dug. "I'm only here for the music," I'd state when approached. "That's what they all say," came the reply.

CCR did not offer high priced rarities, fast turnover being what Cording wanted. Where the other second-hand shops in nearby Berwick Street would sniffily sort through the review CDs hacks like me brought in, accepting some, rejecting others, CCR took everything. And the price they paid was far better than R&TE offered. Chrissie Hynde, in her autobiography *Reckless*, writes, "I went immediately to three record companies, announcing myself as 'Chrissie Hynde, *NME*.' I walked out with as many albums 'to review' as I could carry, took them straight to Cheapo, Cheapo's in Soho, sold the lot and was on the next hovercraft to the city of love." Thus, CCR helped finance Hynde's baby steps towards stardom. Danny Baker also mentions Cheapo in his sophomore autobiography as where *NME* staff unloaded review copies for beer money. If any other UK record shop undersold CCR I'm yet to find it.

Entering CCR, I'd always greet Cording with "Hi Phil" which, at best, was acknowledged by a grunt. His three employees all wore a uniform of jeans and black T-shirts (emblazoned with metal bands), sported spectacles and fulsome locks swept back into pony tails. Their ghostly pale complexions added to the sense of gloom. A small, intense fellow called Harris manned the front counter. Here he would get into screaming matches with certain customers (and, on the phone, with his girlfriend). Out back was Goth Mick, a very tall, very thin, Irish man with a winningly droll wit. Downstairs in the basement resided a chubby chap called Roger who could be unbelievably bad-tempered. These three miscreants were classic record shop clerks and all conveyed a gloomy intensity as they sold, stacked and priced product under Cording's mournful eye. If ever a record shop existed as an example of bleak Beckettian pathos it was CCR.

I don't recall music playing in CCR, the only accompaniment being a transistor radio that Cording kept close to follow cricket Test matches. Being based in the loins of the Soho sex industry – strip clubs, gay bars, massage parlours, X-film cinemas and hot sheet 'studios' – meant the shop's clientele could be colourful, and Harris would rant loudly about the junkie riff-raff that darkened Cheapo's door. Perhaps this, the day in, day out encounters with Soho low life (and the lost tourists asking for directions), was why CCR staff would, at times, act like Pozzo from Beckett's *Waiting for Godot* in their outbursts and wild, impotent furies. For some, CCR was the record shop from hell. For myself, once accustomed to its rituals, I found it an enjoyable asylum.

If nothing about CCR seemed to change across the years (beyond stock), the tensions were surely taking their toll. Harris hated the job and openly spoke of his disdain for Cording. Inevitably, he was let go when things began to get tight around 2006. Roger kept on gaining weight, was hospitalised, returned and then, not long after, vanished forever. Goth Mick told me that Roger had been jailed (apparently for attempting to rob a newsagent of liquor bottles in a quest to feed his addictions). The last I heard, Roger had embraced sobriety and now counsels other lost souls; let's hope he's pursuing a happier, healthier vocation. Goth Mick and Cording continued to run CCR and, with Mick up front, Cheapo became quite a winning place to rummage. Even the Ebenezer Scrooge of Rupert Street began to act in a friendlier manner: I once entered CCR and found Cording saying, "I've saved this for you." He then handed over a VHS of Memphis country blues musicians (Furry Lewis and co.) featuring footage I've never found before or since. How did he know that Memphis music was among my obsessions? Excellent record shop etiquette.

In January 2009, I popped into CCR and found Gothic Mick asking "to have a word". I stepped over, wondering what the latest Roger gossip could be, only to be informed "Phil's dead"! In late December 2008, Cording complained of severe stomach pains, and tests revealed advanced cancer. Goth Mick disposed of the remaining stock and Cheapo, Cheapo Records disappeared. Soho is, undoubtedly, poorer for the absence of this bleak house.

Reckless Records

From the 1960s to the 1990s, Berwick Street in London acted as the UK's music foundation, with at least 30 record shops having existed either on or just off the fabled Soho street. In 2017, only two record shops remain: Reckless Records and Sister Ray (once an indie rock specialist, now largely stocking used vinyl). Across four decades, Reckless Records has weathered retail storms (opening and then closing branches in Camden, Angel and San Francisco, and downsizing in Soho) to soldier on. Having bought from, and sold to, Reckless for 20 years, I asked Duncan Kerr to tell me the story of his shop: "Reckless opened its first store in Islington in 1983, then this store in Soho in 1984. I'm a musician and was between gigs when I started working at Reckless in September 1984 and, in no time at all, I was managing the place. Charlie, the founder of Reckless, had worked for Record & Tape Exchange so knew how to succeed with second-hand and only ever made one real mistake – that was opening a Reckless in Camden that was towards Mornington Crescent. Turns out everyone gets off the tube and walks towards the market and never considers venturing in the opposite direction. We were in a cast-iron lease for that shop and it punished the business.

"A real estate agency made us a great offer on the Angel Reckless so we accepted that and have focused on Berwick Street, which has long been the heart of London record retail. There have been all manner of record shops on Berwick Street over the years and it's changed quite a lot. There were a lot more record

Berwick Street Survivor: Reckless Records. Photo Garth Cartwright

167

shops, prostitutes, film companies, PR companies, bike boys doing dispatches, the pavements were always crowded. Now it's a lot more upmarket, not as rough and ready as it once was."

Kerr emphasises that the survival of the Berwick Street shop is due to three things: *stock, stock, stock*: "As a second-hand store we live and die by stock. We advertise quite heavily and reply to every email. Good stock, fair prices and being nice to customers. We regularly have items that sell for four figures: Nick Drake, Pink Floyd, Beatles. Our best sale ever was a Rolling Stones album called *Necrophilia*. Apparently, there were only three copies of it issued. We sold that 20 years ago for £7000. A man from Germany flew over and paid for it in cash. He had his girlfriend with him and she was livid that he was spending all this money on a record!"

Reckless entered pop history in 1995 when its window appeared on the cover of Oasis' *(What's the Story) Morning Glory?* With some 22 million copies sold. Reckless now keep *Morning Glory*'s cover in the window, an arrow marking the shop's spot: "If you look closely, you will see a man standing outside Reckless holding a tin and in it is the master tapes of the new album. The story I heard about why he's there – and this came from an Oasis insider who told me over the counter – is that they finished the final mix of the album and were out in Soho with it celebrating and got so out of it that whoever was supposed to be holding onto the tapes put them down to rest on a rubbish bin or something in Berwick Street and forgot about them. And they never saw the tapes again! So, they had to do the final mix again. Interesting story! Every day we have dozens of people taking photos and selfies with Reckless behind them."

"It was pretty crazy!": Dan, Beanos, the 2 Two Bills of Notting Hill, Cob and Violet

Used record shops were once seemingly everywhere, as British as damp bank holidays. The following traders all enjoyed a status beyond mere local renown.

Birmingham's Dan Reddington launched Reddington's Rare Records in 1964, expanding into bigger shops as he serviced local and international collectors. In 2006, Reddington closed shop to focus on mail order. In August 2014, he announced the sale of his entire stock of 75,000 records across one weekend, with every item – no matter how rare – going for £1. This attracted much media attention (Dan loved being in the news, boasting about being a pen pal with Reggie Kray) and, on the final day, queues stretched for a mile outside the industrial estate where Reddington kept his collection.

Croydon housed Beanos, Europe's largest second-hand record shop. Spread across three floors, Beanos housed a small café, tiny cinema and thousands and thousands of LPs/CDs. Founded in 1975 as a market stall by David Lashmar, Beanos grew into a labyrinth that allowed for hours of exploring. Having relatives in Croydon gave me the excuse to travel out there a few times a year, and I never left without some interesting purchases, my favourite of which is Stoney Edwards' 1976 *Blackbird* LP. *Blackbird* might not command premium prices but it's a lost gem (never reissued on CD, unavailable on Spotify and iTunes). In 2006, Beanos announced they would be both downsizing and focusing on vintage vinyl, but this failed to resolve ongoing cash flow problems and Lashmar closed up in 2009.

London's Ladbroke Grove has hosted many record shops, but Plastic Passion (2 Blenheim Crescent, W11) is remembered for its famously dysfunctional duo, 'The 2 Bills of Notting Hill'. Opening Plastic Passion in 1984, they loaded their shop with collectable LPs and championed their icons (Dylan for Bill 1; Love for Bill 2). By 1990, the Bills had fallen out bitterly. Instead of closing Plastic Passion, they divided the long, narrow space into two circumscribed shops: Minus Zero Records and Stand Out Records. Sixty-one centimetres stood between the two traders. Cornershop's guitarist Ben Ayres recalls that whenever he entered this psychotic psych rock temple, he could feel a silent animosity bubbling away and, having found an LP to purchase from one Bill, the other Bill would call out, "something like, 'I've got that LP at a better price' or 'in better nick'. It was pretty crazy!" This odd couple continued running their separate-but-shared business space until May 2010. By then, the internet had become the place where much old vinyl was sold and the Bills chose to follow Fleetwood Mac's advice and go their own ways.

Porthmadog's (population 4185) Cob Records began selling used jukebox 45s as a sideline to the Cob Café in 1967. Ousting the café and – by stocking plenty of US cut-outs alongside new and used records – developing an international presence, Cob became the Welsh heavyweight champion: by 1971, Cob was mailing out, on average, 7500 albums a week and had 5000 customers in Yugoslavia alone. So deep was Cob's stock that John Peel became a customer, mentioning on his radio show how he'd sourced The Five Americans' 1966 LP *I See the Light* through Cob. Cob's Bangor (population 18,808) branch opened in 1979 and closed in 2012. In 2017, Cob in Porthmadog continues to operate both as a shop and mail order service focusing on used LPs, 45s and CDs.

Sheffield's Violet May (1910–95) has both a book about her (*Shades of Violet: Remembering Sheffield's Vinyl Goddess Violet May*) and an indie band named after her (The Violet May). Not bad for a chain-smoking harridan who managed notoriously unkempt shops. From 1956, when she first began selling used 78s in her junk shop, until her late 1970s retirement, Violet helped music fans (including aspiring local stars Dave Berry, Joe Cocker and Chris Spedding) get their hands on otherwise unavailable jazz and blues records. In the book's Foreword Richard Hawley wrote, "I never had the pleasure of meeting her but my father did and some of the music he bought in her shop still informs many of my ideas to this day. She widened the sonic palette of thousands of people from Sheffield and other places in Britain."

Chapter 12

Groove Me: 1970s Soul, Jazz and Funk

Shops dedicated to soul, funk and disco serve up dance music delights. London's Mole Jazz and Ray's Jazz create jazz's Bermuda Triangle. In Manchester, northern soul creates an underground scene of shops and stalls. Cameos from Robert Elms, Lloyd Bradley and Henry Rollins.

"Shame, shame, shame – *hey!* – shame on you (if you can't dance too!)." So shrieked Shirley Mae Goodman in 1975 who, having first invited the world to let the good times roll some two decades earlier, knew that dancing 'til dawn was the way to happiness. In 1975 many agreed and, with the UK experiencing unprecedented peacetime dread – the Troubles were engulfing the mainland, the oil crisis exacerbated inflation, racial violence escalated, industrial disputes led to electricity rationing – dance music entertained, engaged and brought people together in joy. One nation under a groove? When the kids got it together at discos across the land you might almost believe it possible. The rise of club culture was facilitated by several remarkable oracles, the first of which occupied a tiny space in a grimy London alley running between Oxford Street and Tottenham Court Road.

Contempo Records

Dave Godin, the godfather of British soul music, was anything but a businessman and, as 1970 got under way, he was forced to close both his Soul City record shop and label. Into the void stepped a Godin disciple: John Abbey. While still at school in 1965, Abbey started a fanzine called *Home of the Blues* where he enthusiastically covered blues, R&B and country. *Home of the Blues* received such a positive response that, by early 1967, Abbey had renamed it *Blues & Soul* and saw the first issue sell more than 10,000 copies. The first British magazine dedicated to soul/funk was up and running and, in 1970, Abbey shifted *Blues & Soul* into the upstairs premises at 42 Hanway Street, London W1, a narrow alley north of Tottenham Court Road tube station. As he was importing large quantities of soul 45s to sell via *Blues & Soul*'s 'Contempo Record Club', Abbey opened Contempo Records shop, each 45 slipped into a bag branded 'The Home of Soul'.

Contempo Records made no effort to attract custom, yet the soul boys – as the youths who loved to dance called themselves – flocked there in such numbers that crowds sometimes spilled out of the shop, down the stairs and into the street. Abbey focused on keeping Contempo open mainly on Friday afternoons and Saturday mornings, leaving him the rest of the week to oversee *Blues & Soul* and, from 1973, run Contempo's record label. He released suburb soul, funk and disco records on the label, enjoyed Top 5 chart success with Dorothy Moore's 'Misty Blue' (1976) and helped launch Al Green and Barry White in the UK. The Contempo Records shop may have been tiny but its impact was enormous and two former customers,

West End jazz giant: Ray's Jazz exterior and interior, 1980s.
Photos Wendy Smith. Courtesy of Mike Gavin.

Robert Elms and Lloyd Bradley, have both eulogised it in books.

Elms, now a broadcaster on BBC London radio, describes in *The Way We Wore* (2006) how he and his teenage soul boy mates would travel in from north-west London to Contempo Records for the tunes that soundtracked the clubs they frequented: "Leg it over the road to Hanway Street, a charismatic, piss-smelling dogleg alley, where up the stairs of an unmarked doorway was Contempo. Contempo Records was the epicentre of the London black music world in 1976, entirely contained in a room about eight feet square above a Spanish bar with an Irish name, in a forgotten street. On Friday afternoons it was the only place to buy the records the DJs had been spinning over the road at Crackers. So, punters literally queued up the stairs, shouting out names of songs and artists, or listening intently to the sides which had arrived in crates from the States that day, deciding whether that was the one to invest in."

Lloyd Bradley, then a black teenager growing up in Wood Green, recalled in *Sounds Like London* (2013) how the London West End import shops served as youth clubs for like-minded funkateers: "Before the bands, the scene was all about records, American import records, available from a few ultra-specialist outlets that carried US imports within days of their American release dates. The West End shops were the scene's entry level, where people accessed the music, got their faces known and found out where the cool clubs were."

Singling out Contempo, Bradley writes: "To call Contempo a 'shop' is to flatter it – it was a tiny room above a bar called Bradley's, reached by a creaky, windy staircase that, today, would be some sort of health and safety cup final. Inside, there was a counter across the middle, with a booming sound system beneath it and shelves stocked with funk behind it. Friday afternoon was when the new music arrived, and punters could spend hours anxiously hanging about while the guys who ran the place took phone calls and tried to reassure the packed room: 'The boxes have just cleared customs, they should be here in an hour or so'."

The arrival of new imports carried an excitement that little else in life matched (for the music fan), and Bradley mentions One Stop on Dean Street, Ray's Jazz on Shaftesbury Avenue, Cheapo, Cheapo on Rupert Street, City Sounds in High Holborn and Dobell's in Charing Cross Road as the West End arc the soul boys would hit as they sought out funk. Further afield, he notes, were Sunshine Records in Turnpike Lane, Moondog's in Manor Park and the mighty Record Corner in Balham (he overlooks Black Wax Records in Streatham – John Peel and his producer John Walters were regulars there). "In the same way that Stern's served as the hub of London's African music community, these shops were vital to the cohesion of the funk scene, probably more so than the clubs," writes Bradley. "The shops, however, were more accessible, conducive to conversation and focused entirely on the music." As Dobell's had done in earlier decades, Contempo provided a network for musicians, writers, DJs, promoters, hustlers, collectors; and these characters went on to help shape Brit funk and late 1970s clubbing.

Abbey shifted to the USA in 1978, settling in Atlanta where he founded noted soul (then rap) label Ichiban Records in 1985. Contempo Records ceased trading in 1979; without Abbey at the helm the oracle had lost its leader, although *Blues & Soul* magazine remains in print, soon to celebrate its 1100th issue. By opening in Hanway Street, Contempo had turned a narrow alley into one of Europe's most vivid vinyl hotspots – All Change Records opened a black music outlet directly beneath Contempo that morphed into Daddy Kool, the West End's only reggae shop, and many other oddball record shops would follow. Alongside Crackers nightclub and Sevilla Mia flamenco bar, these vinyl caverns transformed Hanway Street from squalid alley to Soho hotspot. *Soul power!*

Bluebird Records

Bill Russell and Billy Carruthers opened Bluebird Records on 155 Church Street, Paddington, London W2, in the late 1970s. With a strong inventory of soul and funk, reggae, and rap, Bluebird succeeded Contempo as if by proxy. Immediately successful, Bluebird expanded into the shop next door – where US cut-out LPs were offered at bargain prices – then opened Bluebirds across London and in Luton.

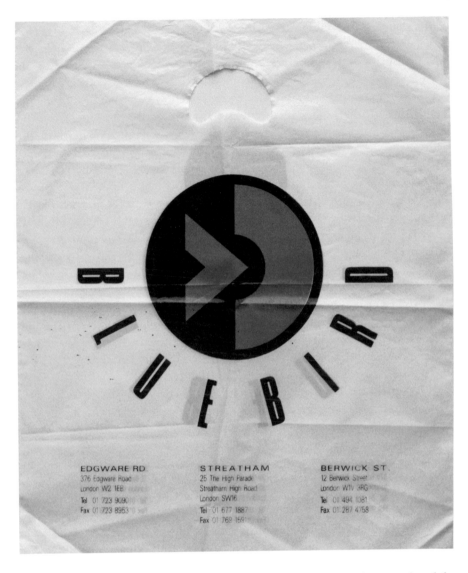

EDGWARE RD.
376 Edgware Road
London W2 1EB
Tel 01 723 9090
Fax 01 723 8953

STREATHAM
25 The High Parade
Streatham High Road
London SW16
Tel 01 677 1887
Fax 01 769 1591

BERWICK ST.
12 Berwick Street
London W1V 3RG
Tel 01 494 1081
Fax 01 287 4758

Bluebird had great stock and a real sense of what the kids hitting the clubs wanted to hear. With radio and TV giving dance hits by The Bee Gees, Village People and Donna Summer plenty of attention while ignoring a huge stratum of funk, soul and disco, Bluebird acted as an outlier, a radar station of sorts, constantly sourcing fresh new tunes and ensuring a new generation of DJs and dancers were never short of American hot wax.

If the disco era saw huge sales of records designed to get people dancing, they occurred mostly in record bars at Woolies, Boots, WHSmith and Our Price. Virgin Record shops and *Melody Maker* might have ignored disco but, just as post-Second World War youth preferred dancing to trad jazz over chin stroking be-bop, the kids were oblivious to such prim prophets. An anti-disco backlash saw the genre's stars fall off the charts but the dance scene, now comfortably underground, only grew in strength. Iain Scott, who managed central London Our Prices in the late 1970s, notes: "With the West End and City shops it was dance 12-inch singles and jazz-funk albums that we sold and sold. In comparison to punk, jazz-funk and club dance records of this period didn't seem to get many mentions from music journalists. But, on the front line of many Our Price shops, punk was an also-ran in comparison to funk when it came to sales."

Where Our Price stocked largely Top 40 music, shops like Bluebird and Balham's Record Corner catered expressly for those who loved contemporary black American music. When Simon Grigg arrived in London (from New Zealand) in 1983, he entered Bluebird and felt awestruck: "DJ Norman Jay told me many years later that he and Joey used to trek across to the States and bring back thousands of old soul albums and deleted singles to sell (in Bluebird). It's where I discovered the likes of Mantronix, Salsoul and Prelude. For a pound or two you could acquire sealed US pressings of albums that you'd only read about. It was my Mecca."

In 1983, the Bluebird record label launched. By licensing tunes from the USA, the label helped turn the likes of Lonnie Liston Smith's 'Expansions' into a UK club classic and issued everything from disco to go-go. Bluebird released records by several British artists, the most successful being 'Fool for You' (1983) by Julie Roberts and 'Rain Forest' by Paul Hardcastle (a Top 5 hit on the US R&B charts in 1984), before closing the label in 1988 to concentrate on the shops. Carruthers sold his share in Bluebird in 1992, shifting back to his native Scotland and transforming into a leading peony grower and nurseryman. Russell kept the chain going, enjoying the boom times brought about by acid house, before quietly shutting up as the new millennium started.

Cranked Up Really High: Manchester's Northern Soul Shops

By the 1970s, the northern soul scene had developed a fierce identity, with its own specific drugs, dance moves, gear, haircuts, slang and, most importantly, clubs and record vendors. Manchester's The Spin Inn, originally in Cross Street and described by one London aficionado as "the only shop that mattered north of Watford", developed into the foremost northern outlet for soul and funk. When DJ Ian Levine presided over a split in the northern soul scene – he began spinning contemporary soul and funk at the all-nighters – the youths who shared his enthusiasm shopped at both The Spin Inn and at Global Records on Manchester's Princes Street. Global opened around 1970 and was owned by Ed Balbier, a US citizen who used his Philadelphia contacts to bring in choice releases on Phili International and other US labels.

For the scene's zealots, who only wanted obscure 1960s 45s, Ralph's, situated near Manchester's Victoria Station, served as the first port of call. Ralph's opened in 1967 and never wavered from its primary mission of selling rare US 45s to DJs and dancers. That this involved the first dedicated bootleg 45 label, means it gets disparaged by some, but the northern soul scene was awash with fakes (many manufactured by Nottingham's Selectadisc). Stuart Cosgrove began shopping at

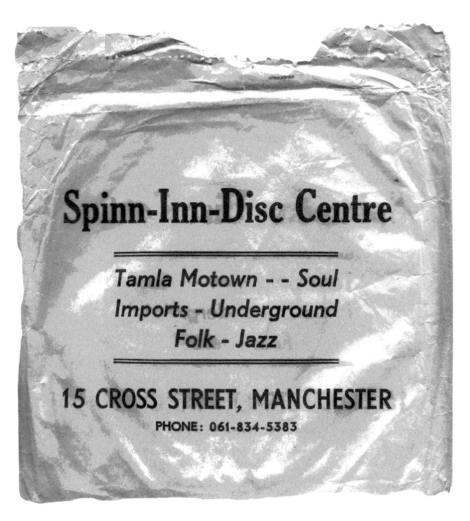

Spinn-Inn-Disc Centre

Tamla Motown - - Soul
Imports - Underground
Folk - Jazz

15 CROSS STREET, MANCHESTER
PHONE: 061-834-5383

Ralph's in the early 1970s and writes in *Young Soul Rebels*, his personal history of the northern soul scene: "Ralph's was northern soul's answer to Hut 8, the wooden shed where Alan Turing led the cryptographers that finally cracked the German Enigma machine. Ralph's Records was a tight and claustrophobic shop with rows of vinyl banking up to the tills. It had curious homemade devices that stopped shoplifting, four thin brush shanks were driven through the holes of imported records and then padlocked on the counter end … I spent months of my life in Ralph's, looking at labels, gazing at credits and listening to conversations."

During the 1970s, Manchester's Underground Market Centre offered several soul music stalls, the most notable being John Doe Records (JDR). JDR was owned and run by two collectors, Rod Shard and Dave Withers: Withers' pedigree as a record dealer involved selling 45s at northern soul's holy grail, the Wigan Casino, and running his Out of the Past stall in the upstairs area of the Arndale Centre. Teaming up, the duo opened JDR in Affleck's Palace, a hippie market housed in the old Affleck and Brown department store. It took an IRA bomb – which destroyed the Arndale Centre in 1996 – to bring an end to JDR.

The youths who devoted their weekends to dancing to obscure US soul 45s were, back then, ignored or ridiculed by rock, reggae and funk fans. Indeed, getting cranked up really high, spilling talcum powder on the dance floor (facilitating spins, backdrops and high kicks) for obscure 45s meant the entire northern scene tended to get dismissed as a playground for 'wurzels' who had swapped cider for speed. Yet from this arcane passion would develop an embryonic gay DJ and dance scene, a blueprint for rave parties, pop impresario Pete Waterman, Soft Cell's 'Tainted Love' (1981) and a 45 appreciation society that helped reissue and re-evaluate many under-appreciated US soul records and singers: deep crate digging discovered innumerable overlooked gems. DJ Greg Wilson, a face on Manchester's 1980s club scene, wrote how northern soul's Saturday night fever offered "a completely different kind of ritual taking place, more spiritual than carnal". The record shops where youths invested in 7-inch singles that encouraged them to dance and dream were small oracles, places where specific 45s offered transcendence. Beatin' Rhythm (originally at 108 Tib Street), Manchester's final northern soul emporium, closed in 2015 to concentrate on mail order. Yet whenever a northern soul all-nighter occurs, the record stalls come out.

Mole Jazz

In 1978, London's King's Cross was home to a grimy transport terminus, a multitude of budget hotels, and plenty of drug dealers and prostitutes plying their intertwined trades. The Scala Cinema, a celebrated grindhouse that Stanley Kubrick would later force out of business, and *Time Out* magazine also existed here. Into this intensely urban milieu burrowed what would prove to be London's last exalted jazz shop, Mole Jazz at 311 Gray's Inn Road, WC1.

Mole Jazz, while never as assuredly funky as Contempo or Bluebird, shared those shops' devotion to cutting-edge African-American music, albeit of the jazz rather than funk spectrum. Initially operating out of a dank building surrounded by heavy traffic, Mole opened as a jazz dance scene began bubbling away in Camden while post-punk bands (The Pop Group, James White & the Contortions) directed their listeners to seek out Albert Ayler and Eric Dolphy LPs. For those who wanted jazz to dance to or jazz to create noise terror with, well, Mole Jazz proved a perfect fit.

"Dobell's was a shadow of its former self while Ray's was stuck in the past," says Mole's Graham Griffith of his shop's hip cachet. Having co-founded All Change Records, the second-hand chain that succeeded brilliantly across West London in the first half of the 1970s (see Chapter 11), Griffith determined that London lacked a record shop that was keyed into the energies abundant in contemporary American and European jazz. He says: "Mole started as a jazz mail order list in 1976. I met Ed Dipple, who was lecturing in maths at Luton Polytechnic, over the counter at All Change and, initially, he helped me run the mail order. The Mole name came about from Ed's wife saying he looked like a mole as he was a huge man with poor eyesight. I left All Change on May 1, 1977 with £3000 in

LPs in exchange for my share of that business. We initially ran things from Ed's spare bedroom but, once records started spilling into the hall, we had to find a premises and the building on Gray's Inn Road proved ideal as they were right by King's Cross Station, near Euston and a host of tube lines and bus routes. We opened in June 1978 and, from day one, we were successful."

Cartoonist Robert MacCauley designed the shop's distinctive logo (a mole wearing braces and check trousers blowing an alto saxophone) and both partners worked their international contacts: they sought out deletions and cut-outs in the USA, and Japanese reissues of rare Blue Note albums and obscure European jazz releases from warehouses and shops across the Continent. This enabled Mole to build the richest jazz album stock ever seen in the UK, and their regular mail order auctions of rare titles attracted bids from across the globe. "It wasn't uncommon for certain albums to attract bids of £200 pounds," says Griffith.

"We did well because we were doing things the other jazz shops weren't. We had imports no one else in the UK stocked. We made sure that Mole's interior was striking and our record label issued excellent albums – we reissued Tubby Hayes' finest recordings. The live Art Pepper recording, *Blues for the Fisherman*, was made when he played Ronnie Scott's and it remained at the top of the *Sunday Times* jazz chart for over 18 months, becoming one of the best-selling jazz albums released by a British jazz label, with over 10,000 sales. And we realised early on that CDs would be huge so stocked all the jazz CD releases while certain shops ignored them."

A Bermuda Triangle: Mole Jazz, Ray's Jazz, Dobell's (and Honest Jon's)

As the 1980s began, a loose assembly of young British musicians – including Courtney Pine, the Jazz Warriors, Loose Tubes, Pigbag, Rip Rig & Panic, the James Taylor Quartet, Ronny Jordan, Galliano – ensured myriad jazz styles commanded youthful audiences for the first time since the 1950s. Once again, London's West End jazz shops were thronged by music-mad urchins full of attitude, and Mole took over James Asman's, the small jazz shop that had existed on New Row in Covent Garden since the 1950s, while retaining the King's Cross shop.

Covent Garden proved a perfect location as Westminster Council's enforced demolition of the building that housed Dobell's in 1981 saw Europe's most celebrated jazz record shop shifting from Charing Cross Road to nearby Tower Street. Moreover, Ray's Jazz was at 180 Shaftesbury Avenue – Ray Smith, who had run Collet's jazz department since the 1950s, had broken away and set up on his own in 1982. Close by sat Honest Jon's free jazz record shop in Monmouth Street. Music critic Richard Williams would note in *Time Out* that having Dobell's, Ray's and Mole Jazz so close together made "for a Bermuda Triangle of West End jazz shops".

Beyond the hassle of relocating, Dobell's remained a jazz hub, and the shop celebrated its fortieth anniversary in 1986 with artists including Spike Milligan and Slim Galliard attending a raucous party. Then Doug Dobell died suddenly while attending the Nice Jazz Festival in 1988. Without Doug running things, Dobell's began to fray, the shop struggling on until Doug's widow chose to close Dobell's in 1992.

Smith now presided over the big daddy of West End jazz shops and he, a former drummer and lifelong roisterer, enjoyed his status. Smith ended up in Shaftesbury Avenue when the redevelopment of New Oxford Street in 1974 forced Collet's record department to move. When Smith came to an agreement with Chris Barber to store and sell a vast number of mint condition 78s in 1975 – discs by Charlie Parker, Dizzy Gillespie, Dexter Gordon and others on the Savoy, DeeGee and Bop labels, still boxed in original packaging from the late 1940s – it attracted much media attention, Smith's brusque nature making certain his interviews were never dull. This and his habit of regularly shooting Russian 78s with an air rifle in the back room of the basement – stating that his favourite disc for target practice was 'I'm in Love with My Tractor' – ensured he enjoyed a larger than life reputation among Soho's denizens. Smith amicably split with Collet's in 1982, setting up Ray's Jazz in the Shaftesbury Avenue shop, while Gill Cook shifted back to Collet's Charing Cross Road base, running the record bar there with blues musician Dave Peabody ("I looked up once to see who was waiting to be served and it was Julie Christie," says Peabody).

Collet's was forced to close after a 1989 arson attempt by Islamists who suspected the shop might stock Salman Rushdie's *The Satanic Verses* (1988) (it didn't) led to extensive water damage. The fall of the Berlin Wall and subsequent collapse of the Soviet Union followed not long after: appropriate then that this fountain of radical thought and music crumbled alongside the Marxist-Leninist ideology that Eva Reckitt (1890–1976) so believed in (see Chapter 2). The beloved Gill Cook did

not far outlive Collet's, her passing in 2006 signalling the end of an era.

Honest Jon's Monmouth Street jazz shop shut when the small chain's two partners split. Former employee John Williams wryly notes, "more people play free jazz than want to buy free jazz LPs". Ray's Jazz, which thrived with the CD boom, watched its contemporaries close and felt a chill wind blowing. Smith had opened his shop's basement up as a Blues & Roots department, and artists like Henry Rollins, Bjork and Joe Strummer would all venture in to seek out old and new music. Rollins recently recalled such on BBC Radio 6 Music, stating:

"Ray's Jazz in beautiful London town – I'd always jam down there and the guy behind the counter knew I was a real nut for music and he really had my number. Whenever I'd be down there within two minutes he had like a 5-inch stack of CDs and vinyl records for me to check out. And one time he pulled out a CD of the Reverend A.W. Nix's sermons and said, 'I think you might like this,' and put on the 'Black Diamond Express Train to Hell – Part 1' and I said, 'Oh! Done!'"

The 'guy behind the counter' was Mike Gavin, son of Bob Glass (a face on the jazz scene who worked in many of London's jazz shops). Gavin loved running Ray's basement yet admits a changing West End made things increasingly fraught for the specialist shops: "The closing of Dobell's and Collet's wasn't good for us as it meant less people were heading into central London to buy jazz and blues. There was a period when all the shops were open [so] that Saturday was just crazy as you had music fans who worked Monday to Friday coming into central London on a Saturday and traipsing around the jazz shops on a mission to buy music. Serious shoppers! Back then the Virgin Megastore and Tower Piccadilly both also had serious jazz sections – the Tower selection was just incredible, they truly had every jazz album then available – so you could spend a day shopping for records without even considering the second-hand shops.

"180 Shaftesbury Avenue was owned by the GLC [Greater London Council] and when Thatcher got rid of the GLC the London Residuary Body was put in place to flog off all the titles to property developers who immediately cranked up the rents. We met them and said, 'We've improved your building: look at the basement – we put in a staircase and a counter!'" but they were uninterested in what we had to say and the rents went up. It got to the point where Ray's had to take £10,000 a week just to cover expenses. That's impossible with a specialist record shop. Ray retired in 2002 and died in 2011. He hadn't been in good health in recent years but, I imagine after decades of selling jazz in central London, he felt this was a bitter end. They scattered his ashes in Soho Square – surreptitiously as it's apparently illegal. I'm pretty sure as that happened there were some bemused tourists wondering what the drummer of The Rolling Stones was doing wandering about the Square looking shifty with an envelope full of white powder..."

Ray's Jazz did find an afterlife of sorts when Foyles bookshop on Charing Cross Road – once Collet's main competitor – bought the name and established a Ray's Jazz outlet within its multi-storey book mart. I enjoy popping in here – they have a fine magazine selection, impressive books (new and used), 78s, vinyl and CDs – but it is a shadow of the giants that once bestrode the West End.

Mismanagement forced the closure of Mole Jazz's New Row shop in 1997, and the King's Cross store appeared on shaky ground. New Note Distribution stepped in to shore up the business but Griffith soon discovered that a manager had systematically looted Mole's stock of valuable vinyl to fund his kids' private-school education. Griffith closed the King's Cross base in 2004, transferring the remaining stock to a space above Harold Moore's classical record shop in Great Marlborough Street, Soho, but he soon realised Mole was irreparably holed. "I made a decision to fund Mole based on sentiment," says Griffith, who continues to run New Note Distribution, "and that was a mistake." With Mole's cessation, the era of the independent Soho jazz shop finally came to an end, much great music and good times passing with it.

Chapter 13

Word Sound Power: Reggae's Sonic Shrines

Roots natty roots! As the 1970s get underway reggae shops reflect heightened racial tensions. Desmond's, Webster's, Intone, Daddy Kool, Dub Vendor, Don Christie, Mango, Summit and Black Wax. Cameos from Alex Paterson, John Peel, Lee 'Scratch' Perry, Dennis Bovell, David Katz, Robin Campbell and UB40.

In April 1970, when Desmond Dekker, a prince among singers, took the stage at the Empire Pool in London's Wembley, a coronation of sorts appeared to be taking place. Having topped the British charts and entered the US Top 10 in 1969 with 'Israelites' – a song of mysterious, awesome majesty – he was the most celebrated Jamaican alive. As this, the first major, multi-artist Jamaican music concert was under way, the music that had shape-shifted across the decade through 'blues', 'blue beat', 'ska' and 'rocksteady' before establishing itself as 'reggae', looked set to rule.

However, it wasn't to be: the 1970s saw rock ascending while reggae and soul were sidelined. Reggae went underground and, reflecting new attitudes among the black British community, emerged harder, angrier and less interested in integration.

The 'Ten-Second Rule'

Coming of age with reggae in the late 1960s was as natural as breathing for Noel Hawks: "I grew up on a council estate in south-east London, and the hippie stuff was mainstream, marketed at you every which way. Rock fans had three weekly music papers telling them all about these bands while reggae and soul got no coverage. Black music was underground, not the hippie bands! I never ever understood how the whole history of Jamaican music got written out of white working-class history as it was our music. You heard it in youth clubs and everywhere else. I bought my first records as a teenager at Maple Radio on Penge High Street. It was run by an old white couple. They'd have the TVs in the front and the most unbelievable selection of reggae records in the back because there was a huge local demand for it. Blue Beat, Island, Studio 1, Pama. They'd do packs where they would seal up one of their carrier bags and sell five records for ten bob – 50p! – and I still have some of the records they sold back then."

I wonder if Maple Radio employed the 'ten-second rule.' British record shops used to be driven to distraction by the request to "play the record" by the Caribbean clientele (ten seconds' play was what Jamaican traders allowed). "Black people would want to hear the record," says Ian Hingle of his time in Musicland and WG Stores, "but it was crazy – 'You're asking me for Al Green's 'Call Me' and saying you want to hear it but you know this is the record you want to buy?' But they'd want to hear it. Ten seconds of each track."

Dub Vendors: left to right – John MacGillivray, Martin 'Redman' Trenchfield, Donald 'Papa Face' Facey, Noel Hawks. Photo taken by Chris Lane. Courtesy of Noel Hawks.

By 1970, the UK was the world's leading consumer of Jamaican records, and with dozens of new titles released every week, countless stalls, shacks and shops operated to supply demand. As the 1970s started, reggae and British racial tensions heightened, and certain outlets decided that the 'Babylon system' wasn't simply the British government but also white customers.

It Dread Inna Inglan

The 1970s was the nasty decade that made Gary Glitter a star, put Margaret Thatcher in Downing Street, and accepted racism as common currency. From *Love Thy Neighbour* on the BBC to Eric Clapton endorsing Enoch Powell on a Birmingham stage, expressions of fear and loathing towards black and Asian people were commonplace.

In turn, reggae, once so dynamic and optimistic, now adopted an often bleak tone while the rhythms slowed, reflecting the strong marijuana now considered an essential part of creation. If Jamaica was riven with gun violence, poverty and political unrest, British reggae artists offered their own forbidding observations on the society in which they lived. Linton Kwesi Johnson articulated inner-city anger and despair, while Steel Pulse, hailing from Birmingham, answered Clapton with 'Handsworth Revolution' (1978), a song professing the streets would soon run with blood. Certain reggae shops also reflected the anger and alienation evident in the black community – a hostility towards outsiders, which had been absent from the ska shops, taking bitter shape. Dread, as the Rastas liked to sing, dread in a Babylon.

When I arrived in London in 1991, living in Tottenham then Brixton, there were plenty of reggae shops – some stank with marijuana's sweet odour. By the 1990s, race relations had calmed somewhat but tensions remained and, entering every reggae record shop I came across, my experiences were mixed. Some were welcoming, others less so. One Brixton shop on Atlantic Road would blare out hate speeches by Nation of Islam leader Louis Farrakhan, the clerk behind the counter glowering as if I was stealing his oxygen. Nearby Blacker Dread seemed to find a perverse pleasure in menacing customers who were not part of the clique. When, in 2014, Blacker Dread's owner was jailed – for money laundering (if there was a law against surly shopkeepers they would have banged him up for that too) – no one hurried to launch a campaign to see him freed.

However, others were brilliantly scruffy oracles, with Brixton's Supertone Records and All Tone Records – the latter owned by rocksteady singer Alton Ellis – being joyous shops in a 'hood then blighted

by riots, crime and poverty. I would drop into All Tone and just ogle Ellis as a fan boy, "There stands the man who sang 'Cry Tough'"! Alton truly was the cool ruler and I miss him and his shop. Super Tone and All Tone were intent on celebrating Jamaican music, and these and other such shops were sonic shrines. Admittedly, often extremely elemental shrines with records in plastic crates resting against stained walls. Yet, when the needle dropped onto vinyl, massive rhythms rolling forth while sweetly intoxicated voices called out to "Jah Ras-ta-far-IIIIII", these distressed trading posts became places of prophecy, the chants and rhythms conveying a reality both here yet also far removed from grey London town.

Desmond's Hip City II

Desmond's origins are discussed in Chapter 4, and by 1970 Hip City enjoyed an iconic status as the sonic heart of black Britain – an Afrocentric palace of sorts where reggae and soul were constantly played at loud volume, LP sleeves hung from the ceiling and posters of Angela Davis, Che Guevara and Muhammad Ali decorated the walls. The British Black Panther Movement (BPM) had a branch nearby and many of the youths involved with the BPM would hang out at Desmond's – on 15 November 1969, violence erupted in front of the shop as youths belonging to the BPM intervened when police tried to arrest one of their associates. In 1974, a sense of black Brixton being under siege intensified when Desmond's became the target of an attack from National Front thugs. No one was hurt but, just as reggae records were increasingly filled with dread forebodings, so were British race relations.

Accordingly, certain white customers became aware they were less than welcome at Desmond's. An online post about Desmond's states that in 1977 the shop was "a very intimidating place for a white person to venture into". Ace Records' Tony Rounce, who has entered manifold reggae shops across England and Jamaica, recalls the Hip City staff actively practising discrimination: "Living in Brixton, as I did in the mid-to-late '70s, Desmond's was my local shop, but I seldom used it. Didn't matter what time of day or what day you went in there, if you were white the atmosphere was oppressive and frequently hostile. Even if you were in there with no other customers present, early in the morning, the staff would frequently ignore you. If you asked for a record that you could see on display, you would frequently be told 'tune finish' and when you pointed out that there was a copy/copies in plain sight behind the counter, the answer was usually 'dem all save.' I went in there maybe half a dozen times throughout the whole decade and I don't ever remember getting good service or a single record. A pal of mine was ejected from the shop with force by reggae singer Dandy Livingstone, who, at one point, was shop manager, for pursuing a similar line of questioning."

Rounce notes that Desmond Bryan, the owner, and his brother Popsy (at Starlight Records) were both delightful men but the Hip City staff were another matter. This noted, there were white customers who enjoyed more positive experiences. Leading reggae DJ David Rodigan recalls, "When I first came to

specialists in Black Music from the roots, Reggae, Heavy funk. **PRE RELEASES FROM JAMAICA** All at: **48 RYE LANE, PECKHAM RYE, LONDON, SE15.** Tel. 732 7758 Buses: 12,63, 37.

London I was buying these records in Muzik City in Lewisham, Desmond's Hip City in Brixton." While Alex Paterson of The Orb says: "I went down to Desmond's Hip City, which was the reggae shop in Brixton in '75 and '76, and I was one of the only white boys in there. By chance, one of the girls from my youth club was working behind the decks and just called me over and said, 'Come play all the tunes you want.' That was that."

Desmond's existed on the frontline for the Brixton riots of 1981 and 1985, and both uprisings intensified the racial divide. When combined with obnoxious staff, the shop likely helped alienate even more customers – white, Asian and black. Having a bad attitude achieves little in the long run and Desmond's closed in 1989, the original 'Blue Beat Centre' having lasted for a quarter of a century. In its time, Hip City became a landmark black British music shop and the 1977 movie *Black Joy* – following the comic travails of a Caribbean immigrant (Norman Beaton) in London – acknowledges such with a scene shot in Desmond's, the record shop that once embodied Brixton's troubled heart.

Intone Records & Tapes

Intone advertised itself as "Rockers dub King Tubby's style. Pre-releases & import soul. New selection of Singles every week going fast!!!" Situated at 48 Rye Lane, Peckham Rye, London SE15, it was owned by Lloyd Coxsone, a major figure in British reggae who ran a sound system, produced numerous records and set up and ran the following reggae labels: Safari, Tribesman and Outernational. Intone was, appropriately for a shop run by a major player, filled with great stock. So much so that John Peel became Intone's most vocal champion – venturing into Peckham in the 1970s was not an activity many of Britain's rock aristocracy would willingly have done – and, in his *Sounds* column in November 1975, Peel described Intones thus: "The noise within tends towards the deafening, with extracts from current releases being played at considerable volume and without pause. This, although it means that all communication must be by hand-signals and shouting, helps the customer to decide which records to buy."

With Peel, John Lydon and The Clash endorsing reggae as *the* rebel music of choice, many of the new rock audience were converts; even Bob Marley sang of a "punky reggae party". Not that Intones always proved welcoming to Caucasians, as Hawks recalls. "I went in there one morning asking for an Errol Dunkley record only to be told, emphatically, 'We don't sell pop records'. I asked again and said it wasn't a pop record only to be told again 'We don't sell pop records'." Such were the tribulations of the 1970s – although Hawks says such experiences were rare and not just related to race: when he attempted to enter

the back room of Tipples, a Peckham newsagent that stocked lots of Jamaican 45s to sell to the local community, the fearsomely grouchy (and white) Mr Tipple refused Hawks access. Intone closed in the mid-1970s, and Peel would soon be found shopping for reggae at Daddy Kool.

Daddy Kool

Initially tucked away on Hanway Street, minutes from the throb of Tottenham Court Road tube station in London, Daddy Kool existed for three decades as the West End's only reggae shop. Its origins find East London mod Steve Barrow getting a job at used record shop All Change Records. He says: "This is spring 1974. All Change had shops all over London and their shop in Hanway Street was underneath Contempo Records, who used to give me all their promos. We called it 'the black music shop' as it was full of soul and funk records. People came in asking if we had any reggae and then the son of Pecking's (Shepherd's Bush reggae distributor and record shop) came in with these Studio 1 releases

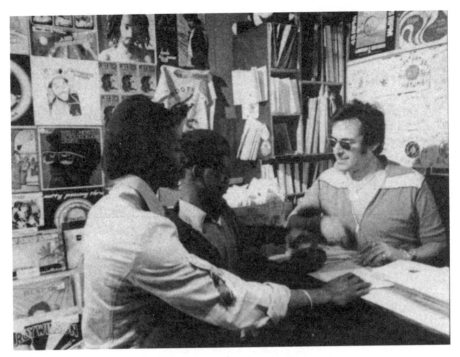

that Coxsone was putting out early 1975. All Change's owner said, 'Why don't you take over?' I met Keith Stone, who wanted to get into the music biz, and said to him, 'We could turn this into a reggae shop!' Keith borrowed the money off his mother to buy the lease. We opened Daddy Kool in October 1975."

Daddy Kool immediately made its mark and every Jamaican musician who landed in London dropped by. When new tunes were being DJ-ed, revellers would pack the shop, huge cones of ganja got sparked and everyone had a very merry time. Barrow remembers: "Until we started Daddy Kool, reggae shops were small, local. We were getting stock from all around London – Brixton, Brockley, New Cross, Peckham – the shops there were often pressing stuff: Morpheus in Croydon, Count Shelley up in Stoke Newington, Klik Records in Harlesden."

As Daddy Kool gathered heat, the partnership between Barrow and Stone grew frosty. "After a year, Keith accused me of ripping him off and dissolved the partnership," says Barrow. "Keith didn't know any black people. I took him around the reggae shops, taught him everything."

Solo, Stone proved a quick learner as Daddy Kool kept trading, shifting into Soho – first to Dean Street and then on to Berwick Street – for almost 30 years. I occasionally ventured in, admiring the myriad 45s hanging on the wall (wire looped through them to make sure none went missing), but always found Stone so sour that I never spent long there. Barrow, meanwhile, helped out at Honest Jon's Camden shop: "I worked for them from 1978 to 1980 in the Camden shop and in the shop in Monmouth Street. At that time, Honest Jon's also owned Maroon's Tunes reggae shop in Greek Street. Rae Cheddie was the manager and Leroy 'Lepke' Anderson worked there. I would cover for them.

Rae bought thousands of records in from the USA. Leroy was a pirate DJ for Dread Broadcasting Corporation and often in trouble with the law. When the partners behind Honest Jon's split the business, they closed the West End shops. I then went on to set up the Blood & Fire reggae reissue label."

Dub Vendor

"Dub Vendor was *the* London reggae shop," says Barrow, and his opinion is echoed by many. Founded by Chris Lane and John MacGillivray, two Londoners who met at school in 1970, Dub Vendor served everyone and commanded international respect. Lane says: "In 1968 a few rocksteady tunes got into the national charts and then the skinhead fashion kicked in and me and my mates were into that. Reggae and soul and Motown were the soundtrack at the youth clubs in 1969 and 1970. Reggae was really, really big. It was a fashion thing – it went along with the clothes and stuff. But, by the end of '71, people changed their wardrobe, they grew their hair and got flares and hippie shit. John MacGillivray was in my class at school and when everyone else dropped reggae he still loved it. We'd take an extended lunch hour and go around the local shops. We bought records from the Muzik City and WG Stores in Shepherd's Bush.

"Saturdays we would get a Red Rover bus pass and jump on the first bus that came along and, if it went past a record shop or junk shop, we'd jump off, have a look. We were looking for ska and reggae and there were lots. There was a great shop in Brick Lane, run by a Jewish couple, called Kominsky's. They had shelves full of Coxsone 45s and blue and red Studio 1 45s, and loads of old records.

"John and I used to go down to the Four Aces Club in Dalston, and we'd often be the only white guys in there. You don't know how rough it could be at dances back then. In those days, everything was more racist and less tolerant. If we went along we'd often know someone running the sound system and they'd come over and talk to us so that everyone could see they knew us. A couple of times we've been in dances and heard that people thought we were coppers! There was a lot of hostility, always a potential for violence.

"Junior's Music Spot in Stroud Green Road, Finsbury Park, was a great shop, that was the headquarters of Bamboo Records and they used to release Studio 1 records on Bamboo, Banana and Ackee. Trojan and Pama were the big reggae labels with Bamboo third. They did good records but had poor distribution. I got friendly with the guy who worked there and, as I had been writing in *Blues & Soul* magazine, got a job there.

"While I was working at Junior's I had access to some rhythms and was messing around with them and sold a few dub mixes to a couple of the young sound system guys. That's how I came up with the name Dub Vendor. I'd been to Jamaica for four weeks just after Christmas '73 and at the session in Black Ark when Horsemouth voiced 'Herb Vendor', so Dub Vendor seemed like a good name. I stayed with Lee Perry when he'd just built his studio in his back garden. Scratch and his missus Pauline treated me really well.

"In 1976, John and I started selling records as Dub Vendor. We started a stall in

Portobello Road market on Fridays and also a shop in Lewisham Model Market on a Thursday. Lewisham Model Market was an amazing place for reggae record shops. When I first went there they had a Muzik City shop in the corner, and at least another two shops all within yards of each other. It's hard to imagine now but record shops were everywhere. You think of reggae as niche, but there were dozens and dozens of reggae shops.

"John had the idea, 'Why don't we set up a stall in Clapham Junction market?' We got a lot of people who would have otherwise travelled to Brixton. We opened the Dub Vendor stall on Saturday 2nd October 1976 and things were very encouraging. We made sure we had all the top new tunes, and made a point of stocking Studio 1.

"Later on, we had a Dub Vendor stall in Petticoat Lane for a few months. It went very well but the trouble was when we were playing music and attracting a crowd you'd have these kids come in pickpocketing the punters and stealing girls' handbags so we got moved to progressively worse locations and it just got to be more trouble than it was worth.

"John and I were draymen – working on lorries delivering beer to pubs – while still doing the Clapham stall and decided, 'Let's get a shop.' We found one under the arches off Peckham High Street. We opened it in December 1977 but only lasted a few weeks as all our stock was stolen along with record deck and amp. That really disheartened me. Thing is, I was thinking, 'I shouldn't be in a shop selling records – I should be making records.' Which is what I decided to do. John kept the stall, then opened in Ladbroke Grove."

MacGillivray hired noted reggae DJ Martin 'Redman' to run the tiny Ladbroke Grove shop. Its success led him to open a large shop at 274 Lavender Hill, Clapham Junction, London SW11. Here he employed Hawks, a regular customer with an encyclopaedic knowledge of Jamaican music. Hawks says: "The first time I went to the Dub Vendor stall I couldn't believe they had those records. And Chris and John dressed like me: they had Fred Perry's on, straight jeans, looked like normal people! They'd all these classic records and I went back for more and more and more. I worked for Dub Vendor for 25 years and loved it. Delroy Wilson and Alton Ellis would come in the shop! Alton was a gentleman! Yabby You too! We were always friendly to customers as we've all encountered the record shop asshole. I ran the mail order: we sent out a list of new releases every month.

"John Peel was the only radio DJ who played reggae in 1979. We used to get letters from Brixton prison saying, 'Do you have this record John Peel played?' It had to be on cassette, you couldn't send vinyl in. One day the phone rang and I answered and this familiar voice said, 'Hello! This is music loving John Peel; can I buy reggae records off you?' He had been using Daddy Kool but had been treated so rudely there that he came to us. John didn't have time to come in the shop so asked to be sent new releases. He said to me, 'How will I know you don't send me rubbish?' I replied, 'Well, I can only do that once, can't I?' He was an absolute gem. Kid Jensen was also a lovely Radio 1 DJ who would buy from us. And David Rodigan worked for us before he went on to become the UK's leading reggae DJ."

With the cool rulers of punk and 2-Tone bands all championing Jamaican music, the late 1970s proved a boom time for Dub Vendor. This, alongside increased black British enthusiasm for local reggae and lovers rock artists, allowed Lane to open a recording studio in the basement of the Clapham shop. He and MacGillivray then launched Fashion, a label that would issue many of the recordings they made beneath Dub Vendor. With Fashion releases climbing the charts (Smiley Culture's 'Police Officer' reached UK No. 12 in 1984, selling far more than its chart position indicates) and Dub Vendor running the world's leading mail order reggae operation, it seemed that nothing could go wrong. Inevitably, it did.

"Throughout the '90s the shops started to go," says Lane. "By the end of that decade reggae really went into a slump. Young black kids weren't interested any more. Then the internet came along. Everything conspired to ruin the business."

Lane closed down Dub Vendor's studio and Fashion record label in 2000. The Ladbroke Grove Dub Vendor closed in 2008. The Clapham Junction branch continued until the 2011 riots: Dub Vendor survived but its next-door neighbour was destroyed and the proprietor made MacGillivray an offer he chose to accept. In 2017, he runs Dub Vendor as a mail order reggae company.

David Katz: An American Dubwolf In London

American reggae historian David Katz – author of *People Funny Boy: The Genius of Lee 'Scratch' Perry* and *Solid Foundation: An Oral History of Reggae* – settled in North London in 1985. He immediately found a vinyl mine literally on his front door: "I landed in Kensal Rise and was amazed to find at the bottom of my street the Seven Leaves record store based in the old station master's office at Kensal Rise Station! Seven Leaves had issued Lee Perry's *Megaton Dub Vols 1 & 2* and *Heart of the Ark Vols 1 & 2* – all great albums! – so I couldn't believe they had a shop so close to me. Tony Owens, a British Jamaican, ran the label and the shop and was initially very suspicious of me: at the time, there still was some level of hostility between the Jamaican community and outsiders; you didn't often see white people in reggae shops.

"Harlesden was rough then. The Stonebridge estate was a byword for problems. There was a big Jamaican community there, and a lot of reggae labels and shops. Starlight was one that had great stock. Hawkeye Records & Tapes was run by Roy Forbes-Allen, a British-Jamaican guy, and he released some brilliant Augustus Pablo albums. Sonny Roberts' Orbitone Records started as a label, Planetone Records, in the 1960s and shifted to Harlesden in the '70s. An old sound man called Count Shelley opened a branch of World Enterprise Records in Harlesden as digital dance hall became the rage. At the bottom end of Harlesden was Jah Observer, a fantastic shop run by Austin Palmer, a totally nice guy.

"All these shops started disappearing in the '90s. This was before the internet. It was more the youth lost the connection with the music. Then, when downloading arrived, it killed things."

Dennis Bovell: Master Blaster

Musician, producer, sound system operator, Dennis Bovell is the hardest working man in reggae: "I would go to reggae shops around the UK. Not just London but Birmingham, Leeds, Manchester, Bristol, as these different shops would have different selections of tunes as the owners would each have their own connections to different producers in Jamaica. So, I'd go around looking for records that couldn't be found anywhere else. I once was in the Bamboo record shop in Stroud Green Road and Junior put this record on that I wasn't too keen on so I passed on it and Fatman, who was also running a sound system, bought it. He shut his system down that night and told everyone that he was going to play this new tune that I didn't have and he really let me have it! Later he told me, 'Let that be a lesson to you – buy everything you hear. Play for the public, not just for your ears!'

"One shop that was special to me was DEB Music in Clapham Junction as I did quite a lot of music for them. That was Dennis Brown's shop and he and Gregory Isaacs were always hanging out there. Body Music in Seven Sisters was, for me, the last bastion of great reggae shops. It was originally called Third World Music as it was owned by Count Shelley and he ran the Third World record label. At some point, it changed its name to Body Music. It used to be a really big record shop, just massive, the best reggae record shop going. Now, well, it still exists but it's been downsized while Costa Coffee has been upsized. And that's it – people today will pay for coffee but not for music. The internet killed the reggae shop. If people can download a tune to their phone they won't ever buy a record. The internet providers make money out of this but the creatives don't."

Birmingham Massive

Birmingham, home to Steel Pulse, UB40 and the largest Afro-Caribbean population in the UK outside London, once hosted several celebrated reggae record shops. Don Christie's and Brian Harris Records both started out as Blue Beat shops and developed into roots reggae specialists. Harris changed his shop's name to Mango Records in the 1970s (not to be confused with the Island Records imprint), and issued many superior Jamaican 45s. Christie ran the biggest reggae shop in Birmingham – a great red rectangle of a building at 116 Ladypool Road – with a smaller outlet in the city's covered Bull Ring market. Both Christie and Harris were white men who set up to serve the city's West Indian community and, in doing so, helped make Birmingham a reggae hub. Robin Campbell, guitarist in UB40, says: "Don Christie's shop in Ladypool Road, Small Heath, was close to where we grew up. I used to live in there. It was always packed and they just kept playing tune after tune and, if you wanted one, you'd put your hand up and they'd pass it to you and this would go on until you had about half a dozen records under your arm and then you would pay for them. I stood out as a white kid as it was very much a black shop but there was never any trouble. It always felt like a blues party in there – the music was blasting and so much ganja was being smoked you could smell it from 100 yards away! It smelt strong! Yet I never saw a copper there. They must have decided to leave them alone."

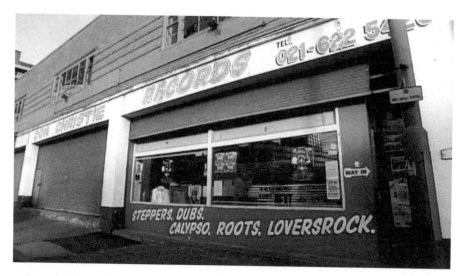

Campbell laughs at the memory and adds: "On a Saturday they would put the speakers out front of the shop and blast the music so loud you could hear it streets away. Legend held that Don Christie only had one leg – he certainly walked with a limp – but I never dared ask him if it was true. He'd nod at me as a regular but I never got to speak with him. I believe he sold the shop to his staff in the early '80s and shifted to Devon or Cornwall. A lot of the records that shaped UB40 were bought there."

In the 1970s and 1980s, Birmingham had numerous reggae shops – Campbell notes that the Handsworth area had at least half a dozen – and among the most distinctive was Black Wax Records. Opened on the Lozells Road in the early 1970s, Black Wax is remembered for the distinctive gorgon's head that featured both on the shop window and on the label of the excellent 45s released on their Black Wax imprint. London-based reggae fan Paul Coote visited relatives in Birmingham as an excuse to shop at Mango and Black Wax: "I don't think I have ever enjoyed being in any reggae shop as much as Black Wax. I first went in Black Wax in 1974 and bought lots of records there and a few in Brian Harris's shop. Brian's shop was in a rather bleak side street so I didn't like going in there as much as Black Wax which was always very friendly and the walls were covered in Jamaican LPs.

"I had been buying from Black Wax previously for a year or so from their mail order as they were the only shop I knew who did mail order of the latest "pre-release" Jamaican imports – they had a seriously tough selection of all the latest imports from Jamaica. I recall the walls were painted dark purple and black and the shop being dimly lit. And they had a Leak Delta amplifier! It was run by Keith Thornton, a white man, and a black guy called Fred. Both were very friendly and helpful."

Christie, Thornton and Harris all got out of the reggae store business in the early 1980s. Coote says: "I don't know when they ceased trading but most of that part of Lozells Road where Black Wax was located got burned to the ground during the riots in 1985. What you have to bear in mind when considering reggae shops is that, in the early '80s when Thatcher's economic policies devastated whole communities, young black people were much more likely to find themselves unemployed and the impact was disproportionate on black businesses like reggae record shops."

Harris moved on to run Icicle Records while Thornton chose to focus on managing Tempest Records, a large general record shop he had opened on the Lozells Road in 1968. Shifting Tempest Records to Bull Street allowed Thornton to develop it into one of Birmingham's finest record shops (Tempest closed in 2010). With the closure of Christie's shop, Campbell returned to The Diskery, the city's longest standing record shop and one his brother David once worked in. Campbell notes: "When I was researching the *Labour of Love* albums, and needed an old reggae record, I'd go into The Diskery and Jim, who had worked there for ever, not only had a copy of every 45 I asked for but he'd know exactly where it was! He had a mind like a computer and was a huge help."

Ian Hingle, who moved from working behind the counter at the Mojo reggae shop ("Harlesden had Mojo, All Ears, Starlight, Hawkeye, Austin's, Orbitone, a surfeit of reggae shops") to driving for Marcus Distribution for 12 years, remembers Birmingham's reggae shops in the 1980s: "As we did 99 per cent reggae music, the bulk of our trade was in London, with a fairly sizeable market in Birmingham. In Birmingham, the two big ones – and not always friendly rivals – were Don Christie and Summit Records. Don Christie was run by a white bloke who could sell sand to Arabs. If he bought a tune off us he'd sell the lot in a week. Summit was run by Winston, who kept a steady trade going, and seemed to cater for a slightly older crowd. Both shops were heavily involved in the local community, selling dance tickets and such. Getting payment was the hardest part of the job – anyone can sell records, it was getting payment from the shops which took a level of skill!"

I visited Birmingham in the summer of 2015 and found Summit Records still operating as a market stall in the Bull Ring. It offered a small, tired selection of reggae CDs, several Jamaican gospel CDs, a few DVDs and a selection of posters. I could barely get to look at the stock as most of the floor space was occupied by plastic containers made for shipping produce (not records) abroad. I hoped for a chat but Summit's proprietor spent all his time on the phone conducting business. While being ignored I thought of the BBC Radio 4 comedy *Rudy's Rare Records*; here Lenny Henry sweats and stresses in a tiny, down-at-heel reggae record shop in Birmingham where the slogan is "If we don't have it, them don't mek it". These days, the new 7-inch singles that are for sale in the surviving reggae shops tend to have been pressed in Germany or Japan as there are barely any vinyl pressing plants operating in Jamaica. *Them don't mek it.*

Dread days: the late Daddy VGO (far left) and friends outside People's Sounds Records, Ladbroke Grove. Courtesy of People's Sounds Records.

Chapter 14

Rough Trades, Small Wonders: Inflammable Materials

The dawn of 1976 finds Comrade Travis opening Rough Trade in Ladbroke Grove, while Geezer Pete establishes Small Wonder in Walthamstow. Together they act as foci for punk's energy flash. Cameos include The Sex Pistols, The Ramones, Talking Heads, John Peel, Stiff Little Fingers, Crass, Bauhaus.

BOOM! BOOM! BOOM! As punk detonated in late 1976, two recently opened record shops acted as cells for the vivid militia, clearing ground for revolutionary activity and supplying teenage insurgents with sonic armaments. That these emporiums were in opposite parts of London and run by two very different men mattered little; caught in the furies of the time, Rough Trade and Small Wonder would play significant roles in shaping punk and its offspring.

Geoff Travis, born 2 February 1952, grew up in Finchley's leafy suburbs. Pete Stennett, born 8 December 1948, was raised on a Stratford council estate. Their upbringings were significantly different – Travis, a religious child, ate kosher food and regularly attended synagogue; Stennett, an archetypal Cockney urchin, learned East End lore on the streets – and where Travis is tall, Stennett is small. Yet both, at a very young age, found salvation in rock 'n' roll.

Travis recalls his Canadian uncle visiting with EPs by The Everly Brothers and Freddie Cannon when he was eight; immediately smitten, young Geoff played them over and over on his parents' radiogram. Stennett suggests that Elvis's influence hovered over the East End, permeating the bomb sites he played on. Both youths were swept up by The Beatles, avid John Peel listeners and devoted record collectors: Travis would explore Soho's record shops during his school's lunch hour while Stennett relied upon Stratford's Co-Op store, ordering *Freak Out* (1967) by The Mothers of Invention there.

Travis went on to study at Cambridge University before hitchhiking across the USA, while Stennett stayed put in East London, working for Phono Disc, a record distributor. Travis arrived back in London in 1975 with a vast collection of American LPs he had picked up in charity stores and, initially, gravitated towards a friend's health food store. By then, Stennett was editing the in-house magazine that Phono Disc published but, in late autumn, he was made redundant. As 1975 drew to a close, both men felt an urgent need, a calling of sorts, to open a record shop.

"We decided to give it a go"
Stennett says of that time: "I took redundancy, and thought, 'What the fuck am I going to do now?' All I knew was music. All I cared about was music. I was married to Mari and we were living in Forest Gate and it made sense to put the redundancy

Small Wonder Records.

© CRASS 1978.

Watch out for the quiet ones at the back
All they want in the smallest crack
Everything's happening down the front
Innocent bystander you're the biggest cunt

WE ALL KNOW

IT'S SO BAD

BUT WE SAY SO

WHAT A SHAME............

162 Hoe Street, Walthamstow, London. E.17 4QH.

"The sound of free speech..." Courtesy of Crass.

Punky afro: Geoff Travis at the controls, 1977. Image courtesy of Rough Trade Records.

money into opening a record shop. The East End wasn't well served by record shops and I was listening to John Peel and aware that kids had to go into the West End if they wanted to buy the records he was playing so we decided to give it a go."

Geoff Travis was experiencing similar symptoms: "I had no interest in a career and, unlike now, there wasn't a great deal of pressure put on you to follow a career. My parents must have been worried sick about me but, thankfully, they never let it be known and were always supportive. We came back and we started squatting. That's important – if we hadn't squatted there would not have been a shop. Back then it was easy and the law was on your side. I was determined to start a record shop and borrowed the money off my father and, right away, made a false start."

Both men were consumed with a spiritual hunger to work with music and set off on their quests: Travis sought out premises in West London while Stennett stuck with the East. Travis remembers: "The first premises we rented were towards Harrow and Wembley. A label rep dropped around and he said, 'What are you doing here? There's no passing trade!' And I was so naïve I had to ask, 'What's passing trade?' I realised he was right. It was a suburban dead end. That was a wake-up call. While we couldn't afford to be on Portobello we guessed that setting up on one of the streets parallel to Portobello might bring in some people. The place we found on Kensington Park Road [in Ladbroke Grove] turned out to have been an old head shop."

Stennett says: "There was no definite plan to set up in Walthamstow, but we came across a place there, a children's wear shop where the owner wanted to retire, so they sold us the lease. I only had about two grand in redundancy money so we had to do everything on very little. We went to the local bank manager and pretty much begged him to lend us money to buy stock."

Small Wonder opened to little fanfare. It was named after a Victorian era photo that Stennett had of a black and white couple displaying their mixed-race infant, and this became the shop's emblem ("and 'cos I'm pretty tiny"). He recalls: "At the start we didn't have a lot of records. Prog rock, kraut rock and heavy metal were still popular and I was well into dub and reggae. Sold new and second-hand. Initially, the stock was, more or less, my record collection. We had a sign up saying, 'We will be fully stocked by Christmas' but that was never going to happen. Mari was still going to work at her job every day. I sold my motorbike to buy stock. I was trying to do something different, stocking dub and reggae, checking the new music Peel was playing."

Travis opened Rough Trade – "I stole the name from a band I saw in Canada. They weren't very good so in all my arrogance I thought, 'I'll have that!'" – spending his father's money on stock.

"There was a one-stop (an independent record distributor) called Lightning Records up on Harrow Road. We used to go there and you could buy all the labels. We had opened accounts with all the major labels but there wasn't really that much stuff we wanted to stock until punk got under way.

"The shop started picking up foot traffic when people began realising we had stock that no one else had. We were in a West Indian community and we didn't want to be tourists in the neighbourhood so we stocked reggae records from the start. There were reggae record shops on All Saints Road but you didn't go on All Saints Road back then. Too rough."

"I'd heard of The Sex Pistols . . ."

Stennett says: "I knew things were changing in music because there had been all this attention towards The Ramones and Flamin' Groovies, American bands that were outside the mainstream. I'd heard of The Sex Pistols so when they came to play Walthamstow Assembly Hall [17 June 1976], I went along to check them out. I mean, I was 27, too old to be startled by anything new – or so I thought – but, seeing the Pistols, it was eye opening. They were just so exciting and in your face and just *fierce*. Like they really did *not* give a fuck. Things had gotten really dull in music and here were the Pistols and I'm hearing about this movement called 'punk' and I signed up for it straight away. It wasn't a business decision – back then it's not like there were any punk records to sell beyond Patti Smith and The Ramones – but I was excited and I wanted to be part of it. From there things just evolved."

Travis recalls: "We knew all about Stiff and Chiswick. We used to stock The 101ers' single 'Keys to Your Heart'. And 'Brand New Cadillac'. All that stuff. Strummer and all those people were coming by. Mick Jones would always come in the shop. Steve Jones would come in the shop with records he nicked and try to sell them to me. We immediately started ordering the new music coming out. When The Saints' debut single 'I'm Stranded' came out and got a rave review in *Sounds*, I ordered 400 copies from Australia. Same with Ork Records in New York. I ordered a few hundred copies of 'Little Johnny Jewell' by Television. And 'Blank Generation' by Richard Hell.

"This was instinctive ordering. There was no movement known as 'punk' back then but I was tuned into this undercurrent of new rock music coming out. And part of the fun was tracking the records down and ordering them. Contacting David Thomas in Cleveland and ordering several hundred copies of Pere Ubu's debut single 'Final Solution', that felt great. Same for Alex Chilton's 'Bangkok' single. We sold hundreds of that!"

Punk coincided with a souring of public confidence - the Troubles were toxic, white majority governments across Africa were losing power to Marxist guerrillas while the South African regime increased apartheid's brutality, the Cold War heated up, military dictators crushed Latin American democracy, industrial strife intensified, inflation ate wages, unemployment kept rising, neo-Nazis openly and aggressively agitated, Tory politicians smeared James Callaghan's Labour government as ruling over "the sick man of Europe" - and both Rough Trade and Small Wonder served as tuning forks of sorts for youth discord, these small shops echoing to abrasive rock and militant reggae records. A call to arms? In August 1976 Notting Hill Carnival descended into a violent riot as black youth battled the police. Rough Trade was on the frontline yet unlike many neighbouring businesses survived unscathed.

"We didn't get smashed up," says Travis. "We had a van driver, Austin, who was a dread, and he had a sound system set up outside the shop so we were thankfully spared."

Yet Rough Trade was robbed by gun-toting local thugs in 1978. Travis wasn't in his shop when this happened, but he admits that urban tensions meant incursions involving surly youth tribes found Rough Trade living up to its name: "The shop was small and could get incredibly crowded. And, back then, you had skinheads coming in intent on causing havoc. London was extremely tribal and we acted as a magnet for a lot of youth. Most came because they were interested in the music but others were looking for trouble."

Small Wonder, being at the top of the London tube's Victoria Line, didn't have the same crowd control problems but the local police force took a dislike to what Stennett describes as: "This spiky little punk rock shop. They tried to blame us for kids wagging school and thought we must be selling drugs 'cos so many kids were coming in and out of the shop. When *Never Mind the Bollocks* came out we put it in the window display and these coppers came in claiming they could do us for obscenity. I rang up Branson and he said, 'Hold tight, we're fighting it' and they did. Meanwhile, I covered up the 'o' in 'Bollocks' and these coppers came back and I could see them scratching their heads as they tried to work out if the display was still 'obscene' or not. Idiots!

"They didn't get me on that but they did their best to disrupt us; one time they sent this undercover female cop into the shop and she's flicking through the albums and I'm smoking a joint and she turns around and says, 'Is that a joint?'

Dirty old town: Rough Trade's original Kensington Park Road shop. Image courtesy of Rough Trade record shop, Ladbroke Grove.

'Well, what do you think?' A few days later they come in with dogs, turned the shop over, looked up my ass, like I was running some drug den out of a record shop! There's this kid, one of my regular customers, and he's outside and sees what's happening so he runs to the nearest phone box and calls the police and says a murder has happened in a street nearby – thinking that all the police in my shop will be ordered out to go and investigate the murder. Well, this obviously doesn't happen. He didn't twig that it was drug squad busting me and some other coppers got sent around to investigate a murder that never happened. That's just one of many bizarre incidents that happened at Small Wonder."

"It was chaotic. But a lot of fun"

Travis, loosely modelling Rough Trade on Lawrence Ferlinghetti's redoubtable City Lights bookshop, put big ideas into practice. Marxist principles ensured all

Rough Traders worked for the same wage, while the shop stocked and supported the new and the unconventional, the unsung and marginalised. Travis says: "We imported hundreds of copies of Talking Heads' debut single, and when the band first came to London we were offered an in-store signing. We leapt at the opportunity and along came the band but no one came to see them. They were still unknown. They just laughed about it and spent their time digging through all the records in the shop. They were music fans so very happy to be in a record shop. We also held The Ramones' first record shop signing in London and that was the complete opposite – mobbed!"

"If punk hadn't happened I'm not sure Small Wonder would have survived as long as it did," says Stennett. Travis echoes this thought: "It was just good luck that punk happened. If it hadn't who knows if we might have survived? Things were very quiet for the first few months. And then, when punk and all the new music kicked off and word got out that we specialised in it, things got really busy. Saturdays were crazy! Just mobs of youths wanting to get into Rough Trade. It was chaotic. But a lot of fun. Really exciting times. Music meant so much to so many people then that they were coming down to get new releases as soon as we had them. People were hungry for the new music and Rough Trade was a focal point.

"We started stocking independent magazines – never the music weeklies like the *NME* as they were available everywhere – but underground magazines and fanzines. I stocked all of Greg Shaw's *Bomp* magazines and *Sniffin' Glue* ended up operating out of our basement [Laughs]. I really liked that Rough Trade provided a centre for alternative ideas and music and publishing."

I wasn't living in London during the late 1970s, but I can imagine just how exciting Rough Trade's Ladbroke Grove shop must have been. Crime writer and biographer John Williams, who regularly hitched from Cardiff to London to visit Rough Trade, confirms this: "I first encountered Rough Trade when they had a stall at the Patti Smith gig at Hammersmith Odeon in October 1976 and I got a flyer from it advertising the shop. I went the next day and it was the first shop that was dedicated to just the new music. It wasn't full of Spooky Tooth and Wishbone Ash albums. It was absolutely amazing. It had tons of fanzines and all the singles that no one else had and the staff were friendly women – which made for a change! Judith, an Australian, was there for years. And Ana da Silva from The Raincoats. It had a notice board that was very important for that early punk period of people getting in touch with one another. I'd come up on a pilgrimage every holiday and breathe in the rarefied air."

Stennett smirks at the mention of Rough Trade. "So serious," he says, "so 'right on'. Small Wonder was just about having a laugh." Stennett then goes on to describe his shop in very similar terms to Travis: "I ordered whatever punk records were available and I'd play them in the shop and promote them, and the local kids got to know that Small Wonder was a place they could come and hear this music and not get a hard time. And the bands got to know about the shop so they would drop in and say, 'We've made a record – will you take some?' I'd have a listen and then make an order.

"I remember when Killing Joke came in with their first single I ordered a hundred copies. I knew straight away that they had something. Small Wonder became a centre of sorts for kids and bands in East London so you'd always have all these herberts hanging about. It was like a little youth club; kids would arrange to meet their mates there. We sold fanzines, had ludicrous murals, it was magic! [He grins at the memory] Because of where we were, because we weren't a big business, we didn't give a shit. One time we got £1000 and I just threw it up in the air around the shop and got stoned. I only stocked music I liked. I never tried to run Small Wonder as a mainstream record shop. When disco was selling massive amounts we didn't stock it. Not what we were about. The freedom was the main thing about Small Wonder."

Freedom and the sense of doing something he loved – Stennett speaks of the shop as if describing family. "I've never had kids," he says, "so records did serve as substitutes in a way." To nurture this 'family', he developed Small Wonder into punk's foremost mail order outlet: "I suddenly decided we ought to try a bit of mail order because there were kids all over the place that just couldn't get this stuff. We advertised in the back of the music weeklies – *Sounds* and *NME* – as they were covering the kind of music we were stocking. One morning Mari got up and saw all these letters on the carpet and thought they must be bills. It turned out they were all from kids writing for records. That's how we became known, by just supplying all over the country and, eventually, all over the world. You didn't have to have a fucking massive shop, you could have a little pokey place like we had and you could sell to thousands of people. And supply them with records they otherwise couldn't have got hold of."

My teenage self first came into contact with Small Wonder via mail order, importing punk 45s to New Zealand. Excellent service, great records; Stennett's passion reached across the globe.

Mucky Pups and Suspect Devices

Small Wonder is remembered today not just for the shop but for the eponymous record label Stennett launched in 1977. By doing so he helped shape London punk's development, a little big man with good intentions and a fearless nature, and the records Small Wonder issued reflect the owner: direct, abrasive, subversive.

"There was no big plan behind setting up Small Wonder as a record label. It was just part of the times. I knew via listening to Peel that there were bands doing it themselves and it wasn't too difficult. We had this 45 by The Desperate Bicycles. It cost 'em about 500 quid, I think, and their slogan was "*It was easy, it was cheap, go and do it!*." So, we went to see them in a sort of smelly teenage bedroom and they told us exactly what to do.

"By then I'd decided that we'd do a 45 by this punk band called Puncture. Colin Faver, who was working for us on a Saturday, took us to a gig behind The Roxy and there was this band called Puncture. It was madness, kids pogoing and gobbing on the band! It just tickled me. I found the whole thing highly entertaining so said, 'Of course I'll put out a single.' We hired a recording studio and did it. They

SMALL WONDER RECORDS

PATRIK FITZGERALD

side A
small four
Ⓟ 1977
Small Wonder
Records
stereo 45
Copyright
Control

SIDE A
1. BANGING & SHOUTING
2. SAFETY PIN STUCK IN MY HEART
3. WORK. REST. PLAY. REGGAE
SIDE B
1. SET WE FREE
2. OPTIMISM/REJECT
(All tracks Fitzgerald)
Produced by Pete

recorded this nonsense song, 'Mucky Pup', and it's great, all about how they fancy this TV news presenter, Angela Rippon. We put it out and the music press gave it good reviews. One of the members of Puncture started turning cartwheels on the tube platform after he read one of the reviews! He was so happy! And that's why I ran the label, to make silly, noisy records that kids like.

"Our second release was a band called The Zeros who were from Walthamstow. They just came into the shop and gave me a demo, as a lot of them did, and you listened to it and if you liked it you thought, 'Right we'll release this.' Our deals were we'd pay for the record, the recording, the sleeve, the artwork, the pressing all of it, and if it broke even, fine, but if it made a profit we'd give them half that profit. And that was the case with every single band. Our contracts were ridiculously simple."

Not long after Stennett became a mini-magnate, Travis founded the Rough Trade record label. He says: "We were really inspired by Chiswick because Ted [Carroll] and Roger [Armstrong] had done it with The 101ers. And Stiff was just up the road – we'd drop in on them to buy stock. And Virgin wasn't far away and we were always going over there for stock, especially for reggae records. But what really got the label going was the French band Métal Urbain. They had issued their own first single 'Panik' and we had stocked it and, to their amazement, sold a couple of hundred copies. So, one day they arrived at the shop with the master tape of their new single and said, 'We don't know what to do with it – will you help us?' So, we looked at one another and said, 'Why don't we help these guys?' It wasn't like we hatched a plan to be the new Stax records. It was just helping out. But then people started approaching us."

Back then, demand for the new music was so strong that, when Rough Trade signed shrill Belfast punks Stiff Little Fingers, Travis found to his surprise that the band's first two 45s both sold over 30,000 copies ('as 'Suspect Device' and 'Alternative Ulster' both did). Then *Inflammable Material*, the band (and label's) 1979 debut album and the first independent LP to break into the Top 20, sold a staggering 125,000 copies. Seemingly born for this moment, Travis morphed into a fully-fledged record man, issuing brilliantly offbeat efforts by Swell Maps, The Raincoats, Cabaret Voltaire and Scritti Politti: "We handled all those copies of *Inflammable Material* at the Kensington Park Road shop. Unloaded them onto the pavement! If it had rained, Rough Trade history might have been different. Same with *Unknown Pleasures* – Factory sent down this overloaded van stuffed full of albums for us to distribute and we had to stack them out front as there was no room in the shop. You have to realise that for many years the shed in the back of the shop was Rough Trade Distribution."

The Sound of Free Speech

In 1980, Travis transferred Rough Trade's label and distribution to nearby Blenheim Crescent, allowing the shop's staff to breathe a sigh of relief that the premises were no longer so hopelessly overcrowded. Small Wonder didn't find a band with Stiff Little Fingers' sales potential, with Stennett happy to issue punk 45s full of snarl and spit. These records were made by and for local youths hungry to express themselves anyway, anyhow. "GLC, GLC," sang Menace about the then Greater London Council's intention to ban punk gigs, "you're full of SHIT! SHIT! SHIT!"

John Peel championed both shops' records on his radio show (although he was unable to play 'GLC'), the music press offered praise and sales ticked over. In 1978, Small Wonder agreed to issue an album by Crass, an anarcho-vegan punk band. *The Feeding of the 5000*, an 18-track 12-inch 45, contained zealous tirades against governments, war mongers, meat eaters and the church. Stennett's outlaw status skyrocketed when he received a visit from the Vice Squad: "I found Crass via a window dresser who came along and gave me this tape. I listened and was staggered. Really angry music, yet really intelligent. Me and Penny [Rimbaud – Crass's founder figure] got on like a house on fire. I did the *Feeding of the 5000* album and the Irish pressing plant said one of the tracks was blasphemous and refused to press it and the whole thing got incredibly fucking heated – it ended up being this blank track on the album and Crass called it 'The Sound of Free Speech'. Then the Vice Squad started threatening to do us for blasphemy. The local coppers really intensified their harassment. One once spoke to me in a very aggressive manner and I asked, 'Is that a threat, officer?' And he replied, 'No. It's a promise.'"

Where Travis quickly developed Rough Trade into the foremost independent record label of the punk era, Stennett preferred to keep Small Wonder as a cottage industry. Even so he gave debut releases to The Cure, Cockney Rejects and Bauhaus, three bands who would win varying degrees of international success. "I never wanted to be Richard Branson," he says. "Never fancied getting all serious like Rough Trade." He even turned down a local band called Iron Maiden. "I thought, 'Nah, metal's dead'," he says then laughs while pondering the potential millions he missed out on.

Rough Trade Distribution began with Travis buying imported punk 45s and wholesaling their stock into other UK record shops, then it organically evolved into the base for a network of tiny record labels that had sprung up to service the new music. This attracted like-minded record shop owners from across the UK (and beyond) to use Rough Trade as a one-stop: Mick Tarrant, of Armadillo Records in Bournemouth, would visit every Friday morning to purchase fresh stock, making sure Devon's punks got a vinyl fix on Saturdays. In 1978 Richard Scott, formerly manager of reggae band Third World, agreed to run distribution. Travis notes: "Richard Scott came in to work at Rough Trade, and he had the idea that we were stocking all these records that other shops in the UK didn't have so why didn't we distribute them. That's how Rough Trade Distribution came about. We also had the Marxist concept that if we controlled the means of distribution we would also have more say in the music that got heard. If you went into a high-street shop, all you had access to as far as music was what the major record labels were putting out. By getting into distribution we were providing an alternative to this."

The punk era coincided with the manufacturing of records becoming far more affordable for independents. Rough Trade's willingness to act as a distributor – empowered by the success of several Rough Trade, Mute and Factory releases – meant Our Price, Virgin and HMV all began stocking labels that Rough Trade distributed, a compassionate gesture in an industry more noted for greed than principles.

"The whole atmosphere was getting nasty . . ."
By the early 1980s, Rough Trade ruled the alternative rock universe: an iconoclastic shop, label and distribution network all pumping out urgent music and ideas – a brand with a brain, a conscience and an international audience. Travis's success found both *The South Bank Show* and *The Sunday Times* profiling Rough Trade. Yet such rapid success, aligned with decision making and management that continued along a co-operative credo, ensured problems arose and, by 1982, Travis found his business in trouble. Accountants were called in, with one insisting Travis close the shop. He refused, instead selling the shop's stock (and gifting the Rough Trade name) to its staff. Travis says of the events that saw the label and shop split: "There was some kind of palace coup by distribution. People came in to work at distribution who were not part of the early days and did not share that culture. Okay, I was in charge to some degree but I was, for many years, on the same wage as everyone else, very much the co-

operative model. Then there was a guy working for the shop who went on one of those business courses and came back talking all kinds of nonsense jargon – we couldn't see eye to eye – so it got to loggerheads. There was a bit of a rupture but it all ended up okay. By that time, I had long stopped working in the shop."

As Rough Trade wobbled, Small Wonder shrank. The label stopped issuing new records in 1980, Stennett finding fewer artists that engaged him as post-punk rock splintered into myriad genres. Instead, he kept pressing Bauhaus's 'Bela Lugosi's Dead' (1979) 12-inch 45. "We sold thousands and thousands of copies of that. One time the band came in to collect their royalties and Pete Murphy was so happy when I gave them this big, fat cheque he kissed me right on the lips!" As tensions in Walthamstow escalated, Stennett and Mari decided to shut up shop: "The thing that really spurred us to shut the shop was this poor Pakistani family, their home got petrol bombed and they died [Yunus Khan Close off Queen's Road in Walthamstow is named in honour of the Khan family, four of whom died in the arson attack in July 1981]. That happened nearby. So, there's this big march organised by the Asian community and anti-racists, and the National Front turn up to confront them. And lots of Old Bill. It became a fucking riot and someone sprayed a swastika on our shutters, the cunts. The whole atmosphere was getting nasty.

"Then the lead singer of Menace came into the shop and threatened me with a gun. When I mentioned it to the other band members they were like, 'Oh, don't worry, it's not loaded,' but that's light relief, isn't it? I had palpitations from the stress. Everything got very dour. The fun went out of it. We shut up the shop and the label, and shifted to Suffolk and continued to run Small Wonder as a mail order company. Then our marriage broke up and that was that."

Stennett has worked as a gardener in rural Suffolk since leaving the punk trade, noting, "When I finish a garden I get the same kind of satisfaction I once did from running the shop."

The Rough Trade record shop continued its mission to champion underground rock bands from across the globe, and Travis has run Rough Trade Records through all manner of ups and downs, one of the true heroes of the British music industry.

That Rough Trade's and Small Wonder's "spiky little punk rock shop[s]" achieved so much is a testament to radical vision, personal integrity, good luck, great timing, stunning music and capitalism's insatiable appetite for the new. What Travis and Stennett began, others would develop, our damaged world needing record shops run by desperate spiritual outlaws.

Chapter 15

Rock in Opposition: Vanguard Record Shops

Vanguard record shops open in Belfast, Preston, and on the Wandsworth Road in London. The Cartel takes shape in Bristol, Liverpool, York, Norwich and Leamington Spa. Rough Trade forges forward. Good Vibrations, Action Records, Recommended Records, Red Rhino Records, Probe, Backs, Probe and Revolver Records. Cameos from The Undertones, The Outcasts, John Peel, Pete Burns, Julian Cope, Henry Cow, This Heat, Cornershop, Sun Ra and Massive Attack.

"Here's three chords, now form a band!" Punk's DIY ethos inspired thousands of youths to grab instruments and rock. Countless others published fanzines, designed clothes, put on gigs, wrote manifestos, got politically active and, in some cases, opened record shops. Rock music meant so much to so many that punk – decidedly uncommercial and anti-glamour – could act as a clarion call to all those disillusioned with rock's old guard and desperate to express themselves. Punk contained huge energies and allowed many to find a voice. From its London origins, punk rapidly spread across the UK and, in Belfast, a spiky little punk rock shop arose. Behind bomb-blasted doors, Good Vibrations extolled a spirit of creativity and unity in Europe's most sectarian and deadly city.

Good Vibrations

The Sex Pistols may have sung about anarchy while The Clash roared of wanting a riot but, in Belfast, these were everyday affairs: *soldiers roamed the streets, paramilitaries ruled through fear and terror, car bombs wreaked havoc, youths fought pitched street battles, rubber bullets and tear gas ripped the air.* Stiff Little Fingers' second Rough Trade 45 called for an 'Alternative Ulster' (1978) and, among the fear and loathing, Belfast rock fans began to look to punk as offering, if not a solution, some kind of salvation.

Before the Troubles took hold, Belfast stood as one of the UK's foremost music cities, with Van Morrison's Them and Rory Gallagher's Taste both roaring out of the Maritime Hotel bar to win international acclaim, while everyone from The Beatles to Cream came through to rock the port. During this 1960s golden age, several record shops served Belfast, the main one being the historic Gramophone Shop. Atlantic Records, where young Van learned his lore, was long gone by the decade's end, but Michael Clifford's Heroes & Villains is fondly remembered by those who made use of it. Caroline Music is less eulogised but local musician Martin Cowan recalls this as the shop where he found The Ramones' debut LP and The Sex Pistols' debut 45. Moreover, it is punk rock that re-established Belfast as a city with more to offer than bombs and bigots.

The Belfast Cyclops: Terri Hooley outside his fortress.

Belfast's punk bands created something remarkable out of chaos and Good Vibrations, a ramshackle punk rock shop, channelled those energies to emerge as the most celebrated shop of Irish rock lore. The antics of Terri Hooley, the face of Good Vibrations, and bands associated with the shop, inspired the biopic *Good Vibrations* (2012), a superb movie that, along with *The Commitments* (1991) and *Once* (2007), proves the Irish make the best rock 'n' roll films. The film employs Hooley's struggle to get the debut 45 of a spotty Derry band called The Undertones heard as the dramatic arc (alongside being threatened by the IRA, Loyalists and skinheads – more challenges than most record store owners ever mercifully face). Finally, John Peel plays the 45. *Then he immediately plays it again.* The only time Peel ever did so. 'Teenage Kicks' is a perfect record and only a moron would have failed to hear this – the music industry being full of such people - and Hooley had been blessed with the good fortune of being approached by a band with a great song.

In *Good Vibrations*, Hooley's passions make him a hero, albeit a flawed one: his crusade for Belfast punk ensures he loses his house, his wife, his friends and, inevitably, his shop and his label. Even before opening Good Vibrations, Hooley was cultivating his own legend. Among his many tales are being told to "Piss off" by Bob Dylan in 1966 (Hooley suggested he withhold paying his taxes as a protest against the Vietnam War); having a punch-up with John Lennon in 1970 (Lennon assumed Terri and mates were IRA supporters and supposedly offered them a stash of guns); snogging Cilla Black ("Did you know she was on Elvis's jukebox?"); befriending Bob Marley ("His dad's Irish"); and being admired by Kurt Cobain ("When he got sick in Belfast he said, 'I don't mind dying here, because it's the home of Good Vibrations Records'"). Hooley's huge energies, roguish charm and party trick of dropping his false eye into a pint established him as the battered Cyclops of Belfast rock.

Losing an eye as a child as well as being bullied had ensured that Terri took refuge in music. "I always remember that music was where I would hide," he says. Hooley started collecting records early on – "I was always in Dougie Knight's or Mrs Moore's or Smithfield buying records, discovering Ella Fitzgerald, Charlie Parker, Paganini, Tchaikovsky, you name it" – and, after failing to set up a pirate radio station, he worked as a DJ in pubs. Purchasing 1000 old records from a seller in *Exchange and Mart*, he realised many of the discs were valuable and he started dealing records from home before setting up a stall in Ballymena market. In 1977, Hooly and a few idealistic hippie mates transformed a derelict building in Great Victoria Street into a record shop "on the most bombed half-mile in Europe". In sectarian Belfast, in the midst of the murderous Troubles, Hooley and co. offered a sanctuary where anyone of any background could come and share their musical enthusiasms. Why not name it after a Beach Boys 45 that stands as one of pop music's true symphonies? Good vibrations, indeed.

The film *Good Vibrations* suggests Hooley was brave to the point of being foolish, and his passion for punk becomes what the French call *'amour fou'* ('mad love'). It's this quality that often animates the best record shops and record labels. Hooley – reckless, possessed, crusading – was aged 29 in 1977, easily a decade older than most punks, and volunteers to start a record label. Then, few musicians dared perform in Belfast – Rory Gallagher and Horslips notably continuing to come and share the one thing that brought the city's tribes together and soothed their savage, sectarian souls: *music*. Hooley did all he could, believing punk to be youth's revenge on a society that refused to listen to the hippies.

"New York has the haircuts, London has the trousers, but Belfast has the bands," was Hooley's mantra. He also said, "Good Vibrations is not a record shop or a record label – it's a way of life!" That was true of many a record shop, but Good Vibrations offered refuge from the barbarians outside, a safe space for dreamers and those seeking freedom through records rather than weapons. Here then existed an alternative Ulster.

Among the bands benefiting from Good Vibrations' existence were The Outcasts, who released several 45s and an LP via Hooley's shop. Martin Cowan who, emboldened by his Ramones and Sex Pistols purchases, had formed The Outcasts, says: "Good Vibrations was chaos. Terri never cared about business or money, he was always in debt, drinking and partying too much. The shop was always full of punks, ex-hippies, all sorts of 'weirdos', very few having the money to buy anything, so requesting records to be played. Anyone who was in a band went there to meet up with similar minded people and discuss all sorts of rubbish. There were homemade posters on the walls advertising upcoming gigs and, later when the Good Vibrations label took off, there were professional posters advertising the label's releases.

"The label was just as chaotic as the shop. It was a miracle that anything was released, operating on a shoestring as it did, but Terri did have some good friends that believed in what he was doing and together they always seemed to muddle through and the recordings got released and, of course, John Peel playing the records did help. I think *Good Vibrations* the movie does an excellent job telling this story – it captures the spirit of the time and it is very accurate in telling what happened! I think it is one of the best music films ever made with a great soundtrack."

Hooley opened and closed Good Vibrations several times over the decades. In 2011, he surely was bemused to read an editorial in *The Guardian* that called for Belfast council to provide arts funding for Good Vibrations after he announced he was having to downsize due to falling record sales. The paper noted, "If the Arts Council can fund loyalist marching bands, it can surely support someone who united rather than divided youth for decades". Hooley never got the funding but he did get the movie – and a mural, and a tree! – and he (*somehow, some way*) managed to keep Good Vibrations going until health problems finally forced the 66-year-old chaos monkey to retire in 2015.

"The Good Vibrations story is an amazing story because it's about somebody who hadn't a clue about what he was doing and just wanted to do it", Hooley said of his fine, foolish self.

Action Records

If Rough Trade, Small Wonder and Good Vibrations represent the royal triumvirate of punk record shops, each of them launching bands that would enjoy lasting acclaim, there were plenty of others that joined in the excitement. Action Records began as a Blackpool market stall in 1979, owner Gordon Gibson noting that there were many outlets for northern soul but few for the new rock music. Local demand encouraged him to open in Preston, and soon after he established the Action record label, releasing new music from artists such as The Fall, Mark E. Smith, The Boo Radleys and the woefully monikered Genocides. As with the other punk rock shops, Action found John Peel supportive of its releases, helping the new music find an audience.

Peel's role as British radio's resident rock guru ran from his 1967 debut on pirate station Radio London to his sudden death in 2004 (aged 65). His importance in introducing new music – unconventional rock, reggae, rap and electronica – to the British public cannot be understated. With punk and post-punk, Peel truly came into his own, breaking ground and promoting all kinds of artists, several of whom were connected to the aforementioned shops. Yet Peel was not just enthusiastic about the records he received in the post, he was a lifelong crate digger. While researching this book, Peel's name turned up more often than that of any other individual – for more than half a century he trawled record shops, and his last major discovery was The White Stripes (whose debut LP he came across in a Dutch record shop, purchasing it purely because the cover's colours matched those of his beloved Liverpool FC). When Peel passed away, there was an outbreak of public mourning: HMV's stores marked his death with a minute's silence and, more appropriately, every Virgin store played 'Teenage Kicks' at

Preston pride: Action Records. Photo Garth Cartwright

the same time. John Peel was gone and, not too long after, so were many of the record shops he frequented.

That said, in 2017 Action Records continues trading, a tough little rock shop in a tough little city, and Gibson remains the drollest of proprietors. Cornershop, who formed when they were students in Preston, made good use of Action and recall Gibson with affection. As do all who have encountered him: there's a great short film about Action on YouTube, where Gibson admits that on his worst day of trading he didn't even sell enough records to cover his bus fare. Preston is one of those post-industrial cities that still appears to be reeling in decline – with divisions of income, religion and ethnicity – and Action provides a rare enclave for locals who like their rock raw.

Recommended Records/These Records

Opening in 1978 behind a permanently shuttered shop front on the Wandsworth Road, London SW8 – one of London's grimmest thoroughfares – Recommended Records was not a punk shop but it shared a wilful desire to stock music that challenged convention. Recommended served as a hub for experimental rock, musique concrete, noise merchants, free jazz, outsider music, the baffling, the brilliant and the simply bonkers. For a long time, Recommended was the only UK stockist of Sun Ra's Saturn label, and served as distributors of The Residents' and Pere Ubu's catalogues.

Recommended's founder is Chris Cutler, formerly drummer of Henry Cow, the experimental rock band that released several albums on Virgin in the early 1970s. Henry Cow founded the 'Rock in Opposition' movement to champion bands and composers that existed outside the music industry. Once the Cow split, Cutler set up Recommended Records as a combined record shop, record label and distribution network to bypass as much of the British music industry as possible. Cutler notes of his years on the Wandsworth Road, "Our policy was to collect what I thought was interesting and generally unknown music from Europe, America and Japan, mostly. Nearly all our stock was pretty much unavailable elsewhere then."

To visit Recommended Records involved considerable effort – it was isolated from public transport terminals – and, upon arrival, there was always the chance that the damn shop might be shut. Kiwi journalist Russell Brown purchased Sun Ra LPs there in 1987, recalling Recommended as, "being like another world, quite separate from everything else that was going on, outside of fashion". Other observers have described the shop as resembling the base for a Maoist group or religious cult than a record shop, so spartan and unwelcoming were the surroundings. Financial shenanigans – "The shop's accountant ran off with all their money" – eventually forced Cutler to divorce the label and distribution from the shop. He chose to concentrate on running Recommended Records as a label and distributor, while the Jacques brothers took over the shop.

With the Jacques brothers in charge, the shop relocated to 112 Brook Drive, London SE1, opposite the Imperial War Museum, and began trading as These

Records. The location proved more user-friendly, but everything else remained the same: music that confounded genre, the odd opening hours, and a lack of external markings to let anyone know a record shop existed behind a permanently closed door (customers had to ring a buzzer to gain entry). Former customer Carl Glover recalls: "It was always a challenge to go to These Records. First, you had to ring the buzzer to gain entry, and this was like going to one of those exclusive nightclubs where someone inside has a look to see if they want to let you in. Then, when you entered, there was a bathtub in the middle of what felt like someone's living room and the bathtub was full of old reel to reel tapes. And when you went to buy records they might well give you a bollocking for your choices! 'What you want this rubbish for?' type of thing. Done in good humour. But it was unlike any other record shop I have ever been to. They had a great selection of jazz LPs there and field recordings, avant-garde soundtracks, lots of crazy stuff that you would never find elsewhere. I believe the shop had strong ties with the London Musicians Co-Op and with This Heat, the post-punk band."

These Records continued to trade until 2004 when Lambeth council sold the building to property developers, who promptly evicted the Jacques brothers. So ended the 26-year legacy of a London record shop that defied all retail convention while making sure that music largely unavailable elsewhere was heard.

The Cartel

It was the worst of times, it was the best of times: as 1983 dawned, Geoff Travis had lost his beloved Rough Trade record shop but, one afternoon at Rough Trade Distribution, a 19-year-old Manchester musician pressed a demo tape on him. Travis listened and agreed that, yes, his struggling record label would release a 45 by The Smiths. This signing would not only enrich Rough Trade Records' fortunes and take indie rock into the mainstream, it would galvanise the network of independent record shops that Travis and Richard Scott had built into Rough Trade's distribution network.

"Distribution was really important," says Travis. "As word got out that we had stock, shops outside of London got in contact and this became the network that became The Cartel."

The Cartel initially took shape organically. In York, there was Red Rhino Records. Opened in early 1977 by Tony K (Kostrzewa), who, inspired by the music he heard on Peel's BBC Radio 1 show, rang the DJ and asked how he could get stock of said 45s for his shop. Contact Rough Trade, said Peel, they have the records. Tony K did and a beautiful friendship began. Other shops followed a similar trajectory and Scott set about building both Rough Trade Distribution and The Cartel network of independent record shops – Red Rhino (York), Backs (Norwich), Nine Mile (Leamington Spa), Probe (Liverpool), Revolver (Bristol), Rough Trade (London) and the independent record label Fast Forward (Edinburgh). While Travis is sincere in talking about The Cartel representing independents "taking control of the means of production", Rough Trade Distribution simply didn't have the funds to cover all of the UK; by working with partners they managed to achieve this. Travis says: "We ended up distributing Mute, who had huge hits with Depeche Mode and Yazoo, and Factory had New Order who also sold incredible numbers. The distribution, in the end, got too big. Even Crass, who insisted their records be priced so low we could never make any money off them, sold a lot of records! My forte was that I never wanted to be Richard Branson. I never wanted to oversee some huge operation."

The Cartel's core shops all made a strong impact in their home cities. Tony K of Red Rhino, easily the most distinctive record shop in York's history, set up the Ediesta and Red Rhino Europe (RRE) labels, his focus being on new bands from the Midlands and the north of England. His labels went on to issue 125 albums and singles, including efforts by The Mekons, Red Lorry Yellow Lorry and Pulp's debut album *It*. Probe Records, founded in Liverpool in 1971 by Geoff Davies (with the help of soul DJ Roger Eagle), served as the leading independent record shop of the north west of England. When located next to Eric's nightclub in the late 1970s, venue and shop served as a nexus for Liverpool's punk scene.

Punk fitted Probe Records perfectly. This Liverpool institution had been championing the raw and the marginal across the 1970s and, although much smaller than the city's Virgin shop, it conveyed a transgressive energy that attracted the best and the brightest. Among those who would work behind the Probe counter were three youths who went on to find fame and fortune fronting The Teardrop Explodes, Frankie Goes To Hollywood and Dead Or Alive. While Julian Cope, being an obsessive record collector, surely made for the perfect record store clerk, Pete Burns must have been terrifying, his famously waspish tongue lashing customers if he disliked their music choices (or clothes or haircuts). Burns, who would serve in full make-up, black contact lenses and whatever outfit took his fancy, was a sight to be seen, and only the foolish or savage attempted to confront him. Instead, many found getting 'shaded' by Burns something of a spectator sport, his pout and repartee both being Scouse classics.

"I'm not lettin' yer waste yer money on that shite," he announced to one customer trying to buy a Half Japanese LP, while telling another "Put that back and get something decent" when they presented him with a Japan 45. Requests for Kiss or Dire Straits LPs would be greeted with silence. A brave lad asked for a Julian Cope album and watched as Burns curled his lip then said, "He's a prick but he's our prick. Go 'ead." Burns' behaviour was encouraged by Davies, who already had a reputation for sneering at customers (Cope recalls Davies refusing to sell a youth a Rush LP), yet Burns' wild self-belief and acerbic delivery won him admirers. BBC radio producer Graham Robertson has fond memories of Burns' turn at Probe: "Probe records really was a lifeline for music fans in early '80s Liverpool. Some kids were scared to go up to the counter when Pete was serving as he was acerbic and scathing but, overall, he was really funny. I personally relished going up to pay as it was always entertaining. My mates would often give me their records to pay for and I would place our selections on the counter and attempt to catch his eye – he was usually permanently immersed in an animated conversation and would often serve you without breaking from it! On one occasion, I got full attention: he came over, cast his usual nonchalant eye at my attire and then on what I had placed on the counter – a copy of *Easter Everywhere* by the 13th Floor Elevators

– he didn't make a comment but had a look of 'Alright yer little shit' on his face before disappearing in the back to fetch the vinyl, handing it over with a wry smile upon return. When I got home I went eagerly to play my new purchase only to find *12 Gold Bars* by Status Quo in the sleeve … Twenty years later I got Pete in as a guest on a radio show I was producing and told him this story. He said, 'Yeah, I was shite. Geoff only employed me for the glamour!'

"Once I was walking towards Probe Records when the door burst open and a huge skinhead who was often around the shop making trouble came flying out backwards closely followed by Pete Burns in what can only be described as an eighteenth-century shepherd's smock, an upside-down straw top hat with his dreads cascading out of the top, full make-up and massive heeled boots. He shot down the steps sideways like a crab and, before the skinhead could get up, lifted his leg up and, fast as a snake, pierced him with the stiletto of his boot in the centre of the chest! That skinhead was truly massive and was a real nuisance, we were all slightly scared of him, but I will never forget his shriek of pain – like something from a slaughterhouse! At the time this happened, I was going to the same very rough boy's school Pete had gone to – locals called it 'Chegger Road' – and to see a huge, malevolent force dispatched with speed and precision by a lad from Chegger in a dress gave me a new definition of strength and confidence."

Robertson chuckles then says: "I always remember two American girls who seemed to be eternally camped at the bottom of the steps of Probe, surrounded by empty cider cans and hammered. A dark-haired one who was the most vocal and her mate with a red Mohican who was always too smashed to stand up straight or even speak. They were banned from the shop but would harangue anyone entering – including my 12-year-old self! Years later I was flicking through a biography of Courtney Love and there was a photo of her with long dark hair around the time she moved to Liverpool!"

Following Rough Trade's example, Davies set up the label Probe Plus Records in 1981, issuing what he called "music to drive you to drink". Releases included such Peel faves as Half Man Half Biscuit and The Mel-O-Tones. Yet Davies found handling Cartel distribution overwhelming – trying to get payment for records distributed, especially to market stalls, causing all kinds of problems – and so eventually he sold the shop on. Probe Records continues trading in the 2010s. It has a new location, no Pete Burns types behind the counter, and lots of classic rock and Third Man Records releases. Along with the most recent Half Man Half Biscuit CD.

Norwich, although home to a university, had been starved of good record shops. When Backs opened on Swan Lane in 1979, it provided Norfolk youth with access to the new rock music. Run by the Appel brothers, the shop's walls were covered in graphic, polemical images provided by the likes of Crass and the Dead Kennedys, and the music stocked proved equally confrontational. Impressed by the Appel brothers' work ethic, Richard Scott invited them to join The Cartel after a mere 18-months' trading: the deal was to handle Rough Trade Distribution's south-east England accounts, Backs receiving a 15 per cent

discount on records they would sell on. Unlike Tony K and Geoff Davies, the Appel brothers rose to the challenge of distribution, closing Backs in the early 1990s to focus on distribution.

Revolver Records, situated on The Triangle in Bristol, is the only record shop in the UK to have a work of literature devoted to it (Richard King's 2015 memoir *Original Rockers*). King began working in Revolver in the 1990s, so missed The Cartel era, but he memorably describes the intensity of this windowless, upstairs emporium where West Country music freaks – punks and dreads, hippies and crusties, the intense and the eccentric – would come to shop for new tunes.

Opened by local musician Tony Dodd in 1971, Revolver was soon sold on to Mike Chadwick and Dodd went on to run Tony's Records in Clifton, a much-loved second-hand emporium. Chadwick developed Revolver into the city's foremost specialist record shop, set up Recreational Records – an indie label that issued a dozen 45s of local bands – and hired Jeff Barrett, now boss of the

Heavenly Records label, in 1984. Barrett recalls: "To me, when I worked in Revolver, it was the most amazing record shop in the world. Record shops can be scary places and this was the scariest of them all: in a windowless building with fag butts on the stairs and Mark Stewart shouting at people! One of our best customers was Grant Marshall. He was part of a firm called Wild Bunch and they were buying electro and reggae from us. Grant was such a good customer – he helped me out many times and would even end up doing his time behind the counter at Revolver. Nellee Hooper and Robert Del Naja were also members of the Wild Bunch and they would, with Grant and Andy Vowles, go on to form Massive Attack. But that was much later. Back then they were youths running a cutting-edge sound system and crazy for records.

"Things were so exciting musically – the first Smiths album came out, the Cocteau Twins, Aztec Camera – and as we were in distribution I had access to all the new releases! And out back there were boxes and boxes of records stacked everywhere and I would go through them and find lost treasure! So, I learned a bit about distribution and learned a lot about how a shop worked."

As with Backs in Norwich, Revolver's owner became so engaged in distribution that he sold Revolver to 'Roger', an obsessive character King describes working for (Revolver closed in the late 1990s, too specialist in vinyl to survive the CD age). While Backs and Revolver both revelled in their roles as distributors, Probe and Red Rhino were overwhelmed, with the York shop declaring bankruptcy in 1988. This, combined with Rough Trade Distribution's increasingly fraught business practices, brought about the downfall of The Cartel and, in 1991, flattened Rough Trade Records and Distribution.

Once the dust cleared, all that remained of Travis's original vision of a holistic Marxist alternative to the corporate music industry was the original Rough Trade record shop. Having divorced from Travis and co. in 1982, Rough Trade had been forced out by their landlord and shifted a few hundred metres to 130 Talbot Road. Here, the three core staff – Nigel House, Pete Donne, Jude Crighton – took control, making sure that Rough Trade continued to serve as the outlier record shop for alternative rock. This trio oversaw Rough Trade's expansion to Covent Garden (here hosting in-store appearances by the likes of Nirvana, Jeff Buckley and The Beastie Boys), Paris and Tokyo, then retreated from all three to its Portobello base, before rolling out to Rough Trade East in Brick Lane in 2007. While other rock shops lost their focus and crashed, Rough Trade held on tight to its punk rock roots and, in doing so, established itself as the leading rock record shop of the twenty-first century.

Travis, who successfully relaunched Rough Trade as a record label in 2000, says: "I buy records every day. I'm probably Rough Trade's best customer. And I have shares in Rough Trade New York. I really believe that a record shop can still be the hub of a community. It can still be a place to hang out. Obviously, they've had to adapt to survive – a lot of shops are now acting as cafés and performance spaces as well as record shops. But that's good. It extends their purpose."

"No Irish, Blacks, Dogs": Minority Music Marts

The UK's minority communities flex their musical muscle. Jewish shops move from East to North London. Stern's African Record Shop enlivens London's Tottenham Court Road. Bhangra rules Southall, Birmingham and the Midlands. Latin Americans bring salsa to Soho. Greeks and Turks divide Haringey. Albania flies its eagle flag over Covent Garden. Cameos from Brian Eno, Cornershop and Cigdem Aslan.

There are certain irrefutable truths: Boris Johnson is an awful liar; Ken Livingstone is a nasty bully; The Stone Roses are ridiculously overrated; the Premier League is awash with grifters; the ice caps are melting; the Holocaust did happen; and music and food both travel brilliantly. My concluding truth is demonstrated by migrants adding spice to life on the British Isles, enriching British cuisine and opening ears. Food and music are made for sharing and have brought plenty of people together to engage in creativity, concord and – for the fortunate - coitus.

That said, in these post-Brexit times it's worth noting how racially divisive the last century in Britain often was. In 1919 thousands of demobbed soldiers attacked black communities in the port areas of Liverpool and Cardiff; in the 1930s Oswald Mosley's fascist brown shirts intimidated Jewish communities in East London; in 1958 gangs of Teddy Boys terrorised Notting Hill's black community; Bristol Buses proudly had a Whites Only employment policy until a successful, four-month long boycott broke the race barrier in 1964 (Harold Wilson would introduce the Race Relations Act in 1965); Enoch Powell's predictions of race war and call for 'repatriation' in 1968 drew voluble public support- 'Paki-bashing' skinheads bullied, harassed and intimidated immigrant communities while the neo-Nazi National Front's thug rallies were an urban blight across the late 1970s and early 1980s. Things may have improved immeasurably over the last quarter century, but Belfast mob attacks on Romanian Gypsies and boneheads bullying Muslim women who wear the hijab stain a nation that now likes to put forward a harmonious multiculti face to the world. 'No Irish, Blacks, Dogs' signs may have vanished from guesthouse windows in the 1970s – and 'No Travellers' from pubs in the 1990s – but the likes of UKIP (UK Independence Party) and Britain First ensure fear and loathing lingers.

Against such ugliness, music balms wounds, soothes souls, and provides more immediate comfort and spiritual rejuvenation than alcohol or religion. Moreover, the stalls and shops that sold records to Britain's minority ethnic populations played a central role in those communities. West Indian record shacks are documented in earlier chapters, so my focus here is on emporiums that served other migrant communities.

The West End's unofficial African Embassy: Stern's. Courtesy of Robert Urbanus.

Yiddish Cocktail

Many pioneering UK record shops were Jewish businesses; considering Emile Berliner was Jewish while Thomas Edison is believed to have been an anti-Semite, this is poetic justice of sorts. A century ago, when London's East End served as the Jewish community's base, the likes of R. Mazin & Co. could advertise that they stocked 'Hebrew, Yiddish, English & Foreign' 78s, adding they had both 'Jewish Home & Synagogue Music'. Mazin was based at 141 Whitechapel Road, London E1. A nearby competitor was S. Goldstein & Sons at number 160. Goldstein & Sons advertised "Complete Stocks of English & Hebrew Records" as well as all kinds of pianos, and announced they were established in 1822 – what London tales that shop could tell!

Levy's of Whitechapel (see Chapter 1) served as Jewish music's foremost shellac shetl, its labels issuing records for home, synagogue and beyond. One of the latter is a personal favourite: Stanley Laudan's 1957 10-inch LP *Yiddish Cocktail* (Oriole) finds the remarkable London-based Polish vocalist performing 'Rock 'n' Roll Kozatsky' alongside attempts at samba, klezmer and Gypsy. A celebrated Warsaw crooner in

the 1930s, Laudan (1912–92) fled from the Nazi invasion to Moscow, yet conditions there were so unsafe he somehow made his way into occupied Europe, joined a pro-Allied army unit, and fought in Italy up to and including Monte Cassino. Wounded, Laudan was transported to the UK and, with an anglicised name, kept on making music. If *Yiddish Cocktail* didn't catch on with the kids who were then buying Elvis and Tommy Steele, no one can fault Stanley for trying or the Levys for blending mitzvah spirit with music biz grift.

In 1996, Bloom's restaurant shifted from Whitechapel High Street to Golders Green, London NW11, after 76 years of bad-tempered service. This signalled a finale of sorts for East End Jewry, the community now based in the area from Finchley to Stamford Hill. In North London no record retailer as remarkable as the great Whitechapel emporiums came to the fore but plenty of small Jewish stores sold records and other goods. "There were Chassidic shops up in Stamford Hill," says Ben Mandelson, leader of the Yiddish Twist Orchestra, "that had simcha [wedding tunes], chazanut [cantorial synagogue music] and niggunim [East European wordless melodies] LPs."

Local resident Marc Engel adds: "You will still hear this stuff played as muzak in the kosher stores in Golders Green/ Hendon or Stamford Hill. It mostly sounds bloody awful! They would have sold this stuff on vinyl back in the day, but probably only in Judaica/Jewish book shops which are slightly less prevalent and sell books and ceremonial items such as candlesticks, yarmulkes, etc. Israeli folk and pop LPs were also widely available. They still sell this music, as do all the food shops, but, of course, it's on CD now. And Steimatzky Hasifria, the Golders Green branch of the Israeli chain of book stores, closed in 2015."

Country and Irish

Pre-WW2 the Irish were Britain's largest immigrant community and, if there's one stereotype acceptable about them, it's that they love a song. For decades, Kay's Irish Music Centre, situated right next to Our Lady of Hal, the Catholic church at 161 Arlington Road, Camden, London NW1, served as a congress for London's Irish population, experiencing its busiest times on Sunday afternoons once mass was over. Kay's stocked not only records but Irish newspapers, flutes, tea and such. However, it was the record bar that generated the greatest excitement because Kay's had LPs, 45s and cassettes reflecting all manner of Irish music making. That said, Reg Hall – musician and chronicler of London Irish music making – recalls Kay's offering a conservative selection of Irish records in the 1950s and 1960s: "When Topic Records tried to sell Kay's 78s by Margaret Barry (an Irish Traveller and noted banjo player/singer) they wouldn't touch them with a barge pole! Yet she was regularly playing in The Bedford Arms on the same street!"

At some point this policy changed as Kay's became noted for sourcing records from across Ireland; so much so that Collet's folk department regularly sent staff there for Irish folk LPs they couldn't find elsewhere. Kay's also had lots of Elvis and Jim Reeves LPs, these singers having been unofficially adopted as Irish icons. The new Camden rock underground that based itself around Rock On and Dingwalls also made use of Kay's, with The Pogues researching rebel song that became part of the band's early repertoire. Indeed, before Rock On opened in 1975 (see Chapter 10), Kay's served as the only record shop in Camden, and possibly the only one anywhere with plaster Madonnas in the window.

Hall recalls a record shop in Daventry Street off Euston Road that sold Irish records on Decca that were unavailable elsewhere, and a stall in Shepherd's Bush Market that had good stock. He notes that HMV's Oxford Street shop had an International Department where you could get all kinds of HMV releases

from across the globe – "African, Indian, Trinidadian" – but no Irish. "Because they were released on a Dublin HMV subsidiary that was separate from the British HMV." Hall notes that by the 1970s shops began to open in British cities that catered to the Irish communities, records being sold with all kinds of other goods. Further north, E. V. Silman's record shop in Cricklewood, London NW2, catered for the Irish community in the 1950s and early 1960s.

For those Irish Londoners who lived out west there existed WG Stores, the venerable Shepherd's Bush record shop. Owned by a Jewish family, WG catered to everyone. Ian Hingle, who worked there for most of the 1970s, remembers it doing a roaring trade with Irish imports: "We sold a lot of Irish music that would come in boxes from Belfast, and the covers were always bent up – the Irish customers didn't complain, they couldn't get the music anywhere else so they just accepted them. Big Tom & the Mainliners was a big star then. He played what they called 'country and Irish' and he was a big fat guy who owned his own label, his own pressing plant, everything, and he would do an album every three months and we would order a hundred copies of each one and sell out in a week!"

WG Stores closed in the early 1980s. In Liverpool, The Musical Box once did a roaring trade in 'country and Irish', but this long-standing shop has found its audience diminishing over recent decades as ties to the old country fade.

Redemption Songs

I'm an atheist through and through, but as religious beliefs have inspired phenomenal amounts of great music I've been known to drop into faith outlets in search of a song. Gospel remains a major player in the US black music industry but marginal in the UK, Christian book shops being the major outlet. West African gospel is often sold with Nollywood DVDs at market stalls, and Caribbean gospel now incongruously sits next to reggae CDs in Jamaican shops. Brixton was once home to Red Records – a strong gospel selection as well as rap and R&B – and the Miracle Record Shop, which served only the Lord. Local musician Big Joe Louis says: "The Miracle Record Shop was at the start of Acre Lane [Brixton], just up from where the McDonald's is. This is 1983, '84 that I found it and I would go in there and search through their old stock. They were a gospel record shop set up to cater to the local black community so they had everything, the latest gospel stars from the US and British choirs and records from the West Indies. Just gospel, nothing else. I remember at one point they had a big wicker basket of singles filled with US 45s on Caravan and other gospel record labels. They were priced from 50p to a pound. I found great things there."

Due to the activities of extremists like the Taliban who ban all music, Islam has recently been tarred as an anti-music religion. Yet the Muslim world has produced much beautiful music. For me, life without records by Fairuz, Khaled, Nusrat Fatah Ali Khan and Ali Farka Toure would be poorer (to name but four icons). Where London's Edgware Road runs into Marble Arch has long represented the heart of Arab London, and Ben Mandelson, always on the lookout for music from overlooked regions, recalls it as once having so much music on offer that one shop specialised in Sudanese music cassettes. Times change and it is now bereft of music vendors. In Birmingham, Oriental Star continues to exist as a booking agent for Pakistani musicians, but it shut its record shop and label long ago. Zamzam International on Green Street, Newham, London E13 is an Islamic store that stocks all manner of things (including devotional CDs), while the shop connected to the Regent's Park mosque also carries a selection of devotional CDs from the Muslim world.

Also in London, Turkish shops in Hackney and Bangladeshi on Brick Lane remain stalwarts, selling pop and faith CDs side by side.

Hindu bhajan temple music is – if on record – sold by the Indian shops covered later in this chapter. I'm unaware of Buddhist, Mormon or Scientologist record shops ever existing in the UK. But, you know what? I wouldn't be surprised if they once did.

Stern's West African Record Shop

"I used to go to this record shop just off Tottenham Court Road called Stern's, and that was a place where you could buy records from other countries, so a lot of Africans went there because you could buy West African records there. I used to sniff around there as I was just fascinated by all the covers. All these people with amazing headdresses on and you think, 'Christ, I really want to hear that record, I wonder what that sounds like.'"

So recalled Brian Eno when musing on how he found his way into the music that would inspire his *My Life in the Bush of Ghosts* album (1981).

From humble beginnings selling light fittings and lingerie, Stern's African Record Shop introduced Fela Kuti, Franco and Salif Keita to the West. Initially aimed at supplying London's growing African community with new records from their homeland, Stern's would develop into a mighty African oracle that helped the largest continent's voices be heard.

Based at 126 Tottenham Court Road, London W1, Mr Stern, a Jewish Londoner, thought to turn the back room of his electrical goods shop into a record bar in the early 1950s. He may have initially sold British records but, by the 1960s, Stern's was known as the African Record Shop. What encouraged him to do so? No one knows, although legend has it that African students (studying at the School of Oriental and African Studies, SOAS, nearby) traded records from home for electrical goods repairs. As for the stock of lingerie, well, Mr Stern was always interested in earning a quid and, back then, a thriving red-light district existed in Fitzrovia.

Stern's built up a word-of-mouth reputation as the place to head to for African records; Mr Stern relied both on visiting Africans to sell him suitcases of LPs and 45s and upon the Oti brothers' general goods supermarket in Balham. The Oti brothers ran a classic general goods store, providing the African community with much of what it wanted from 'back home': Nigerian staples such as yam and dried fish were sold as well as boxes of Nigerian LPs and, for a while, the brothers issued African artists on their own Oti record label. Alongside Stern's and the Oti's, there

were little African shops existing off London's Berwick Street in the early 1960s – Georgie Fame remembered regularly perusing their selection of West African 45s.

Robert Urbanus, a dapper Dutch national who loved African music, frequented Stern's. So much so that he and two friends bought Stern's in 1982. Urbanus recalls the Tottenham Court Road Stern's shop as, "a lovely old-fashioned electrical goods shop with African records in sale in the back room. And some country albums: Nigerians love country music". Urbanus went on to develop Stern's into an international platform for African music: label, publisher, distributor, concert promoter and a truly spectacular record shop.

Urbanus arrived in London in the late 1960s, but it took a year in Africa to expand his musical horizons: "I lived in Ghana as a student in 1975 and saw all these great African bands at their peak. On returning to London, I continued my musical education by buying records in the only place you could: Stern's. They stocked new LPs by Fela Kuti, Sunny Ade, French African artists. You could listen to albums there: you can't sell records to Africans without them listening to it first. When I heard Stern's was going to close – the lease was up and Mr Stern wanted to retire, he was well into his seventies – I and Charles Eastman, a Ghanaian, and Don Bey, an Armenian, decided to take over Stern's.

"New Year's Eve 1982 is when we took over Stern's. We bought the name and goodwill and a little filing cabinet full of documents from the mail order service he offered and his leftover stock. Until then Stern's had been known as 'Stern's West African Record Shop'. We dropped the 'West' and kept the rest. It took us a couple of months to find a suitable space. Charlie Gillett played an African record on his Capitol Radio show, mentioned buying it at Stern's and how the shop had now closed. I called up the station and told him 'The old shop has closed but Stern's is reopening soon.' We opened in Whitfield Street [London W1] in April 1983. On the day of our opening party a friend with suitcases full of new releases arrived – the hottest new Franco and others!

"At the old Stern's, if you saw a record that interested you, well, you had to buy it or there was a good chance you might never see it again. There were lots of African students in London and many would arrive with a suitcase full of new LPs from Africa to sell. There were some real characters. One guy would bring over lots of LPs to sell then go to Holland, buy a second-hand car and ship it back to Nigeria. We made contacts with labels and distributors to ensure we had a more reliable stock, started the Stern's Records label in 1983 and set up as distributors with Iain Scott of Triple Earth Records. We started exporting all over the world and found quite a good market in Japan."

A focal point for African music, Stern's shook with the energies it unleashed. Urbanus recalls: "On a Saturday the shop would be full of Africans coming to get the new LPs, and I'd DJ and they would be literally dancing around the shop and shouting, 'I'll have that one!' At the same time, we were attracting English music fans who would pay attention to what was being played and what the Africans were purchasing. We'd get new stock in every week – vinyl and cassettes, initially – and, back then, you could really sell records.

"We started touring African artists early on. One of the artists we booked was Youssou N' Dour. It was his first ever UK concert. Those events really blew minds. People were realising Africa had so much more to offer than war and safaris."

Strong releases by Ivory Coast reggae singer Alpha Blondy and Salif Keita found Stern's on a roll.

"Salif's *Soro* [1987] eventually sold more than 60,000 copies which, while not a lot for a pop record, was huge for an African release. That album attracted so much attention. We had the likes of Carlos Santana calling up and offering to take Salif on tour."

Success saw Stern's shift into a spacious building just behind Warren Street tube station but, by the late 1990s, Urbanus noted a steady decline in sales: "The decline was brought about by piracy. We always lost sales to pirated cassettes but when the CD burner came out, it was so easy for African pirates to burn CDs that it hit us hard. And then the burnable DVD where you could store several albums on a single DVD hit African music even harder. I knew the pirates. They would come in and buy one copy of each new release. Then downloading hit. And that was that."

Urbanus added a café – one of the first record shops to do so – its rich coffee and cake adding to the ambience created by the bright music bursting forth. But it wasn't enough to save Stern's. Urbanus closed the shop in 2010 to focus on handling the label's publishing and back catalogue, while issuing superb CD compilations of vintage African recordings. Stern's represented the best of London: progressive, inclusive and exciting, a shop that brought cultures together to celebrate and share adventures in music. Where Stern's once operated there is now a bookie: instead of the mellifluous tones of Franco and Tabu Ley, you can hear the 3.15 from Haydock Park and observe the glum faces of punters losing their savings. *Plus ça change?*

The Indian Subcontinent

In Southall in London, there once stood two legendary record shops: ABC (established in 1965) and Indian Record House (established in 1967). These magnificent emporiums, with incense burning and every surface brighter than everything else, were palaces of Punjabi music.

Iain Scott, who ran Triple Earth Records and worked as a distributor for world music labels, dealt with both shops: "The guy who ran ABC was Anil Puri. I think the Hussein brothers ran Indian Record House. Anil didn't speak to me for more than two years after I unintentionally insulted him by saying, 'Indian business is small business' – I meant in terms of the price per unit. The Indian records and cassettes that were sold in the UK matched the price in India, so were cheaper than other albums here. He took it that I was saying he ran a small, insignificant business – this is a guy who now drove a Rolls Royce being insulted by a skinny white youth! – and wouldn't speak to me until, finally, somebody put in a good word for me and I was forgiven.

"While a lot of the music they sold was imported, The Gramophone Company of India had an office in Hayes in the EMI building so, if demand was big enough, some Indian albums were pressed here. When I distributed Gramco, Stern's and Triple Earth I remember I was supplying Harrods and they catered to a very wealthy Asian clientele who would not be caught dead in Southall but wanted to buy Indian music! Things tended to move very quickly in the Indian market and it is a market that was really punished by piracy – this is way before digital downloading – bootleg cassettes stole an extraordinary amount of sales. Birmingham's Oriental Star Agency, who launched Nusrat Fatah Ali Khan in this country, grew out of a record shop."

Tjinder Singh, Cornershop's vocalist and songwriter who hails from Wolverhampton, recalls: "I didn't start buying records until I was about 15. I grew up in an Asian household where the music we listened to at home was Hindi film music, Sikh devotional music and Punjabi folk music. I hate terms like 'Bollywood' and 'bhangra', we never called it that when I was growing up. To buy Indian records you'd get them from the back room of a sari shop. Soho

ABC MUSIC SHOP
7 THE BROADWAY
SOUTHALL MIDDX. 4BI 1JR
TEL: 01-574 1319

Road in Wolverhampton had a lot of Asian shops. Me and my cousin were raised on devotional music at the local Sikh temple. We used to record some of the performances. This was before I got interested in pop and rock music.

"My older brother got into metal and had Deep Purple and Rainbow LPs. Very Midlands music. I started buying records at Max Millward Records in Wednesfield, Wolverhampton. I got into northern soul and reggae through Max's shop. And then I started buying pretty standard indie stuff. I was pretty ad hoc about what I would buy as I was filling in for the record collection my parents never had. That got me into going to charity shops. And newsagents also had ex-jukebox singles for sale that were very cheap. I'd still go to Asian shops to buy music. Leicester has the Belgrave area with lots of shops. Even in Preston there were places like Deepdale that had Asian shops and some of them would stock music."

Down in London, DJ Ritu was also buying Indian music while starting to sample the sounds of other cultures: "I bought my early Bollywood albums in sari shops in Green Street, Forest Gate. I then started using the bhangra shops in Southall: Virdees, IRH, Metro and ABC. Eventually, I went closer to home at DVD Zone in Turnpike Lane and outlets in Ealing Road, Wembley, for Bollywood, whilst Haringey was my oasis for purchasing Greek and Balkan music at Trehantiri on Green Lanes and Greek City in Palmers Green. For Middle Eastern CDs, Edgware Road was the prime hunting ground. I used to walk miles to get the tune I wanted or needed."

Ken Hunt, a London-based journalist who has written widely on Indian music, notes: "Sound of Asia on Bell Road, Hounslow, was the first Indian record shop I came across. Before that I would buy imports at Collet's. George Harrison regularly dropped in to Collet's to purchase LPs of Indian classical music. By the late 1960s, there were at least four Asian record shops in the Southall/Hounslow area serving a primarily Punjabi population. I found that you had to be cautious when buying Indian LPs as they were often pressed on atrocious Indian vinyl and the sound quality was really bad. For Tamil music I'd go to Tooting Broadway. The high street had a whole bunch of shops that sold South Indian food, clothes and Kanatic music. The Tamils weren't as pop obsessed as the Punjabis so I could still find good South Asian classical music on cassette and then CD.

"In the mid '90s I would still head out to Southall as there was a shop going strong that sold CDs and books and magazines from India. Thing is, you could haggle with them. I'd haggle! It was Little Punjab and so, just like in Punjab, you haggle. I once went into a shop and asked if they had the Wadali Brothers CD – they are a fantastic qaawali outfit – and was told 'We don't have it' so I said, 'Do you know someone who does?' And the shop owner sent out a runner who came back with a copy! I visited Bradford in 2000 and, looking around, I found that the sari shops tended to have a music section out back. By then it was largely pop stuff they were selling, bhangra, which I was never very interested in. I still bought CDs in Mitcham as recently as 2007. Alperton is a good area to visit as it is very Gujarati and you can find Indian classical and Bollywood there."

Ninder Johal

In 1989, Ninder Johal launched the Nachural record label in Birmingham to promote bhangra, the music that fused Punjabi folk dances with electronic beats. Bhangra quickly came to dominate the British Asian music market, fusing with rap and dance music, crossing over to a wide audience and allowing Nachural to enjoy international success with Panjabi MC in 2002. Johal says: "Bhangra was part of the British Asian experience, and running a bhangra label meant selling the music to all the little Asian shops and stalls. This meant not simply having one distributor but lots of distributors – I needed local distributors who knew the Asian market and would go and supply all those little shops and stalls. I'd have the distributors competing against one another. Bhangra was hot, people wanted it, so I'd have distributors selling it everywhere. I had three distributors in Leicester alone! Distributors in Bradford. In London. Up north. I did go and see Virgin and HMV and provided them with some stock but I never had much faith in them selling bhangra. Asian people tend to buy music when they shop for food and other things so they're far more likely to buy it in an Asian market – pick up rice and dal and a bhangra cassette! – than take a bus into a city centre and go to an HMV or Virgin.

"There were some big Asian record shops back in the '90s – ABC, Planet Bollywood, Oriental Star Agency – and they all stocked bhangra, but the reality of it was making sure that all the stalls and mixed goods shops had bhangra cassettes and CDs. Bhangra was huge: on one high street in Birmingham there were eight retailers of bhangra, four stalls and four shops. Everyone wanted bhangra! There were even these little bhangra music shops that some of the youth set up. Places that were like clubs. Bhangra was the sound of British Asians and it was very exciting.

"2008 is the year that digital kicked in and that killed the Asian market as far as selling CDs. The shops that sold bhangra have gone. Or, more correctly, they're still there but they don't stock CDs and cassettes any longer."

Latin London

John Armstrong, London's leading Latin DJ, has been buying salsa, samba and son records for longer than he cares to remember: "The earliest Latin shops were actually stalls on Berwick Street and a couple on Lisle Street in Soho, late 1960s. I can't remember the dealers' names; they'd have jazz mainly, with Latin jazz and a little Cuban, Tito Puente, Machito, etc. as a sort of sideline. Usually the records would be lacking the Mecolico sticker and hidden under the counter – so illegal imports! [Mecolico was import duty, not VAT. Each retailer had a code which appeared on the sticker, to prove they'd paid import duty].

"The marvellous Collet's on Charing Cross Road would gamely try to get any obscurity you'd care to name, including tejano, Cuban, etc. The Colombian shops around Elephant and Castle would occasionally get a concession of LPs (and later CDs) along with all the other goods. And there was an amazing second-hand record shop in Bishop's Castle, Shropshire, which carried the best selection of rare folkloric Latino and Arabic second-hand stuff I've ever seen anywhere.

"Undoubtedly the most significant establishment was Hitman Records. Hitman was owned by Clive and Stan Chaman, two Trinidadian musician brothers. They first set up shop near the Hammersmith roundabout in around 1978, moving to Lexington Street, Soho, by around 1984. It soon established a rep as one of the best all-round black/dance music shops in the West End. Stan had good direct contacts with NYC and Miami distributors and ordered the very latest salsa LPs every couple of months in batches of four or five pieces each title. When he had new stock, Stan would hit the phones and it became a question of who could get to the shop first got the records. Those were the days to own a Soho record shop! Stan and Clive closed the shop around 1992 and moved to Miami.

"Mr Bongo was a great shop in Berwick Street. It was founded in the basement below Daddy Kool in Berwick Street by Dave Buttle who developed Mr Bongo into one of London's leading shops for Brazilian, Cuban and Colombian music. They populated their vinyl racks with trips to Caracas as Venezuela was the only market then reissuing Fania albums and, if you had the right sort of import/ export licence, the product was incredibly cheap. Mr Bongo moved location

WE SPECIALISE IN IMPORTS.
JAZZ • FUNK • SOUL • REGGAE
SALSA • SAMBA • CALYPSO
CORNER OF, BREWER STREET,
and LEXINGTON STREET, W.1.
TEL: 01-437 8708

several times, always staying near or on Berwick Street in Soho and always offering top Latin imports. Dave also set up the Mr Bongo record and film labels where he has made some great music and movies available. He closed the shop in 2003 but still runs the business – online only now, of course – selling 45 reissues of sought-after Brazilian and African tunes as well as his DVD reissue of lost world cinema classics. The days when you could score exclusive Latin records in Soho are long gone but, while they lasted, they were great times."

Balkan Bazaar

After the Second World War, a sizeable number of Greeks, Turks and Yugoslavs settled in the UK. The Yugoslavs tended to sell records in their food shops, while Greek and Turkish record shops set up in north-east London. Ben Mandelson recalls, "Trehantiri in Green Lanes, Haringey, was founded and run by the Pattalis family. I heard a lot and learned a lot thanks to them. I even bought some instruments there. It was a great hang-out."

Cigdem Aslan, the gifted Kurdish vocalist, also found Trehantiri inspiring: "Trehantiri means 'little boat'. They used to sell records, CDs, cassettes, instruments and music scores as well. I discovered it and was very happy to find one of my favourite band's albums there. Finding this shop made me feel like I never left the university band where I used to sing rebetiko songs!"

Even fans of the Eurovision Song Contest found their way to Green Lanes as Trehantiri stocked a plethora of CD singles and albums by past and present Eurovision singers. Former customer Nick Nasev notes: "They had a wall dedicated to Eurovision artists, both CD albums and CD singles. Not just the Greek and Cypriot singers but Israel, Turkey and everywhere else. I'd travel there just to get a single of a specific singer I liked. Of course, the arrival of MP3s wiped out the demand for such."

"Turkish shops were also in Green Lanes, but the Newington Green end," says Ben Mandelson. "The main one was Ercument Plak Evi. They even released vinyls in the 1970s, including a Nigerian juju one."

Through Communist Party links, Collet's (see Chapter 2) always stocked plenty of Eastern Bloc releases. Simon Broughton of *Songlines* magazine recalls: "Collet's had lots of interesting Russian stuff on the Melodiya label, although this was mainly classical. Melodiya simply didn't publish much folk or world. The other eastern European labels from Bulgaria (Balkanton), Romania (Electrecord), Czechoslovakia (Supraphon), Hungary (Hungaroton) were always more fruitful. I got my first album by Georgian duduk player Djivan Gasparyan there. I definitely used to take advice from staff of what was interesting."

One nation from which Collet's failed to get music was Albania, then the world's most isolated state. No matter, only a short stroll away was The Albanian Shop. It may sound like a Monty Python-style skit but, during the Cold War era, The Albanian Shop in Betterton Street, Covent Garden, London WC2, defiantly flogged Stalinist kitsch along with such rare musical treats that even John Peel made use of it (and mentioned it on his radio show).

Mandelson recalls The Albanian Shop "as the only place (back in the 1970s–80s) where you could buy Albanian EPs!" Miranda Vickers mentions The Albanian Shop in *The Albanian Question*, focusing on the role of one William Bland (1916–2001): "... a member of the pro-Stalinist wing of the Communist Party of Great Britain and a great anti-Revisionist. In 1955 the Albanian government invited communist comrades in Britain to establish an Albania-UK friendship society....Aside from his rigid ideological views, Bland was genuinely very fond of Albania and its people and was instrumental in organising that wonderful little shop on the corner of Betterton Street in Covent Garden that contained an array of all things Albanian including the obvious political propaganda but also imported craftwork such as pottery and rugs as well as a rich folk music emporium at the back of the shop."

Jim Potts, who worked for the British Council and collected records, recalls of The Albanian Shop, "they had a small selection of used records (78s) and some CDs produced by the manager of the shop, e.g. live recordings from the Gjirokaster Folk Festival. I bought Greek rebetika 78s there."

The Albanian Shop's window was decorated with the nation's eagle flag, with images of Stalinist stooge Enver Hoxha. Inside you could buy his speeches and Hoxha key rings, miniature statues and other such personality cult trash. However, at times, it appears The Albanian Shop stocked large numbers of records, often at very cheap prices. How did they get such stock – confiscated from 'bad passport' families in Albania? Donated by party members? – I've no idea but it's more likely the former as Greek culture was banned, Albania being in a state of proxy war with the Hellenics.

My love of Balkan music means that I wish I had known about The Albanian Shop. Growing up in Auckland, I did visit an Albanian shop next door to Record Exchange, a large second-hand record shop. Sadly, the Kiwi Albanian shop only sold pamphlets by Hoxha, Stalin and Lenin. I used to drop in after record shopping and chat with the old soldier who ran it and once, when I ventured that Stalin was more monster than saviour, his complexion grew florid and he barked, "If it wasn't for Uncle Joe you'd be speaking Jerry or Jap!" If his shop had possessed an array of Albanian/Greek 78s I surely would have feigned enthusiastic agreement.

The London Albanian Shop was an oddball oracle, one that allowed the world's most isolated nation to communicate across political, geographical and linguistic divides via music. It closed in 1994, communism's collapse having rendered it redundant. I only hope that whatever vinyl, shellac and CDs it held in stock on that fateful day didn't join Hoxha's speeches and statues in a skip.

More than 1 million people from Balkan and East European states have settled in the UK over the past decade, but no new record shops have opened to serve them. Many a grocer sells the pork, puréed peppers and sweet wines they relish but technology has rendered the role of the record shop as a link to "back home" redundant. Today, music tends to be found on the migrants' mobile phones. It's easier to travel with. And it can be downloaded for free.

Chapter 17

Dance Stance: The Rap and Rave Massive

Electro and rap bring a new urban American sound to the UK. House and techno create turbo clubbing. The nation goes raving, pirate radio returns with a vengeance, and dance music shops open across the UK. The new millennium begins, the internet takes over, the end is nigh. Featuring: Groove Records, Deal Real, Spin Inn, FON Records, Black Market Records, Eukatech, Fat Cat, Swag Records, Big Apple Records. Cameos from the Pet Shop Boys, John Peel, Richard Russell, A Guy Called Gerald, David Bowie, Jeff Mills and Skream.

Rap and rave: the hard Bronx rhymes and the soft Chicago dance beats – one an ultra-masculine street sound, the other created in gay clubs. These were the underground engines of contemporary music across the 1980s. Separately (but secretly intertwined), they placed the DJ at the forefront of modern music, encouraged a DIY attitude, and inspired the last great era of record shops.

Chris Lowe of the Pet Shop Boys admitted on 6 Music that, when the duo formed, "We initially thought, 'Wouldn't it be great to have a 12-inch single available in this dance music shop on Berwick Street?' And that's what we achieved with 'West End Girls'." Many others harboured similar dreams.

Groove Records

Over Groove Records' entrance, a painted sign read "Soul-Electro-House-Jazz" and announced "The Dance Music Specialists". Situated on the corner of Greek Street and Bateman Street in Soho, London W1, Groove Records acted as a sonic hinge on which electro, rap and new jack swing would collide with house and techno. Groove was the quintessential 1980s record shop and premier rap retailer: what was heard first in Groove quickly echoed across London, then further afield.

Run by Jean Palmer, with her sons Tim and Chris, Groove opened in the late 1970s selling soul and jazz-funk imports then, as the 1980s got under way, established itself as ground zero for British hip-hop. Jean had years of experience working in record shops and an ear attuned to what the youth wanted. All of this helped her sense that rap was the new urban sound: importing every rap record that such tiny US labels as Sugar Hill, Sleeping Bag, Def Jam and Profile released, the Palmers' New York City contacts ensured they received new releases immediately. Not since the mod era, when new R&B records elicited a similarly visceral response, had a music – and the shop that stocked it – generated quite such fervour. Word quickly spread: if you wanted the beats 'n' rhymes rocking block parties in Harlem and the Bronx, only Groove had them (and a huge mural akin to those staining New York City subway trains covered its exterior so emphasising, "this ain't no Our Price").

The Groove posse: Jean Palmer and friends. Photo by Chris Long. Courtesy of Mike Hall.

As mods had once flocked to Transat Imports a few streets away, the self-styled 'B-boys', wearing baseball caps and Adidas trainers, a few even sporting fake gold chains or VW-emblem necklaces, began descending upon Groove, paying silly prices for 12-inch 45s by artists such as Schoolly D, Spoonie Gee and Roxanne Shante. Groove's influence was such that Mike Allen's weekly Friday night rap show on Capital Radio found the DJ counting down Groove's Hip-Hop Sales Chart while Jean Palmer's fame got to the point where the BBC *Nationwide* TV programme interviewed her, describing Palmer as "the disco granny". She certainly stood out, this tiny grey-haired lady who sat in a corner knitting, yet was capable of reeling off titles and dates of the forthcoming imports.

While Groove got on with flogging the latest rap records, upstairs a more traditional Soho trade continued, signs on the door reading "Large chest for sale" and "French mistress gives lessons". Inevitably, rumours abounded, linking record shop and knocking shop, both being devoted to selling cheap thrills to testosterone-fuelled males. Conjecture? Surely. But the imperious behaviour of Groove's staff surely only encouraged this.

Groove was a small shop but full of fresh stock, its advertisements stating "NEW RELEASES received DAILY direct from the USA". This ability to source the newest hip-hop attracted youths from across the UK: Bristol's Wild Bunch sound system – later gaining fame as Massive Attack – travelled to London just to get 12-inches from Groove. As well as being a hub for the new urban American music, Groove was the record shop where the new street fashions – casual and sportswear – were first noted in London's West End. Wannabe British rappers like MC Kermit, Derek B and Wee Papa Girl Rappers, and DJs, including future Radio 1 presenters Tim Westwood and Nihal, were all Groove regulars. Loud, crowded, full of swagger, Groove served as both vinyl vendor and hip-hop club. Entering meant you had to know your tunes, and any sign of hesitation or dissent could result in public humiliation.

Such bear-pit behaviour proved extremely intimidating to casual shoppers. Two pals of mine recall its intensity: "Groove was bedlam," says Russell Brown. "I once took a visiting friend in and he found it overwhelming and had to go and wait outside!" Simon Grigg concurs, adding, "Neil Barnes [later of Leftfield] first pointed me at Groove. It was overflowing with 12-inch funk, hip-hop and soul platters, all thick and smelling like American pressings only could then. It got so I used to avoid Greek Street to preserve my wallet."

In 1986, Tim Palmer, aware that greater potential profits lay in owning a record label than in running a record shop, founded City Beat Records and entered into partnership with Beggars Banquet. Running the label from Groove, City Beat began issuing electro/rap records, both licensing from the USA and sourcing local talent. City Beat scored lots of minor hits and then topped the UK charts for three weeks in 1994 with 'Doop', a novelty dance hit by Dutch electronic duo Doop. In 1989, Palmer co-founded XL Recordings to release house, techno and trance 12-inch singles, again with Beggars Banquet financing and distributing. Richard Russell, a clerk at Groove, was promoted to running XL A&R in 1991 and, by 1994, was in sole charge of XL. Thus, Russell receives all the kudos for turning XL into the most successful label in the Beggars roster via The Prodigy and Adele (as well as bringing Jack White and Radiohead on board). Groove Records closed its doors long before any of this largesse: Jean retired while her sons chose to work elsewhere in the industry rather than compete with Soho's new dance music shops.

Groove's legacy continued with Deal Real, a Soho rap shop that established itself in an alley off Carnaby Street. Here it hosted in-store performances from Kanye West, GZA and Amy Winehouse (among others), and counted many future grime stars in its community before closing in 2007. Groove Records played a pivotal role in launching hip-hop and electro in the UK. If it hadn't existed, then overwrought Croydon diva Adele might never have gone on to become the world's most popular singer. A blue plaque, please, for this overlooked Soho oracle.

Raving I'm Raving

By 1986, the major US rap stars were commanding large British audiences but their beats 'n' rhymes rarely worked on the dance floor. House music, with its fast-yet-gentle beats and yearning voices, provided the opposite experience and, by the mid-1980s, had transformed clubbing into the de rigueur weekend experience. In 1987, the Chicago and Detroit sound got tagged 'acid house' and gained a smiley face emblem, a drug and an aesthetic. This cast a spell that transformed almost everyone in the UK under 30 – goths and football hooligans, Brit funkers and bhangra fans – into ravers who wanted to dance all night. And hug one another while stating how much they "love you, man".

Such behaviour was viewed by some as terribly un-British. Or maybe not. From the waltz and foxtrot to jiving, disco and *Strictly Come Dancing*, the British public's appetite for music that gets people out on the floor is insatiable. We might not dance particularly well but we do like a boogie. Just as 78s by the likes of Jack Hylton flew off the shelves, 12-inch house and techno 45s sold and sold and sold. Inevitably, dance music shops began opening across the UK to supply demand and, very quickly, there were more specialist record shops than ever before. Dance music rode an unconscious wave of collective goodwill spurred on by the collapse of the Eastern Bloc, peace talks in Northern Ireland and the Middle East, the unravelling of Tory rule and the rise of New Labour, all signalling good times – *high times!* – and encouraging a quasi-mystical belief that by dancing all night you were making the world a happier, better place.

If tunes shaped by DJs in black Chicago and Detroit clubs first fired up the scene, ravers immediately began embracing records made by the British and French, Italians and Germans. House and techno hit hard and this often instrumental, electronic music arose in popularity around the same time as the personal computer took residence in every teenager's bedroom; here was a music anyone with access to the right software could create. Countless youths across the UK did just this: a tidal wave of 12-inch 45s were released between 1987 and 1997 – a decade book-ended by the opening of London acid house club Shroom and Roni Size winning the Mercury Music Award – all aimed at keeping feet moving while creating a distraction in the mind.

Probably as many youths declared themselves DJs as there were rave records released, these aspiring Grandmasters regularly buying new 12-inch 45s. Unlike disco, where the most popular tunes were chart hits on major labels, the records that ravers wanted were more akin to being part of a secret society, often bearing only a white label with meagre credits. No way Woolies could stock them, while Virgin, HMV and Our Price had no idea how to sell a faceless music with rapid releases and fast turnover. Even venerable independents like Rough Trade and Bluebird struggled, staffed as they were by elders largely immune to rave's charm. The last roar of the British record shop thus took place as ravers opened techno temples.

Some of these temples were spacious and emulated a club's chill-out room with sofas, incense and strobe lighting. But many were no larger than a cupboard, huddled in basements where Gollum-like clerks hissed at anyone who appeared ignorant of their vinyl speciality – "We don't sell that kind of music!" one shouted at me when I asked if they had Portishead's debut single – while others existed tucked away up in attics. Pop-up shops appeared in clubs and squats, with London mirroring the Jamaican example of 'record shacks' that set up and shut down anywhere and everywhere. Those running these shops often wore a uniform of black T-shirts emblazoned with rave slogans and possessed the pallor (and manners) of troglodytes. While it's hard to imagine them ever cutting a rug on the dance floor, they certainly were passionate about the sounds they sold.

These enterprises often involved a cottage industry phenomenon where small 'collectives' of DJs, dancers and labels came together to make sure their records were available. *Human Traffic*, a 1999 movie about a crew of Cardiff ravers, effectively parodies the quasi-religious intensity of ravers gathered at DJ Koop's shack: overpriced

12-inch rap and dance 45s being hustled to the guileless, all exchanges conducted in arcane slang, freaky dancing breaking out to particular tunes. Those were the days! Or were they? I was new to the UK then and, being a moth to record shops, found dance music vendors selling their wares almost everywhere: from Soundz in Torquay, through Ambient Soho in Berwick Street Market, Just for the Beat in Tottenham and Global Grooves in Birmingham and Chester, to Glasgow's 23rd Precinct Records. Every high street and side street appeared to have a dance shop, their walls full of 12-inch 45s alongside a small selection of DJ-mix CDs, flyers for clubs and raves and, in certain cases, illicit substances that were kept under the counter and only sold to a select clientele. These shops spread the acid house gospel, pushing pulsing electronic beats – *doof doof doof* – to the faithful as a soundtrack for a new society. Or, at least, for Saturday night.

Spin Inn

As raving grabbed British youth's attention, it wasn't only the new shops that catered to the Ecstasy generation: plenty of black music shops across the UK adapted too, notably Manchester's Spin Inn, which embraced electro, rap, house and techno. In 1988, when 21-year-old customer Gerald Simpson mentioned to staff that he had been recording acid house at home, they suggested he leave his demos with them. He did so and the Spin-staff passed them to Stu Allan (a local radio DJ and Spin customer) who played Gerald on his show the following week. This led to Gerald being signed by Rham! Records, a small indie label near Merseyside, as A Guy Called Gerald. His debut 12-inch 45 'Voodoo Ray' immediately blew up Manchester's Hacienda nightclub and quickly became a rave staple. It went on to reach No. 12 in the UK charts, becoming the best-selling independently released single of 1989. Most of the dance music shops selling 'Voodoo Ray' were not chart return shops, which meant that Gerald sold far more copies than his chart position suggests, hinting at the vast number of dance 12s then being purchased.

FON Records

Of all the dance shops that set up record labels to release music, Sheffield's FON Records leaves the most potent legacy. FON – a recording studio and record shop – forged links between the steel city's alternative electronic music history (Cabaret Voltaire, Human League) and the new dance music. When two FON employees, Steve Beckett and Rob Mitchell, decided to start a dance label based in the shop's back room, they called it Warp Records.

Warp's 1989 debut 12-inch release, The Forgemaster's 'Track With No Name', proved an instant success – kids were hungry for hard techno – and FON changed its name to Warp. Beckett told Richard King of the shop's instant success: "On a Saturday they were literally queuing down the street to wait for the doors to open. All the Transmat releases, or whatever the two or three big tunes were that week, would be gone in an hour. The importer had brought in what he could and there was obviously no digital access to it then, so it was a real supply-and-demand thing."

John Peel started championing Warp releases and the label experienced chart success with LFO and Tricky Disco. The partners then closed their record shop to concentrate on developing what would soon develop into the UK's foremost electronic music label.

As the 1990s got going, the dance-shop-as-dance-label created a unique ecosystem where people from the provinces could put records out that were sold via independent distributors to dance shops. When a tune took off – often after initially being pushed by DJs in a shop – it might sell thousands and thousands of copies without ever needing to deal with London's music industry. Dance music, at least briefly, did suggest alternatives, and the most ardent ravers believed the communities they forged through parties and pills would shape a new society. This wasn't to be, but the tribes who gathered in dance shops and at all-night dance parties – crusties, eco-warriors and hedonistic dreamers – gave the hippies' utopian dream a final flourish.

Pirate Anthems

How did the kids who bought all those copies of 'Voodoo Ray' get to hear it when the likes of BBC Radio 1 and Capital Radio were awash with George Michael, Bon Jovi and Madonna? Through what rising dance hall reggae star Shabba Ranks would celebrate in song: *pirate anthems*. In the 1980s, pirate radio returned with a vengeance. Whereas the 1960s era pirates were posh, white chaps hoping to be at the forefront of commercial radio, the 1980s pirates were primarily black youths from inner-city estates who set up bedroom stations to share the tunes dropped at sound systems, raves and in their local record shops: dance hall reggae and rap, house, techno and jungle. DJ-mix tapes were sold and shared like cigarettes, and certain dance shops made sure they advertised on the pirates. Exciting times and, just as with jazz, dance music was quickly defined by genre – house, techno, trance, deep house, ambient house, tech-house, gabba, hardcore, jungle, drum and bass, breakbeat, bashment, garage – with both DJs and shops specialising in select beats. Two West End record shops reflected this divide.

Black Market Records

For almost 30 years, 25 D'Arblay Street, Soho, was a place of pilgrimage: here stood Black Market Records (BMR), the world's premier dance music shop. BMR opened in 1987 and pioneered the New York groove in London. John Peel popped in to purchase dubstep, while Joe Strummer tended to favour soulful house. Meanwhile, David Bowie, daughter in hand, perused the drum and bass selection. Dave Piccioni, BMR's main man, recalls all this and more: "I was born in Huddersfield, went to college in Liverpool and put on parties. Me and my friend Sven were buying records from Groove Records; even though we were from the North they were known as the best import shop. Back then you had to go to a record shop to find out about new music.

"I then lived in New York City for five years as a DJ. I came back in 1990 and worked in Black Market just before it went bust – it was closed for several months – then me and Nicky Black Market bought it. I'd seen how record shops worked in New York City and they were completely different from in the UK. All had records on the wall and you asked a guy to play them for you or they had decks for you to play. In London, you flicked through empty sleeves. So, we were the first to put records on the wall. People said, 'You're crazy, they'll get nicked.' I thought, 'I may lose a few but it's a better system and the big plus is I'll save staff hours crawling around looking for records.' We put loads of record decks there, Technics 1200s, had a bank of them, and people would grab the record and put the headphones on and listen – or get it played on the system. And it worked really well.

"There were about seven or eight record shops in Soho selling the same stuff as us, with Red Records being our biggest competition. When we opened, we were 50 per cent house and 50 per cent rap and R&B. That changed around '92, '93 when dance music splintered. Our basement became hardcore: jungle, drum and bass.

"We just aimed to sell music we were all passionate about. People loved the

Hot wax hugs the wall: Black Market Records, Soho. Courtesy of BMR.

experience of coming in the shop – we had DJs, wannabe DJs and bedroom DJs and the latter two groups wanted to own a piece of the shop. We had a Bozack valve mixer: the sound was great! At one point, we re-did all the lights in the basement to brighten it up as kids were coming down and dropping E. Saturdays were super-competitive between us and the other dance shops as to who could get the promos first.

"They were exciting times to be in clubs and record shops. Twenty to thirty per cent of our customers were from overseas. Mail order started to kick in around '95, '96. In 2000, we were one of the first places to align online sales with shop stock. We knew our customers were early internet users so we ensured they could find us on it.

"BMR was a uniquely difficult business to run: 90 per cent of your entire stock line would change every three weeks. With dance music, there was no demand for CDs or back catalogue. That makes it a tough business as if you ordered 50 copies of a record and it only sold 40 then you were left with 10 and no profit to be made. The key to success was buying the right records: if your buying was off you lost money. If we had 1000 different titles on the shelf there were another 3000 we rejected. The guy behind the counter could be famously arsey but if they knew their stuff you had to give them credit for that. All these different London tribes related to each other via music and if you didn't know the music then they were rude to you – it was their way of demonstrating their tribal allegiance.

"We were part of the process of shaping dance culture here. I had to be a DJ as I don't think it was otherwise possible to keep up with the music. At its peak on a Saturday we had four guys behind the counter upstairs, three downstairs, the records were flying out. You put a good record on and everyone starts nodding their head and the hands are going up! Sometimes I would have a pile of 50 and say to the guys 'We've got to shift these' and they would play it three or four times and shift them all.

"Our peak era was between 1992 and 2000. We'd get to work on Monday morning and there would be a crowd of Japanese tourists outside wanting to take photos. We sold over 10,000 BMR MA-1 [bomber] jackets. One ended up in a V&A exhibition on black music culture. BMR always went through peaks and troughs: house music went into a real trough at one point and everyone seemed to think it was finished. Then drum and bass went massive and that kept us afloat. Then dance music had another renaissance; the drugs changed, Mitsubishi Ecstasy came in and you had a big house revival.

"The decline started when DJs stopped making dubplates and started making CDs. A big DJ would get a DAT of a tune off a producer or label and then have to shell out £30 to burn a dubplate. Only the bigger DJs could do this, that's how they stayed big. CD burning killed it. The internet hadn't really taken off then. There was a lot of stigma in dance music about playing CDs but as that started to decline we were fucked.

"By 2009 I decided 'enough'. I wasn't living the life anymore. After I got out, BMR became BM Soho and got Dub Vendor into the shop in order to try and make ends meet. It suited both parties. Then the landlord locked them out when they still had six months on the lease. Very sad. I'd have liked a party to celebrate Black Market's legacy. It was a community – we didn't realise that at the time. I think the world is a poorer place for not having these areas of community. I get irritated when I see people talking about the 'online community'. It's not a community, it's a *screen*.

"I now live in Ibiza and run a restaurant. It's similar to running BMR: food, service, décor all has to come together. I love it but I miss the excitement of BMR. That was the last great era for music, clubs and record shops. We'll never see anything like it again."

Eukatech

Piccioni observed of selling dance 12-inches, "Every shop had its own identity. BMR was always perceived that we came from an American black music source while others were very European techno shops." The latter is true for Eukatech, a Teutonic techno specialist improbably located in London's Covent Garden. Or perhaps not so improbable: Covent Garden once came second only to Soho for its remarkable array of clubs (including punk hotspot The Roxy) and record shops. Celebrated jazz and soul shops existed here, as did Rough Trade's Neal's Yard shop. Even London's only soundtrack LP shop once huddled on New Row.

Of Covent Garden's several dance shops, Fat Cat is noted because it closed as a retailer to concentrate on the Fat Cat record label: signing Icelandic band Sigur Ros found them selling millions. Yet the ravers who still have memories intact emphasise that Eukatech was London's premier techno shop. Marco Lenzi, a gregarious Italian, ran Eukatech from beginning to end: "In 1988 I was in Ibiza for three months and met loads of English people there and a French girl. I went to Paris to meet the girl and a friend said, 'Let's go to London for a few days,' and I'm still here! I started going out clubbing and just wanted to stay. I was always into buying records and got into producing – I set up Molecular Recordings with a guy called Marco D'Arcanfelo. He taught me everything. And after a few releases I started getting offers to DJ.

"In 1993 I got involved with Silverfish, a techno shop situated in a building that's now been demolished up the top end of Charing Cross Road. The idea of Silverfish started with Alex Oppido, a very talented guy. Silverfish was on the second floor and not easy to find so we went out flyer-ing at clubs and raves. Silverfish had a café and an art gallery – the first record shop to do such – and we discovered Red Bull when DJing out in Germany. We became the first place in the UK to import and sell Red Bull – the ravers' drink! We wanted to get the licence to manufacture it in the UK but had no funding so missed out on a fortune. We sold house-techno-trance and, in the weekends, we'd strip the shop back and set up sound system and party there through until Sunday.

"We spent two years together and then a disagreement meant we decided to split. Alex kept Silverfish going until 1998 while a German company, Undercover, contacted us, wanting us to set up a record shop and look after its labels. We found this place in Endell Street and that's how Eukatech came about. For Undercover, we distributed 16 labels. Eukatech had a little café with CDs on the ground floor and vinyl downstairs. At the beginning it was tough. We worked closely with clubs and sold tickets to events, just scraping by. Fat Cat were our big competition, they were the don of techno shops, but after they shut we became the main outlet. We specialised in techno and tech-house and were one of the best. There was a house music shop nearby, Plastic Fantastic in Drury Lane, but they were not competition at all.

"Eukatech got really well known and we had two big shows in the shop featuring DJ Jeff Mills. The first was when he launched *Live at Liquid Room* at our place and the second time was when he was selling limited editions of Axis Records for three days. The shop was rammed – especially with lots of Japanese! We had Richie Hawtin, Laurent Garnier, François Kevorkian – you name it, they'd all come in. You had collectors, amateurs, pro DJs, guys from abroad buying for their shops. We had a lot of labels, so people were coming to buy all kinds of quantities. Saturdays were always brilliant with lots of people in and great for contacts for me for DJing. We weren't making loads of money but we survived – people were buying records and merchandise and CDs: compilation and DJ mixes and artist albums.

"You had to judge what to stock. You read about it, got a promo and listened to it and maybe took 20 or 30 copies – or only 5 copies – we tried to be careful. You knew when a record was going to be big. Being a DJ I'd get lots of promos and you test them when you play out. People would come and say, 'Take 10 on sale or return?' We had records that nobody else had. Labels knew our clientele were big DJs so we'd get the best stuff. We'd import stuff direct from abroad. Eukatech was a way of life. Wake up and go to the shop – play records, eat records – it's a record shop! To be in a shop selling electronic music meant I was working in paradise.

"In 2005, the mother company Undercover went down. Before that happened we had managed to transfer the shares to ourselves so we kept the shop going alongside running the label from the shop. It was lot of work. We tried to run it online but it was too hard. Digital was hitting hard and loads of companies and record shops shut. Eukatech's end came about later that year when the landlord decided to double the rent, so made it unaffordable.

"Techno doesn't sell anymore. The kids download it for free. It's not a commodity anymore. Big companies and big artists on vinyl sell but not small artists. It's all corporate now. That said, Molecular Records is still alive and I still DJ in Asia, but I work 9 to 5 now as I've got two children to support. Everything about the rave scene was great. The energy! The vibe! The friends you made! I'm proud to have been part of it and think Eukatech achieved a lot."

Swag Records and Big Apple Records

In the shadow of the Home Office, serving those who exist in the suburban gristle of Greater London and Surrey, there once existed an electronic bazaar of sorts. Croydon, unlovely, much-mocked Croydon, grabbed dance music, stripped it of any pretensions and built a music alive to the rhythms and discontents of this concrete interzone.

Back in the early 1990s, when in Croydon, I would go looking for records. I noted how, while Virgin and Beanos had huge stores, the myriad small shops selling 12-inch dance 45s were where the action was. These shops barely

Big Apple boys: DJ Hatcha and John Kennedy. Courtesy of John Kennedy.

245

registered back then, when the likes of *DJ* and *Mixmag* magazines championed the best places to buy tunes. No Peel or Bowie popped in here to purchase new 12-inch 45s. *The NME* and *The Guardian* never mentioned that Croydon might be where the future of dance music resided. Away from prying eyes, interesting things were gestating out there as, once again, record shop proprietors and their customers came together, not just for an exchange of goods and money, but to create a deeply felt instinctive sound.

During dance music's peak years, kids living in the CR0 postcode were extremely well served by dance music shops, with almost a dozen operating in the mid-1990s. Of those, two made a lasting impression – Swag Records and Big Apple Records. Swag Records, founded by DJ Liz Edwards at 42 Station Road, West Croydon, in 1992, would soon be noted as *the* tech-house (the sound of underground parties in the early 1990s) shop. Swag reflected how the tastes of clubbers had changed since the initial acid house craze in the late 1980s: from dancing to anything – especially if it had squelchy 'acid' sound effects – electronic music had imitated jazz and splintered into countless niches, each with dedicated followers who often dismissed competing alternatives in a manner akin to their granddads clashing over trad or be-bop.

Dance music shops tended to specialise in what the proprietors favoured: as Edwards was a working DJ, she understood what moved the crowd and ensured Swag worked as a space where DJs and producers could test out new mixes. But it was another Croydon shop that played midwife to the future sound of London.

Big Apple Records existed for 12 years, closing in 2004 with little noise. These days it has a phantom presence similar to, say, the acoustic bluesman Robert Johnson who died unknown yet left a handful of recordings that went on to shape blues and rock music. I realise this claim sees me entering Pseud's Corner, but what took shape at Big Apple has become, more than a decade later, the ruling electronic beat music. And this sound is now known internationally as 'dubstep'.

Dubstep began with Croydon kids blunted on skunk creating an often eerie, electronic pulse. In a few years, dubstep would command international audiences and artists such as Beyoncé and Rihanna would hire dubstep producers, Eurovision entrants would employ dubstep beats, and every major club and dance music festival would boast dubstep DJs as part of their line-up. Just as rockabilly took shape through experimentation in Memphis's Sun Studio, dubstep was born out of a nucleus of youths who worked at (or hung out in) Big Apple Records.

Big Apple opened in 1992 when three friends – Gary Hughes, Steve Robertson and John Kennedy – set up Apple Records at 37 Surrey Street as a dance shop spread over three floors. There was house and techno and lots of jungle (Jamaican-flavoured ragga-electro). Competition was tough, with at least eight other dance shops in the area, and, by 1996, Kennedy had bought his partners out, downsized his shop (setting up a recording studio in the upstairs space) and focused on selling the then hugely popular garage sound. He also had to change his shop's name to Big Apple after a legal threat from a representative of The Beatles. Kennedy says: "Everything about that time was intense, and everything

The Croydon massive: ravers pack Big Apple. Courtesy of John Kennedy.

was fun. You're with friends every day, people who love the same music as you do, and while it wasn't a gang it was a youth club. One with new music arriving every day! And we were in the fruit and veg market so there was plenty going on around us. We had a lot of fun and Arthur Artwork was a real joker. So much so we had the Armed Response Unit burst into the shop one day due to one of his pranks backfiring!"

Over the next couple of years, Big Apple employed the likes of DJ Hatcha and Skream, while Digital Mystikz were regular customers – all teenage unknowns back then, but names that inspire fervour in dubstep fans today. These and many other youths were attracted to Big Apple due to Kennedy making sure it stocked cutting-edge garage and jungle tunes. Pirate radio, he notes, was how he got the word out: "South London had so many pirate stations then. Upstart FM, Girls FM, Delight FM. I'd advertise on them and give their DJs a discount if they mentioned Apple as where they bought their tunes. As each station had up to 60 DJs this meant we got a lot of pirate business. And the kids came flocking in! Croydon's always had lots of record shops. It's perfectly situated between London and Brighton and has good transport links and a big shopping area. For years we had people queuing to get in and I'd have to send them home when I was shutting up every night. It was mental."

Being a long way from the glamour of the Soho shops, Big Apple served as a nucleus for local yearnings, and its young customers made beats on their PCs and PlayStations, intent on channelling the sound of the shop. Here they blended Jamaican dance hall and dub, added hip-hop's taut pulse, and kept beats broken and shuffling, creating a sinister, skunk-spiked polyglot, the Croydon mestizo. In 2002, Kennedy launched the Big Apple Music label in partnership with Artwork and DJ Hatcha, to promote both the shop and new local talent. The term 'dubstep' originates from this time and Big Apple was the first label to release tracks by Benga, Skream, Loafer and Digital Mystikz, these teenagers (average age 17) now being viewed as dubstep pioneers. Ahead of the curve, Big Apple's releases initially met a lukewarm response and Kennedy, exhausted from a dozen years of working six-day weeks, decided to shut up shop. He could have continued trading, he notes, but as garage became grime, the pirate stations were forced off air and 9/11 blew a hole in the economy, he saw tough times ahead: "I'd always wanted to travel so I closed Apple and shifted to South America. If I'd stuck it out I might have made a fortune out of dubstep. [Laughs] I needed a break and what Apple achieved was great. I loved every minute of it. I'm pleased I did it."

Both Big Apple and Swag Records closed in 2004: the youth who once enthusiastically queued to buy new 12-inch bangers no longer rolled up in such numbers for they had found out how to download. The dance shops thus acted as canaries in the music industry coal mine, dozens shutting in rapid succession. The closure of Swag and Big Apple marked an era's end of sorts: the youth tribes that had, since the end of the Second World War, used music as a defining part of their identities now had little need for record shops. Croydon represents, if not the oracle's last stand, a retreat from which there would be no return.

Chapter 18

Things Fall Apart: Apocalypse Now for Record Retail

Record shop chains dominate retail: HMV, Virgin, Our Price, Andy's, Woolworths, MVC, Music Zone, Fopp, and American invaders Tower and Sam Goody. Millions and millions of CDs are sold, the music industry is awash with money and then... then it all begins to crumble. Cameos from Richard Branson, Shabba Ranks, Emmylou Harris, George Melly, Bob Dylan, The Moody Blues, Mariah Carrey.

Our Price Records

Opposite Brixton station music blares, champagne corks pop and ribbons are cut: a summer afternoon in 1990 finds Our Price Records celebrating the opening of the chain's 300th UK shop. Head honchos from Our Price and several record labels toast their good fortune. Never had it so good? This depended on who you asked.

For a chain that began in 1971 specialising in selling compact cassettes and 8-track tapes (then heralded as the future of recorded music), Our Price had gone on to open more record shops across the UK than any other chain, now ranking second only to Woolworths in sales of recorded music. While Our Price (and the major record labels) may have felt the opening of number 300 was cause to celebrate, anyone who loved music and record shops viewed the chain's high-street domination as depressing: Our Price's bright, banal emporiums stocked little beyond the Top 40 and a predictable selection of perennial best-sellers. The chain existed along with the Sock Shop, The Body Shop and WHSmith on high streets and in train stations, guaranteeing customers an identikit, palliative shopping experience.

Our Price, in the 1970s and early 1980s, had employed staff with a passion for music and allowed certain store managers to promote the music they loved (an Our Price in Selfridges' Oxford Street department store sold more classical CDs than any other UK record retailer). However, as the chain aimed to dominate British record retail, a numbingly narrow list of titles became its focus. To wander into an Our Price store – living in Brixton in 1994 I occasionally dropped into No. 300 (never, ever finding anything worth buying) – you could sense how those who ran the chain saw music as a confectionery: a selection of new chart flavours with evergreen albums like *Thriller* and *Queen's Greatest Hits* ensuring fast turnover and maximum CD sugar rush.

Our Price's rise reflected how UK record shops, riding a CD-led a sales boom, were devalued of purpose and bereft of occult powers. Such lucre proved a false dawn: the rapid expansion of Our Price, Virgin, HMV and other chains propelled Gresham's Law into action, bad driving out good, setting the scene for a retail apocalypse. Not that the music industry foresaw an impending collapse: in the

This town, coming like a ghost town: Soho 2009. Photo by Garth Cartwright.

1980s and 1990s the chain stores resonated with the sound of cash tills ringing.

The rise of Our Price mirrored the huge UK demand for Top 40 albums that had been growing ever since The Beatles' rise, one that peaked in the late 1990s with artists such as Blur, Oasis and The Verve each selling millions of CDs in the UK alone. The music industry was booming, but this expansiveness involved huge waste and, for the most part, extremely slight music, while the chain record stores often forced out solid local record shops by siphoning off the customers who purchased only Top 40. Our Price, frantic to open as many shops as possible, had a pernicious effect on independent retailers, exemplifying the Thatcherite agenda of filling every high street with banal chains.

In record retail, the chains employed a corporate tactic of buying in bulk from the major labels, so using a number of promotions to undercut competitors. These retail vampires drained independent traders and, in doing so, decimated the UK high street. In Hastings, this led to a tragedy when the city's most beloved record shop, The Disc Jockey, was forced to close after Our Price announced they were opening. Proprietor 'Big Al' Jansen, a man who had provided residents with great records and much joy, committed suicide in August 1985, leaving a note stating "Can't function without DJ".

In building big, bright sheds to mint money, the megastores and their ilk exemplified another strand of Thatcherism, emphasising the functional rather than the personal, pushing uniform product as opposed to the passionate and imaginative. The ideal of a record shop as a communal space where people gathered to share enthusiasms and knowledge, the employees acting as spirit guides, the best and the brightest, the long lost and the weird all being celebrated, had no place in the corporate structure. Entering a Virgin or HMV now offered no pleasure, and these stores – listening booths reduced to a few pairs of headphones on a pole, no seating or public space – seemed to actively discourage browsing, with loud Top 40 music blasting and security staff shadowing those who did not treat buying records in the same was as purchasing a snack. The chains also began employing an unwritten rule of not having anyone over 25 on the shop floor, culling employees with deep knowledge. By ruthlessly chasing the public pound, the chains operated more as record supermarkets than traditional record shops, only lacking the generous discounts Tesco and co. offer. Across the 1990s, a new CD cost around £15 (sometimes more) and this made buying music a luxury for anyone not on a comfortable wage.

The supermarkets decided to enter the music industry seriously in the late 1990s – emulating Our Price in only stocking the Top 40 alongside *Best Of* or *Now That's What I Call Music* compilations, celebrity efforts and a handful of 'classic' albums. They offered their CD stock at considerably lower prices than any of the record chains – music-as-loss-leader – to make sure customers spent more on alcohol and baked beans. In doing so, they torpedoed the record shop chains.

Andy Gray, having built his Andy's chain of record shops into a significant retail force through East Anglia and the Midlands (see Chapter 9), found his small empire under siege at the end of the 1990s: "HMV got really aggressive and the

supermarkets latched onto CDs. The supermarkets hadn't stocked a lot of LPs because of the space they took up but CDs were perfect for them – they fitted easily into a shopping basket and they could cut deals with the major labels to sell CDs at cost, while knowing people would come into supermarkets to buy a new chart album and then buy other stuff too. And the people who managed the supermarkets liked it because selling pop CDs was a lot sexier than selling toilet paper. We couldn't sell the chart albums as cheaply as the supermarkets could, so we lost the casual shopper who would pop in to buy the new *Now That's What I Call Music* CD. This meant our margins were getting ever more squeezed. We'd made mistakes like opening in shopping centres in Sheffield and some other places and when the rent got doubled we had to get out. By 2001, the writing was on the wall. By 2003, I was sick of putting my money into shops so decided to close the chain down. History has proved me correct as all the other chains have gone."

Well, almost all: HMV staggers on, dazed and confused, a blind giant that now appears unsure about why it still exists. The end of Andy's presaged a slow-motion collapse of a kind the UK had never witnessed before: over the next five years every UK record shop chain would either fall apart or, in HMV's case, engage in a radical restructuring that saw many shops close and jobs lost. This wasn't due to harsh economic times or punitive sales taxes, instead the public simply stopped going to the shops that had previously held such sway. If the speed of the collapse stunned most onlookers – hundreds of shops closed and thousands of jobs lost in one retail market – more prescient observers noted that the record chains had grown at such an accelerated rate over the past 30 years that they now resembled retail bodybuilders, so quickly did they expand, get bigger, louder, brighter, with CDs being the steroids swelling their big profits. Inevitably, dysfunction set in and the muscular megastores found entropy overtaking their systems. When the public no longer wanted CDs, the chains were revealed as muscle-bound, impotent.

The Our Price chain, having been horse-traded back and forth since the mid-1980s between WHSmith, Virgin, an Australian retailer and an investment consortium, had been in bad shape for several years. Richard Branson, finding himself left holding the package, desperately tried to diversify the Our Price shops into Virgin mobile phone vendors. The public weren't buying it, and by early 2004 the shutters came down on the entire chain. Beyond the staff who lost their jobs and the record labels that lost a major outlet, few mourned Our Price's demise. The Brixton Our Price is now a Poundland, the discount chain that helped send Woolworths' 807 UK stores to join Our Price in the retail junkyard in 2008.

Woolworths

When Woolies first began selling 45s in 1970, it tapped into the British public's huge demand for pop, dominating Top 40 singles sales for the rest of the century (as well as shifting plenty of LPs by artists likes Nana Mouskouri and James Last). For Woolworths, records, initially viewed as a side business, quickly became among their most lucrative merchandise: by 1990, 'entertainment (music/video)' made up a fifth of the chain's total turnover. That said, Woolworths sold an increasingly narrow selection of titles, the music section serving as little more than where the kids who had outgrown pick 'n' mix would head while their parents shopped. And the parents must have felt that Woolies wasn't offering such great value when the CD single became the only way for tweens to own the latest Take That, Spice Girls and All Saints hits.

Overpriced CD albums and, especially, CD singles – if a new CD album cost £15 in 1992, a CD single often retailed at £5 (the minimum wage was £3.50 an hour) – reflected both the labels' and chains' contempt for consumers. A contempt which fuelled the use of CD burners and then the downloading of music MP3s. Woolies and Our Price sold a lot of CD singles and, for a while, raked in huge profits. The music industry has, understandably, lashed out at pirate websites and howled at newspapers giving away free CDs, but a brutal truth involves the industry's greed – overpricing CDs, signing and hyping mediocre talent, throwing its support behind chain stores, and pumping stock into supermarkets – left the public feeling they had been served a shit sandwich for long enough.

DISC JOCKEY
FOR
RECORDS

2 QUEEN'S ROAD
HASTINGS

TELEPHONE
2031

Many more closures came in the early 2000s and now, from the distance of a decade, it seems impossible that there were ever so many high-street shops shifting huge quantities of recorded music. CDs began to resemble retail typhoid, and the collapse of northern chain Music & Video Club (MVC) sparked a domino effect that toppled record retail.

Music & Video Club, Music Zone and Fopp

MVC was started in 1989 by former Our Price managers (having left after WHSmith's takeover) who saw an opportunity to emulate the London-based chains across the north of England. MVC modelled itself on Our Price, setting up on high streets and selling popular CDs, cassettes and VHS videos. The business changed hands several times, with Woolworths' parent company Kingfisher becoming owners in 1993. By 2005, they were in administration and the Manchester-based record shop chain Music Zone (founded in 1984) took over ownership of 41 MVC shops in January 2006, so leapfrogging to the third largest UK record chain with 104 stores (all branded Music Zone). In January 2007, Music Zone went bust. Yet Fopp, a Glasgow-based chain, purchased 67 Music

Zone shops in February 2007, rebranding them Fopp. Founded in 1981, Fopp had succeeded by cleverly stocking a small number of shops with a select range of discounted products: jazz, blues, soul and rock CDs, cult books, DVDs and full price ephemera (T-shirts, calendars) in cities with universities nearby. The Music Zone acquisition proved a wild overreach and, by June 2007, the chain had collapsed, spelling the end of mass high-street record retail. HMV bought the Fopp name and operates a handful of Fopp shops today, both to rinse 'classic' CD/DVD/books cheaply and to sell a selection of full price vinyl/CD/DVD releases.

Tower Records and Sam Goody

Tower Records and Sam Goody, the two dominant US record chains, both attempted to replicate their American success in 1980s Britain. Goody quickly opened 22 inauspicious shops across the Midlands and the North, while Tower focused on a flagship store in Piccadilly Circus, London W1 – a vast 2322 square-metre building offering wide-ranging stock – with smaller London outlets in Camden, Kensington, Queensway and Kingston, before expanding to Glasgow and Birmingham.

Sam Goody never found its footing and quit the UK in 1999. Tower took over a couple of small Goody shops as it practised a stealthier expansion, yet it would soon find itself in trouble, both at home and abroad. It closed all its UK shops by 2004 (the Piccadilly and Kensington shops were then taken over by Virgin in an act of wild folly). I was a contributor to Tower's monthly *Top* magazine and saw, albeit from a distance, the chain begin to stumble as the same problems that closed Andy's undermined Tower: without selling thousands of chart CDs every day there was no way they could continue to service their shops. Tower's founder Russ Solomon had a genuine passion for music and made sure his shops employed experts: the Piccadilly shop had a depth of selection matched by no other UK record retailer. Those who worked at Tower enjoyed the experience, being assigned to departments that sold the music they loved. Stephanie Pulford, a Californian fresh to London, got work running Tower Piccadilly's Country-Folk-Blues-Gospel department in 1993: "It was a great shop and the freedom made up for being paid peanuts and working all kinds of crazy hours. It was open to midnight and you had to work shifts, 8–4, 10–7, 12–9, 3–12, which were tiring. The manager of the store was Steve Lyttelton, son of Humphrey. I liked him a lot. A nice man and reasonable. We sold some vinyl, not loads, Tower was very much a CD store.

"Everybody that came to the UK would come up – Emmylou Harris, Robert Earl Keen – and do a signing in my section. When we had Emmylou doing her signing, Evan Dando turned up and just pushed to the front of the queue with his Gram Parsons records. He pissed me off! George Melly did a signing in the jazz section and that was really fun. He held court all afternoon. Of course, the big stars were downstairs and they pulled huge crowds in. Mariah Carey did an in-store and she took over a room and had all these demands: the walls had to be draped in white silk and there had to be this number of white roses and other such stuff. I don't think she asked for puppies but she did ask for everything else!"

Tower's muscle in the US market ensured in-store appearances that no other UK chain could match and, during the era of mega CD sales, almost every prominent act was obliged to do a Tower appearance. I once went to use Piccadilly Circus tube and found the station closed due to the huge number of Whitney Houston fans mobbing Tower (and overflowing around the station – whose ticket barriers faced Tower's basement entrance). When Capital Radio announced Bon Jovi were appearing in Piccadilly Tower, crowds closed down the Circus and the local police chief threatened to arrest Tower's management (and the band), so enraged was he by the unsupervised herds of shrieking Jon fans. Shabba Ranks set off another kind of chaos: while waiting in an office before he did his in-store appearance, he spied a young lady among the gathered fans and sent one of his entourage out to make introductions. Shabba and fan then got busy on a desk, the dance hall star being so engaged in coitus he declined to bother with his in-store appearance. Disgruntled Ranks fans rioted, looting CDs and causing much affray. As Solomon encouraged a hedonistic spirit among Tower staff, I hope Shabba's shag didn't lead to any employees being fired!

Virgin Records: End Of Empire

Across the 1970s and into the 1980s, Virgin was the chain in which music-obsessed youth tended to gather (see Chapter 9). Howard Devoto, after quitting The Buzzcocks, put up an ad in Manchester's Virgin store for musicians: Barry Adamson saw it and applied to join what would become Magazine. The Specials used Coventry's Virgin for the same purpose. As did thousands more musicians across the UK. Richard Branson never possessed much interest in music, but his gregarious nature informed the stores, and Tony Rounce recalls Virgin as easily the best of the chains when it came to management–staff relations. Admittedly, Rounce worked for Virgin in the 1980s.

When Lois Pryce got a job in Bristol's Virgin Megastore in 1992, she embarked on a career as 'Specialist music buyer', shifting first to Croydon before joining the head store at London's Oxford Street, experiencing throughout a chain run by number crunchers speaking business jargon. In a 2015 piece for *The Independent*, Pryce observed of her time at Virgin: "Virgin was establishing itself as a corporate music retailer and any cool underground status it had enjoyed in the 1970s and 1980s had been destroyed by a rash of identical Megastores opening across the UK. An aggressive branding strategy was under way, illustrated by the mean-eyed, slick-haired Operations Director who snarled at us new recruits: 'Do you understand it is essential that all our stores look the same and stock the same product?'" And there was a whole new lingo to learn, most of it ending in the suffix '-age'. We didn't use signs, we used 'signage'; we didn't give change in coins, it was 'coinage'; the area of the shop floor was measured, not in square feet, but 'square footage'. Our workplace was a 'store', not a 'shop', but most galling to our young, ideological hearts, was that the music we loved so much was 'product'."

No surprise then that Pryce gave it all up to ride her motorbike to Iran, The Congo and other destinations free of corporate speak.

I arrived in London in 1991 and found the Virgin stores free of the *joie de vivre* that had once made them legendary (and they were no longer stocking bootlegs). Tower offered a much broader selection of the 'specialist' music that engaged me, and had the best magazine selection in the UK tucked away in Piccadilly's basement: every music magazine, all kinds of fanzines, goofy US publications (and more). Predictably, I spent hours there. Pryce notes how, when the Croydon Virgin hired a line manager whose retail background involved selling trainers – he knowing (and caring) little about music – she realised it was time to escape. Inevitably, what once had been the feistiest retail chain ever to grace UK high streets entered retail history's dustbin in 2008.

Branson, scarred by Our Price's collapse and savvy regarding the Virgin brand, feared the UK's high streets would be littered with shuttered Virgin Megastores. To avoid this, he oversaw a management buyout: 130 Virgin shops (and stock) across the UK and Ireland became Zavvi, changing hands for a proverbial £1.

Predictably, Zavvi went bust within 15 months of opening. As with Our Price's collapse, Branson's wealth surely took a substantial hit but he must have breathed a sigh of relief that no forlorn Virgin stores – windows covered in fly-posters and graffiti, iconic logo cracking and crumbling – existed to remind Joe and Joanna Public that Sir Richard's famous brand had succumbed to malingering distempers.

HMV: The Giant Stumbles

First opened and last standing were HMV. The veteran British firm had expanded rapidly across the UK (and then internationally), making it the world's most powerful record chain. Cutting deals with the major record labels, HMV could ensure that a new artist/album received maximum high-street promotion. All kinds of shenanigans went on between the record labels and record chains – this involved deals on prices, the window display, promotions, advertising, marketing, in-store appearances and more – the money sloshing around encouraging all manner of dissipate extravagance. This activity was a long way from HMV staff being told to place EMI LP covers at the front of the bins (see Chapter 6). Inevitably, as the chains formed tighter alliances with the major labels, independent record shops were given less attention, marginalised even though they often promoted the best and brightest releases. Popular music had become a multi-billion-pound industry and a corporate mentality ruled, one averse to art and risk, to outsiders and the odd. The oracle was being poisoned, the circle broken.

In 1986, HMV opened a shop the size of a football pitch (150–4 Oxford Street, London W1) – *covering 60,000 square feet over three floors!* This was, the chain proudly announced, the world's largest record shop. You know what they say about size not being important? Well, this proved true of 150–4 Oxford Street. I did drop in and, on occasion, found an import that I'd long wanted. Yet much of their stock consisted of canyons of chart CDs, hordes of trash books, piles of boxed TV series, *Trainspotting* posters, Cobain T-shirts … not a place to relax and hunt for music. Still, 150–4 did suit the age of spectacle: an in-store by Bobby Brown closed Oxford Street when 3000 fans flocked to see Whitney's beau, while Michael Jackson, dropping in to shop, was followed by 1000 fans (*Thriller* [1982] being HMV's biggest ever selling album). Indie rock icons Echo & the Bunnymen and Blur both played (separately) on the building's roof to promote new albums.

Meanwhile, back at 363 Oxford Street, Elton's Princess Diana tribute sold 1318 CD singles in its first hour on sale. By 2000 it was estimated that 363 had sold some 30 million records (across all formats), making it the world's most successful record shop. In a sign forewarning the bad management that would soon bring the chain to its knees, HMV closed 363 in April 2000, shifting stock across the road to the much larger space of 360 Oxford Street. *Two megastores on London's main shopping street less than half a mile apart! Woo-hoo!* I imagine the suits smirking, toasting one another and saying, "That'll teach Branson and Solomon who's the big gorilla of record retail!" Having emulated King Kong, HMV quickly came crashing down: 360 struggled from the start and by 2010 its lease was sold and the shop closed. HMV then reopened 363 in 2013 to retain a West

Retail ruination: HMV shut up shop 2012.

End base because they shuttered 150–4 in 2014. The world's largest record shop is now a Sports Direct. Many HMV outlets across the UK and abroad were shut down around this time. The chain had become too big, too anonymous, lacking in any kind of character: having been top dog for so long in record retail, HMV found itself relegated to the kennels. Poor old Nipper would find lots to howl about if he entered HMV in this century.

The online marketplace

Amazon and other online retailers (including Play.com and, shamefully, HMV) possibly did more damage to high-street record shops than the pirates. They exploited a loophole that allowed them to sell inexpensive consumer items VAT-free from firms based in the Channel Islands. Until the UK government outlawed such practices in 2012, this meant the online giants could offer new chart CDs at prices that not even supermarkets could hope to match. The hard-fought ruling brought some equality back into selling mass market albums but by then, of the record shop chains, only HMV still existed. The chain's managers must have pondered on how to entice the customers back into the shops; the same customers they seduced online with Adele CDs for a fiver.

Not that they found an answer: the supermarkets won the public vote for CD sales, to be followed by the revenge of the nerds as downloading meant youth no longer even wanted to purchase recorded music. Combined, the hypermarkets and Napster levelled record retail. All kinds of things have been done to try and keep the last major UK record shop chain afloat, with the restructuring specialists Hilco buying HMV for £50 million in 2013, then closing over half of its original stores; today around 125 remain. Those that survive are bereft of magic, and often seem bereft of music, as they attempt to unload stacks of *Amy* and *Game of Thrones* DVDs and *Grand Theft Auto* games. The excitement and musical passion that once surrounded HMV has long gone, but it remains the UK's top dog: with the end of VAT-free internet selling, HMV have overtaken Amazon to, once again, rule the market – or what's left of it – in physical music sales.

Game over: Record Shop Ruination

At the dawn of the twenty-first century, it wasn't just the chains that were crashing: more than half the UK's independent record stores closed up as New Labour stumbled into Iraq. From 948 independent record shops in 2003 to 408 in 2007, the British record shop appeared in freefall, soon to be extinct. The town of Hastings went from having eight record shops to Morrisons supermarket being the only vendor of new music. Piracy, free CDs in newspapers, downloads both legal and illegal, online streaming, Amazon (and other VAT-free online sellers), supermarkets, rising rents, record labels treating independent stores with contempt... the list goes on and every item is valid. Yet there's one thing many never considered: the culture had changed.

The culture had changed. If the golden age of UK rock runs from 1967 to 1997 – *Sergeant Pepper* to *OK Computer* – then the rise of record shop chains mirrored that epoch. And their fall reflects on how rock music is now far less important today than it was across those three decades. It wasn't just HMV and Virgin, the big rock shops, that were closing. Dance music shops were hit harder than any others by downloading at the start of this century, while reggae shops – for so long a lifeline to "back home" – lost their relevance to black British youths who didn't relate to Kingston's sound system culture.

It's not simply that twenty-first-century youths have far more distractions than previous generations (mobile phones, internet, computer games, more access to fashion and travel), but music itself means less to the public. TV shows like *Pop Idol* and *The X Factor* produce identikit pop stars who enjoy the intensity of the limelight, quickly shift a lot of downloads of one (or two) hits, and then tend to be tossed aside. Fast-food muzak. The surly rock band is now a carbon of a carbon of a carbon, as redundant as a Penny Farthing bicycle. No surprise then that the general public embraced smiley, arena anthem merchants Coldplay and Ed Sheeran.

Sales of the music press had been flatlining for quite some time: *Sounds* and *Record Mirror* both ceased publication in 1991, *Melody Maker* died slowly and horribly in 2000, while the *NME* devolved into a banal bible devoted to excruciating profiles of errant indie rockers long before it became the worthless free publication it is today. '£50 Man', who (the music industry determined) would enter a megastore on a Friday evening, grab three £15 CDs and a copy of a classic rock glossy (*Q*, *Mojo*, *Uncut*), stopped venturing in and, while those magazines survived, they all experienced a sales slump. The public became more and more interested in football and less and less interested in music. Even enthusiasm in specialist music faded as new releases by celebrated jazz and world artists failed to come anywhere near previous sales figures. What did remain is an interest in spectacle: Glastonbury (and its imitators) are the English middle-class equivalent to The Hajj, while going to see The Rolling Stones and other classic rockers is akin to visiting a stately home; 'Best of British' and all that. Taylor Swift and Rihanna continue to command much tabloid attention, while the Mercury Prize gets earnest broadsheet coverage, but the way that music soundtracked shifts in British society – from Beatlemania to rave – is no longer trenchant today.

After a century where recorded music often seemed to lay down a challenge to the listener – or at least invited them on an adventure where sound and fury signified all kinds of things – we now live in a post-mannerist age where everything seems available but little holds our attention, and even less commands an emotional engagement. The record shop era involved, for many, constant excitement as we joined this invisible underground empire that trafficked in joy – records as antidotes to boredom and conformity; records as style and spirit guides; records as looking glasses we could fall through into different worlds. As UK culture changed, interest in going for a song became a thing of the past and your average independent record shop – with the emphasis on 'average' – found itself redundant.

In Chapter 8, I noted how The Moody Blues had set up a small chain of record shops called Threshold Records. These shops catered far beyond the band's core fan base, yet during the 1980s the Moodys began to close the shops, keeping only the branch in Cobham, Surrey. Around 2009, when out cycling with a friend, he directed our ride to Cobham so I could visit Threshold Records.

Cobham exists at the heart of the stockbroker belt, south west of London, and Threshold Records, spacious and orderly with a wall of 'Recommended' CDs, felt right at home there. This was a shop where little signs throughout stated "Threshold – serious about music". Serious indeed; it felt like a classroom, and surely no local teens gathered here to check the latest rap or dubstep releases? The Moodys owned the building, basing their operation and fan club there and, not long before I visited, Threshold had enjoyed a major refit, with the band arriving to cut the ribbon at the official reopening. Fans from across the globe flocked to Cobham to get autographs and, I imagine, many CDs were sold that day. Nonetheless, all this did not help to keep Threshold open for much longer. In fact, on the Saturday afternoon I dropped in the shop felt becalmed. My friend briefly chatted with the proprietor and bought a CD (a Candi Staton reissue on Honest Jon's record label, I seem to remember), but there were none of the energies evident that power an engaged record shop.

Home to Chelsea's training ground and many wealthy entertainers, Cobham is "the UK's Beverly Hills" (according to *The Daily Mail*). However, the well-heeled were no longer interested in entering a record shop

The era of mass CD buying reached its apotheosis in 1995 when sales of Alanis Morissette's *Jagged Little Pill* (33 million copies), Oasis' *Morning Glory* (23 million copies) and Hootie & the Blowfish's *Cracked Rear Mirror* (19 million copies) left even jaded observers stunned. Today it is now observed as one of those odd consumer phenomena, similar perhaps to hula hoops and pet rocks. A better comparison might be with the gin craze: in 1743 an average of 10 litres of gin was drunk for everyone in England but, by 1757, this had quietly wound down. Orgies of consumption are often followed by widespread abstinence.

I'm unsure about what caused peak CD sales in the UK to be breached. I like to think it was Oasis' dreadful *Be Here Now* (1997; 600,000 copies sold in the week of release), although the chains might suggest Robbie Williams' *Rudebox* (2006), there being so much unsold stock that EMI shipped container loads to China to be used as ballast in the construction of motorways. Or maybe the public felt it had spent more than enough of its disposable income on CDs. The Moodys duly noted this, and Threshold Records crossed the threshold into retail oblivion in February 2011.

Small record shop chains had been quietly folding since the 1990s, many like Andy's Records simply found themselves unable to compete with supermarkets, Virgin and HMV. The mighty Vallances chain (40 stores across Yorkshire, the Midlands and Lancashire, each selling electrical goods, musical instruments and records) was sold to the Rumbelows electrical chain in 1987, only to find its parent company (Thorn EMI) closing the entire chain in 1995. L&H Cloake, a family-run chain of independent shops founded in the early 1950s that stretched from Brixton to Brighton, also disappeared in the 1990s. Harum Records operated five branches across North London, and their Crouch End shop, being near The Eurythmics' studio, had many a celeb drop in (including Bob Dylan, always on the lookout for old gospel LPs). But by the new millennium all were gone. Record bags, the occasional photo, a local newspaper mention and memories are all that tend to survive of these lost shops.

Where opening record shops had once, in the words of veteran retailer Steve Bronstein, "been a licence to print money", they were now, in many cases, losing money. Even with the chains gone, plenty of independents couldn't survive. Selectadisc, Dub Vendor, Black Market Records (BMR), Red Records, Revolver Records, Beanos … the list goes on and on as eulogised shops shut down. *The culture had changed.* Around this time, EMI did a day's market research with a group of teenagers, digging deep to find out what music meant to them, the styles they liked, and how they heard about and followed artists. When the afternoon's interrogation was over, EMI told the teens to help themselves to any CDs they wanted from the considerable catalogue on display. What did the teens choose to take home? *Nothing.* None of them wanted a single CD.

Those still working in record retail also noted the absence of youths entering their shops. For now, nothing flowed and everything abided.

Aftermath: Remnants of an Underground Empire

Perched above Brighton Station, The Record Album is at once an anachronism and ultramodern. Opened in 1960 by George Ginn, the shop has only ever stocked LPs, 45s and 78s, its content and direction shaped by Ginn's passion for film soundtracks. An alcove is packed with classical LPs ("But young people show little interest in classical these days," sighs Ginn), while markers in the bins designate everything from Light Orchestral and Exotica through Judy Garland and Liza Minelli to Country and Western. And there are drawers full of 45s. *What a delight!*

The Record Album is a treasure chest for the odd, the obscure, the marginal and, obviously, the movies. John Wayne's spoken word album is here. As is Gary Stewart's *Slippin' Around*, a lost gem from the doomed country crooner. And Morricone's *Maddalena*, an inspired soundtrack to a 1969 Italian B-movie. Ginn plays me Craig Safan's *Warning Sign*, an album of dense, paranoid, Hollywood electronica. He then lightens the mood by playing Erich Maria Korngold's *Kings Row*, a lush, orchestral extravaganza that Ginn announces is his favourite ever soundtrack, and the one he credits with firing his passion. The movie, by the way, is a 1942 Ronald Reagan effort, well received then if largely forgotten now. Due to Ginn and his fellow aficionados, the *Kings Row* soundtrack lives on.

"Korngold was an Austrian Jewish prodigy who composed his first opera when he was about 15 or 16," explains Ginn. "Very highly thought of. He escaped the Nazis to Hollywood, as did many European composers. You might hear echoes in his style of composing in John Williams' soundtracks." As *Kings Row* fills the air, I listen and then glance at Ginn. Eyes closed, head nodding, fingers conducting, he's lost in music.

Running The Record Album makes Ginn Brighton's longest established record dealer and one of the few anywhere to be trading after more than half a century. "I've recently renewed my lease for another five years," says the 86-year-old. "So, you could say I'm an optimist."

Droll, charming and immaculately dressed – few record shop staff today serve customers in a collar and tie, while even fewer address me as "Old boy" – Ginn is a marvel of decorum and musical knowledge. His turntable is a solid steel Technics from the early 1970s while the cash till is 60 years old. "With age it has lost its zing. Like me," says Ginn. Being the only specialist soundtrack shop in the UK means The Record Album attracts customers from far afield and many a celebrity. "Nick Cave and Warren Ellis both regularly drop in," says Ginn. "Who else?" I ask. He lists noted actors, musicians and DJs alongside film, TV and record producers, BBC staff and collectors from far and wide, all of whom come looking for specific LPs.

"I don't do anything special", Ginn says. "I'm just a chap who has followed his hobby, really."

Vintage vinyl veteran: George Ginn of Brighton's The Record Album. Photo by Garth Cartwright.

This 'hobby' allows Ginn to observe the music industry's peaks, troughs and many foibles with a wry eye. He remembers when HMV dominated Brighton ("Nondescript") and describes wandering into Virgin, when it opened in Brighton circa 1971, as if entering a Bosch painting: "They were playing extremely loud rock music and the air was heavy with incense, and flower power bods were lying about on bean bags smoking God knows what! I turned around, left and never returned! It's now a Boots store." The vinyl revival (that began quietly in 2007 and has risen exponentially since) has benefited The Record Album – the issuing of 'classic' horror movie soundtracks on vinyl is just one of the ways Ginn finds his shop a youth magnet. By staying true to his vision, The Record Album is more 'hip' than all the boutique shops now desperately displaying vinyl.

Across the decades, George has had to move shop three times. He's never considered retiring but he suffered life-threatening injuries several years ago when he was brutally robbed and attacked by a junkie parasite, and this forced him to take several months off. "I was determined to not let it shut me down. So, I recovered with my wife riding shotgun. And I'm still going strong."

By entering The Record Album I've engaged in conversation with Ginn and a young Czech customer, found vinyl artefacts and learned about music, movies and Erich Korngold. On occasions like this, record shops continue to serve as oracles where knowledge is shared and friendships forged. Brighton is overcast and squally but, inside The Record Album, I feel as if I'm in an exotic locale, some fantastic place. A sensation the best record shops have always inspired.

Ginn runs The Record Album with the aim of making a living while serving a specific community; reaping intensive profits from bulk sales of Coldplay or Adele CDs simply doesn't fit his manifesto. Which, in this age of late capitalism, could be seen by some as akin to heresy. He agrees that shops like his strengthen a city's character. This is true of all the great UK record shops, throbbing with ideas and energies and music, glorious music. Small wonders, indeed. Such temples facilitate conversation, creativity and community, as well as laughter, gossip, enthusiasm, empathy and knowledge. In short, they enrich existence.

Plenty of music fans – and people who value independent retailers – started realising this as record shops began vanishing en masse around the turn of the century. In the USA, where an even greater levelling took place, Record Store Day (RSD) was launched in 2007 by a group of Baltimore workers who wanted to draw attention to the surviving shops. In doing so, they succeeded far beyond their wildest dreams.

RSD has become a big deal in the UK, and is now run by the Entertainment Retailers Association (ERA) who relentlessly spin stories of a 'vinyl revival' (as if product fetishism suggested a healthy industry). However, the actual sales figures for vinyl remain tiny (around 2 per cent of all UK recorded music sales). Still, many independent shops report a huge sales spike on the day. It even launched a free mini-festival in Soho's Berwick Street: for several years, both a sound system and a stage entertained (inevitably headlined by punk era veterans – Adam Ant, Gang of Four, Ruts DC – so emphasising RSD's nostalgic appeal), while the public crowded into Sounds of the Universe, Phonica, Reckless and Sister Ray.

RSD 2015 found Berwick Street more packed than ever before with a small contingent of youths shattering alcopop bottles and scrapping on the street, attracted not so much by the event but by the free street party. Westminster council were not amused. Unsurprisingly, RSD 2016 found no stage or sound system occupying Berwick Street. Several hundred people still arrived to queue for limited edition vinyl releases, or just to purchase something, *anything*, on what is now akin to Mother's Day or Christmas, a consumer orgy where unscrupulous traders snap up 'limited edition' vinyl releases and then rush them onto eBay.

Much as I love record shops, I'm not an RSD devotee. The event has helped independent traders, but RSD is the one day a year when I'm highly unlikely to go record shopping. That the major labels now issue everything and anything on vinyl means the best independent labels – you know, those who have championed vanguard music across the decades and kept vinyl alive during Peak CD – struggle to get access to pressing plants.

No new vinyl pressing plants have been built and this means Universal, Warner and Sony block book the existing ones to ensure they have plenty of vinyl Ed Sheeran LPs for Tesco's and HMV. These same independent labels are also finding their releases increasingly relegated (when it comes to shelf space) by the very shops they have always supported: vinyl reissues of The Beatles and Blur will always generate far greater sales than a new LP consisting of ancient 78 era recordings from Epirus or a 12-inch 45 created in a Croydon bedroom.

Moreover, retailers can't survive on being busy one day a year. Or on fashion, which the vinyl revival might turn out to be.

Observing the UK's surviving record shops today, I wonder how many occupy a position similar to those that started in the years following the Second World War, being run by aficionados who cater to a specific community. Rough Trade have brilliantly succeeded with their in-store cafés and stages, and the likes of Pie & Vinyl, in Southsea, have made a success of selling LPs and meaty treats. Such boutique outlets have led the much talked about 'record shop revival'. The revival first began being noted round 2013 as HMV closed 80 of its UK chain stores as new independent record shops sprang forth, often focusing largely (or solely) on vinyl. These tended to be small shops akin to vintage clothes stores or niche cafes who aimed at a certain demographic and never considered stocking Top 40. They tapped into a generation who had grown up on downloading music and now wanted something both solid and chic – vintage music, of sorts – as well as a middle aged audience who had always bought music and appreciated vinyl for its superiority to CD and MP3 (warmth of sound, design aesthetic). Canny marketing allowed Rough Trade, Pie & Vinyl, Sister Ray, Sound Of The Universe and others to mount large, noisy Record Store Day celebrations that attracted crowds and the media.

Still, it's worth noting that many record shops lack the space or ambition to do this: I can't imagine Ginn wanting to host an in-store event, even if John Carpenter announced his availability. First and foremost, a good record shop is about having great music available. If running a café and promoting events takes over, and the records end up as secondary, emblems rather than the essence, then it's game over.

'Game over' being how much of the UK's high streets now appear, having lost their butchers and bakers and record shop makers, until the shopping districts resemble either places of privation (wastelands of charity shops, fried chicken shacks and Pound stores) or opulence (innumerable skinny soy latte vendors cohabiting with luxury brand outlets). Wandering through London's Covent Garden and Soho in 2016, I now find it hard to conceive how these glossy neighbourhoods once contained energies that shook the globe; the 2015 lockout of Black Market Records (BMR)/Dub Vendor (see Chapter 17) quite possibly signalling the end of Soho as a place where, for centuries, myriad bohemian dreams took shape. Equally unsettling is to stroll around Liverpool

and Birmingham, these proud cities that once produced musicians who shaped popular music. Today record shops – indeed, much independent retail – in both appears flattened, hollowed out.

Admittedly, the loss of record shops and bookshops, of the fish monger, and greengrocers, may appear inconsequential when compared to events currently overwhelming the UK. Yet the celebration of individual skills, vision, ability, hard work, trade, and the hustle and flow that go into running a small retailer, is one everyone should engage with. A network of independent traders energises areas, build bonds, create jobs and help set the mood, a commercial climate, of a community. And this plays a part in shaping the soul of our cities.

Deprived areas come in all shapes and sizes, and when your neighbourhood no longer supports independent retailers, it enters into a decline that may, initially, appear invisible. A good local record shop tends to be proudly provincial. This could be Spillers stocking all kinds of releases by Welsh artists. Or the Drift Record Shop making sure Totnes is now the dream Devon destination. While Rye Wax, in the basement of Peckham's Bussy Building, channels the energies of the club events upstairs. These emporiums all attract people to a locale, encourage communication and investigation. Asda might offer discounted Iron Maiden LPs, but entering a hypermarket rusts the soul.

Shopping is a quintessential human activity, and how we go about it says plenty about us, our society and the future we envisage. Across the last century, Brits often led the world both in creating popular music and in running distinctive record shops. Today, Rough Trade's fresh presence in Brooklyn and the eclectic nature of our greatest surviving shops – from Honest Jon's and Sound of the Universe through King Bee to Soul Brother, via Coda and Supertone, Rat and RK Bass (to name a select few) – means they still do. These remnants of the 'underground empire' continue to traffic in joy and are worth far more than whatever 'turnover' gets posted. The spirit guides may have, largely, been banished, the temples almost completely desecrated, but Mr Sifter continues to sell songs to the people of Didsbury. Well done, that man.

Rave On – Twenty-First-Century Closure and Renewal

Across England, Wales, Scotland and Northern Ireland there remain several hundred record shops and stalls. While Greater London has dozens of record shops spread across its vast circumference, other major UK cities often feel bereft, almost as if the music's over. Yet small towns – and even villages – are also home to remarkable outlets. The following listings are by no means comprehensive, covering shops I've entered or that have been recommended to me. Obviously, these listings can change rapidly and radically so those who go and seek shall find.

Funky Stuff

As with jazz and soul, a handful of specialist dance music shops continue to exist. Peckham and Hackney are home to new record shops that often sell a solid selection of new dance vinyl. I highly recommend Rye Wax and Lorenzo's Record Shack. Hackney offers Vinyl Pimp (huge selection, high prices), Kristina Records, Cosmos Records and Love Vinyl (all specialist and all good). In **Soho** Phonica Records, 51 Poland Street, is the last West End dance shop and, while specialising in 12-inch 45s, offers plenty of variety. And they still have rows of turntables for listening on. A gem.

Idle Hands at 74 Stokes Croft, **Bristol**, is a new dance shop run by a young veteran and is highly rated by enthusiasts. Eastern Bloc (5A Stevenson Square) is **Manchester**'s premier dance shop and hosts in-store performances from the likes of A Guy Called Gerald – that's celebrating your history! **Edinburgh**'s Underground Solu'shn (9 Cockburn Street) offers a vast array of vinyl alongside audio equipment and DJ kit. In **Northampton** Vinyl Underground, 80 Abington St, is located inside Watts Furnishers and has traded since 1993. They also have an outpost in **Brighton** which is part of a three-storey building at 104 Trafalgar St. Here Rarekind Records, in a pocket of Brighton that exists below and outside The Lanes, occupies the ground floor and deals rap and soul (alongside miscellaneous cheap vinyl), Vinyl Underground's techno and house outlet exists in a cupboard sized space on the first floor (just like the old days), while RK Bass Records, a drum and bass outlet, is up another flight of stairs. RK is run by a young woman who is charm personified. Housing three such specialised record shops in one building is a brilliant idea and, with its huge urban mural out front, 104 promises a music retail space full of sound and vision.

Jazz and soul have few outlets today: Eric Rose's Music Inn in **Nottingham** is the oldest and most traditional still trading. Ray's Jazz in Foyle's bookshop on **Charing Cross Road** is run with love and deep stock. Turnstyle Records in **Streatham** and If Records in **Soho** are the only new jazz shops in the UK and well worth a visit. Both Soul Brother in **Putney** and Crazy Beat Records in **Upminster** are serious soul and funk shops. They keep the faith.

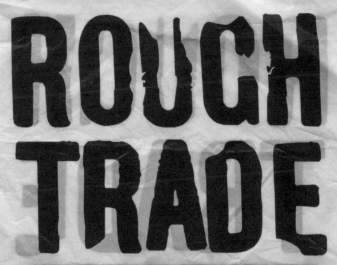

ROUGH TRADE

E A S T

DRAY WALK, 91 BRICK LANE, LONDON E1 6QL. TEL: +44 (0)20 7392 7788

ROUGHTRADE.COM

d&b audiotechnik ■ ■ / SENNHEISER Fender Bowers & Wilkins

Reggae

Only a handful of reggae record shops or stalls survive. Most are based in London: Payback Records in **Bristol**'s St Nicholas Market is the only non-capital stall I can think of worth noting. In **London**'s **Ladbroke Grove** there's People's Sound Records (11 All Saints Road W11), founded by the late Daddy Vego – whose rotund figure, beaming features and huge head of dreads made him resemble a Rasta Buddha – home to a mighty Carnival sound system and now it stands out like a holy Rastafarian relic of sorts in an extremely gentrified neighbourhood. **Shepherd's Bush** is home to two veteran shops. Peckings Studio 1 (81 Askew Road W12) is run by Chris Price, the son of Peckings' founder, the late George Price, and continues to offer a wall of reggae 45s and a dynamic atmosphere as 7-inches get spun. Webster's Record Centre (established 1966) stocks reggae (and gospel and Ed Sheeran) at 61 Shepherd's Bush Market. The last time I visited, Webster regaled me with tales of Trojan days and how Dennis Brown was once a very close friend. "Him visit here," he said indicating his small but brilliant stall. Well, of course!

Hawkeye Records & Tapes (2 Craven Park Road. NW11), is the last of the old **Harlesden** shops. Two traditional West Indian record shops are **Peckham**'s Maestro Records (just off Rye Lane) and **Tooting Broadway Market**'s Music Specialist, both offering reggae, soul and gospel as well as flags, stickers, hair oils and much else – the delightfully shambolic Music Specialist even has dozens of cassettes for sale! **Tottenham** is home to Zen Records and Body Music (downsized but still standing). Veteran Jamaican musician Rupie Edwards runs a reggae record stall in Ridley Road Market, **Dalston** E8. Take your copy of 'Skanga' along and ask Rupie to sign it!

Inevitably, **Brixton** remains the best place to find reggae vinyl. Seasoned retailer Supertone Records on Acre Lane is run by Wally, a Jamaican gentleman who is among the most affable of record vendors. Supertone is worth an afternoon of anyone's time (and trades on the net if you can't make it to SW8). There are also two new shops: Pure Vinyl in the Reliance Arcade and Lion Vibes in the Granville Arcade. The formidable prices displayed on some of their records reflect how 7-inch singles that were once produced for shanty town sound systems are now expensive antiques. Reggae historian David Katz notes, "Reggae record shops are as much a part of Brixton as akee and salt fish or rice and peas. They're part of the landscape and, hopefully, they'll remain so."

Rock

Rough Trade's three UK stores – **Portobello**, **Brick Lane** and **Nottingham** – continue Geoff Travis's original manifesto of championing the best contemporary indie and experimental outfits. Banquet Records in **Kingston upon Thames** is not just the last of the Beggars Banquet shops but also the last record shop standing in a shopping area that once had nine. It survives because it always aims to be exceptional. Probe Records in **Liverpool**, Piccadilly Records in **Manchester** and Jumbo in **Leeds** are superb rock shops, eclectic in stock and oozing energy and inspiration. Resident Music in The North Laine, **Brighton**, offers a similar and excellent service (Icelandic chanteuse Emiliana Torrini describes Resident as "My favourite record shop – all it needs is a sofa and a coffee machine and I could shift in!"), while Spillers in **Cardiff** makes sure that not only new mainstream bands are stocked but lots of underground efforts too and, naturally, every Welsh artist going. Hot Salvation Records in **Folkestone** offers Kent's denizens a remarkable array of rock and left-field releases. There are two specialist punk shops – **Camden**'s All Ages Records and **Brighton**'s Punker Bunker – both run by affable rockers; I always enjoy dropping in and searching for a lost 45 ('Mucky Pup' where art thou?) from my lost youth and, inevitably, buying a badge or two. Crash Records in **Leeds** specialises in metal/alt-rock and provides a nucleus for northern hard rockers. **Newcastle**'s Beatdown Records specialises in metal and punk. Something shouty was blaring from the speakers when I visited so I asked the clerk behind the counter who the said noiseniks were. "Saxon," he replied. Rock on, dudes!

Classical

Classical record sales initially survived the internet's arrival unscathed, but the public's rejection of CDs has since hit hard. A handful of specialist classical shops still exist but 2017 saw Soho's Harold Moores and Waterloo's GRAMEX both finally shutting shop. Les Aldrich Music at 98 Fortis Green Road (**Muswell Hill**) has been a north London stalwart since 1945 and offers sheet music and instrument repair alongside a fine selection of CDs and LPs. The owners have started hosting in-store classical concerts. In **Norwich** there's Prelude Records, a spacious and very well stocked classical shop. **Nottingham** has Classical CD. I'm sure there are others, especially in university towns, I'm just unaware of them.

Ethnic Flavours (A London Walkabout)

Two exceptional, long-standing record shops – Sounds of the Universe in **Soho** and Honest Jon's in **Ladbroke Grove** – remain the best places for new Caribbean, African, Latin and Balkan releases. Yet you can still find gems in specific **London** neighbourhoods. What follows are a few places of note that continue to stock music from the Big Smoke's myriad communities. Stoke Newington's 121 Green Lanes (N16) is the base for Melodi Muzik, a large shop with a vast range of Turkish CDs, DVDs and cassettes (no vinyl revival here). It offers lots of Turkish football team regalia, musical instruments, posters of Mecca, Korans and such. **Hackney**

may have become a playground for hipsters but Melodi Muzik continues to serve the borough's Turkish community – community shops offering an array of contemporary music from 'back home' tend to be rare these days. The Afghan Music Centre at 65 The Broadway reflects how **Southall** is now home to a burgeoning Afghani community. Sadly, the great Southall Indian record dens that once stank of incense and featured brighter patterning than any psychedelic rock shop are long gone (ABC may still occupy a diminished space in a clothes shop), but there are grocery shops here stocking Bollywood and bhangra CDs along with cassettes from several Indian regions.

In **Chinatown**, you can find a slim selection of Chinese pop CDs while African and Jamaican stores and market stalls across **Peckham** and **Brixton** quite often offer new CDs (and occasionally old vinyl). In **Peckham**, there also exists Persepolis, a Persian food/goods store and café that stocks Iranian CDs and cassettes: classical, boy bands, techno rock, (most being made in California by the Iranian diaspora). If you fancy a CD of Persia's greatest diva Googoosh (and you do), then Persepolis is the place to go. Tasty snacks, too. By the by, where Persepolis stands was, in the 1930s, a record shop! Sangeeta Ltd (22 Brick Lane E1**)** stands as a fortress against the ongoing gentrification of **Whitechapel**, proudly representing the musical enthusiasms of that neighbourhood's Bengali community: all kinds of CDs (and quite a few cassettes) from Bangladesh, India and Pakistan are on sale here – seeing a whole row of Nusrat Fateh Ali Khan CDs brought a smile to my lips after passing one too many designer cafés. Music lovers across the UK, please add to this list.

Record Recyclers

There are now far more *used* record shops than *new* record shops. As even charity shops tend to overprice vinyl, believing any black wax has worth, all kinds of tat gets marked up. That said, record hunting remains a pleasurable activity - Ray Templeton started 2016 with a great find of jazz 78s in a Balham Oxfam, all going for the proverbial song!

London and the South

Greater London's used record shops have slowly been dispersing from the centre to the suburbs. Outside of Reckless and Sister Ray (with its basement full of tasty LPs) on **Berwick Street**, there is little to be found in Westminster. Music & Video Exchange's surviving record shops are in **Notting Hill** and **Greenwich** (Greenwich also has Casbah Records, a brilliant mod shop with lots of new and used 1960s and 70s era records). **Camden** has Out On The Floor and Sounds That Swing (with Vinyl Boutique in the basement) – all carrying forward Rock On's legacy. **Camberwell's** magnificent Rat Records puts all the new stock out on a Saturday morning, so ensuring queues form for the 10 a.m. opening. Rat is the only record shop I have ever worked in and, while there, I worked alongside Anthony Joseph, a funky Trinidadian orator who has gone on to find fame in France and beyond. Nice one, AJ.

Just down the road in **Peckham**, there's Lorenzo's Record Shack and Sacred Groove (both excellent). **Hackney** has always had plenty of second-hand record shops: worthy of mention are Lucky 7 (with a basement full of dance music vinyl) and Eldicia (good for reggae and soul). Occupying the most exotic location for a used record vendor is The Record Deck, a houseboat that sails the canals of the River Lea and is often found moored near Hackney Marshes. **Angel** is now home to Flashback Records (with outposts in **Bethnal Green** and **Crouch End**). **Crouch End** is home to Audiogold, a hi-fi shop with a record department (largely used, and some tasty new LPs). Up in **East Finchley** there's the gloriously overcrowded Alan's Records – Alan also cuts keys so you can purchase old Chess 45s and a new front door key.

In **Ruislip** is the aptly named Sounds of the Suburbs. A bit further north is Second Scene Records in **Watford, Hertfordshire**. Into the Chilterns and The Record Shop in **Amersham**, Buckinghamshire, offers records, CDs, instruments and sheet music. **West Norwood** is now home to the elegant Book & Record Bar. In **Palmers Green**, the Record Detective Agency remains proudly off line so you have to visit to see what is in stock. The same is true for Monkey Music in **Brighton** (43 Baker Street). Monkey specialises in rare psychedelic rock and psych folk and is hidden away from chic, tourist Brighton. Brighton also has Wax Factor and Across the Tracks, both overflowing with used vinyl. **Croydon**'s 101 Records, full of used bargains, is the last independent record shop in a borough once teeming with them

Slipped Discs in **Billericay, Essex**, sells new and used and has a good café attached. **West Wickham, Kent**, has rock 'n' roll era collectors' shop Rollin' Records, which runs its own label and sells vintage 45s and LPs. **Surrey** is home to Collectors Record Centre in both **Guildford** and **Kingston**. In leafy **Henley-on-Thames**, there's In the Groove with its diverse and often budget-priced stock. Out of Time exists in both **Norwich** and **Ipswich**, second-hand record shops that share the same name but different owners. The Ipswich shop is packed with bargains and – get this! – is possibly the only record shop left in all of **Suffolk**. Beatnicks Records in Norwich is also of note. **Norfolk** is home to the Holt Vinyl Vault, a post office in **Holt** that doubles as a second-hand record shop. Here I bought stamps and a Nick Lowe 45 on Stiff. **Reading** has The Sound Machine, specialising in classic rock, while the Medway Record Centre in **Gillingham, Kent**, and B'side the C'side in **Herne Bay, Kent**, both service their local communities and visiting record collectors. **Bristol** has Wanted Records (an excellent collectors' shop), Centre for Better Grooves (jazz, soul and reggae: very Bristol!) and Plastic Wax (a large, long-established second-hand emporium). Tucked in between Bristol and Bath is **Keynsham**, home to newcomers Longwell Records. The Raves from the Grave shops in **Frome, Somerset**, and **Warminster, Wiltshire**, are both highly spoken of and worth visiting when in the **West Country**. Appropriately at the end of England, in **St Ives, Cornwall**, there is Vintage Gramophone Records which stocks only 78s and gramophones!

Sister ray

London's premier vinyl specialists

Soho 0207 7343297

@sisterraystore

Shoreditch 0207 7293142

@sisterrayace

We will always pay good money for your vinyl

The Midlands

Nervous Records in **Hinckley, Leicestershire**, is a tiny treasure trove of used vinyl that has existed since the 1970s.**Nottingham** is a delight for crate diggers: Langley Mill Records is one of the UK's largest dealers of used vinyl; Big Apple is small but offers a lot of interesting records; Rob's Records is run by a veteran northern soul DJ and jammed with vinyl – from floor to ceiling –quite possibly more than any other record shop in Europe. Rob's resembles a hoarder's cave, boxes of records piled on top of boxes of records, and, if you have the patience to dig, many gems will be found here.

The Diskery in **Birmingham** is one of the UK's longest standing record shops and remains home to all kinds of used 33rpms, 45s and 78s, while Swordfish Records has a long history as an alternative rock shop (mostly used); here I found Johnny Jenkins' *Ton Ton Macoute* LP.

The North

In **Manchester**, King Bee Records is held in very high esteem by all who visit (including Mr Marr and myself). This is the shop for rare northern soul 45s, great reggae and blues, and the best selection of soul LPs I have ever come across in a UK shop (they even had Charles Wright's seminal double LP *Doing What Comes Naturally*). Being Manchester, the shop also has plenty of long deleted indie albums (and much more). Surprisingly, for a city of Manchester's size and musical heritage, it is not particularly well endowed with record shops: Vinyl Exchange appears to be oriented towards indie rock fans, and although the vast Arndale Market has two small used record shops, neither held anything enticing when I visited in 2015. In the southern suburbs, there stands Sifters Records – as endorsed by Oasis.

Liverpool's few surviving record shops include The Music Box (trading since 1950), Cult Vinyl and 3B Records. **Blackpool**'s one surviving record shop is the excellent Records & Relics, housing the best selection of soul 45s I've seen in a UK shop. **Sheffield** has the expansive and excellent Record Collector, which encompasses two shops, one vinyl and one CD. Operating since 1978, Record Collector is a fine place to hunt for bargains and search out collectors' items. Rare & Racy is a Sheffield institution, selling used books, magazines and records, and is much beloved by Jarvis Cocker. A tiny Sheffield shop with a good, small selection of 45s and LPs is LP Records, run by a northern soul fan who, when I visited in 2015 (purchasing the *Three the Hard Way* soundtrack), enthuses about how he has just been to see 82-year-old Tommy Hunt, "and he was great!"

Leeds, always competitive with Sheffield, has no one shop to match Record Collector's size but in the beautifully spacious Relic's Records and the basement Wall of Sound (previously based in Doncaster and Huddersfield) it offers two fine emporiums. In Wall of Sound I found Delbert McClinton's first three ABC albums and a rare James Brown LP. Minster Records in **Beverley, East Yorkshire**, comes highly recommended by Sheffield record shop historian Simon Robinson. Life of Vinyl in **Thornaby-on-Tees** is a north Yorkshire vinyl specialist. Rebound Records is **York**'s long-standing second-hand shop and regulars speak very fondly of it. Vinyl Tap in **Huddersfield** is a long-standing specialist used record shop. **Newcastle**'s Beatdown Records has a big second-hand section out back. Not far away is RPM Music, a tiny shop tucked away up a flight of stairs and behind a pub. RPM is packed with LPs, 45s, CDs and historic gramophones. Their slogan says, "Vintage Vinyl & Audio Furniture", and the owner states that all the old record players have been refurbished by a veteran electronics engineer who grew up fixing these beasts when they were new.

Sound It Out, located on **Teesside**, was celebrated in Jeannie Finlay's engaging 2011 documentary feature (called *Sound It Out*) that drolly portrayed the shop, its affable owner and customers, and their musical passions in a region now bereft of record shops.

Scotland

There remains a handful of impressive second-hand traders across the border in Scotland. **Aberdeen** has One Up Records, **Dundee**'s Groucho's Record Store has been trading since 1976 and counts Johnny Marr as a fan, while **Edinburgh** is home to Record Shack and Backbeat – both old-school shops with no online presence where you can dig for hours. Ian Rankin is a vocal enthusiast for Backbeat, and as he knows Edinburgh's dark corners better than most, I will take this as gospel. **Glasgow**, although a larger city, is not quite so enticing for crate diggers: Love Music, Mixed Up Records and Missing Records are all worth visiting, and reflect the Scottish love of all things rock. You want used Simple Minds, Deacon Blue and Nazareth LPs? Here they rest.

There are many more used record shops tucked away across the UK; overlooked by me but surely loved by their clientele. May these scuzzy citadels shine on, crazy diamonds that these oracles are.

UK Record Shop Directory

This section lists record shops in the UK, unless they have already been previously detailed in the book.

England

Greater London
Cosmos Records London, 324d Hackney Road.
Cruisin', 132 Welling High Street, Welling – surviving suburban shop.
Eel Pie Records, 44-45 Church Street, Twickenham – just opened in June 2017 so making it the UK's newest record shop (as this book goes to press). Run by Phil & Kevin who are extremely passionate music fans, Eel Pie offers new and used and an eclectic selection.
The Little Record Shop, 43 Tottenham Lane – Hornsey-based second-hand vinyl shop specialising in rare jazz, reggae, rock and soul.
Records, 70 Lee High Road, Lewisham – traditional Lewisham record shop.
Sounds Original, 169 South Ealing Road – used records with an emphasis on 1950s and 1960s collectables. Lots of bargains.
Spitalfields Market – a large record fair is often held here on the morning of the first and third Friday of the month (and second Saturday). Many stalls, all kinds of records on display, easily the most enjoyable of the record fairs.
Wood Street Market – Walthamstow's covered market often has several decent record stalls.

The South
Acorn Records, 3 Glovers Walk, Yeovil - West Country shop once frequented by local girl Polly Harvey.
Beatnicks Records, 50 Magdalen Street, Norwich.
Ben's Collectors Records, 5 Tunsgate, Guildford.
Black Barn Records, 15 Burleigh St, Cambridge – opened in 2016 by Adrian Bayford who won £148 million in the Eurolottery.
Black Cat Records, 3B Bridge Street, Taunton – independent shop whose owner, Phil Harding, is a wise fellow.
Bridport Music, 33a Southport Street, Bridport – one of the few record shops trading in Dorset.
David's Books & Music, 14 Eastcheap, Letchworth Garden City – highly recommended book and record shop.
Drift, 103 High Street, Totnes – Devon's foremost new release shop.
Fives, 103 Broadway, Leigh-on-Sea.
Forest Records, 7 Earley Court, Lymington – well-regarded Hampshire second-hand record shop with lots of reasonably priced vinyl and CDs.

Head, 269 INTU Shopping Centre, Bromley – Head is a small chain of new release shops. Other outlets are in Belfast, Leamington Spa, Cardiff, Bristol, Blackburn and Warrington.

Holt Vinyl Vault, 1 Cromer Road, Holt – Norfolk post office that doubles as a used record shop.

Hot Salvation (vinyl café), 29 Rendezvous Street, Folkstone.

In the Groove, 14 Reading Road, Henley-on-Thames – excellent used record shop.

Jam, 32 High Street, Falmouth – very cool coffee, 'zines and vinyl shop with an emphasis on local bands and Americana.

Medway Record Centre, 36 Canterbury Street, Gillingham.

Pie & Vinyl, 61 Castle Road, Portsmouth – what it says.

Rapture Records, Unit 12, Woolgate Centre, Witney – open seven days, this 2011-founded shop attracts much love.

The Record Album, 8 Terminus Road, Brighton – Europe's foremost soundtrack shop.

The Rock Box, 151 London Road, Camberley, Surrey – long-standing shop that does what its name states.

Record Corner, Pound Lane, Godalming – a traditional small town Surrey record shop that has existed since the 1960s and continues to sell sheet music along with a wide variety of CDs, LPs and 45s.

Rise, 70 Queens Road, Bristol – the head shop of a small chain of Fopp-style (see Chapter 18) shops mixing full price and discount records plus books and T-shirts.

Rollin' Records, 6 Station Road, West Wickham – 1950s collectors' 45s.

The Soulmine, 3 High Street, Aldershot – Hampshire northern soul specialist, open Thursday–Saturday and has a stall at many club nights.

Soundclash, 28 St Benedicts Street, Norwich – East Anglia's foremost new music shop.

The Sound Machine, 24 Harris Arcade, Reading – large second-hand classic rock shop.

The Truck Store, 101 Crowley Road, Oxford – opened in 2013, this Oxford shop is connected to both Witney's Rapture Records and the city's Truck music festival.

Trading Post Stroud, 26 Kendrick Street, Stroud – Gloucestershire's longest established record shop.

Union Music Store, 1 Lansdown Place, Lewes – Americana specialist. Not too many record shops where young Texan Cale Tyson is a favourite and Hank Williams is venerated.

White Label Records, 105 Castle Mall, Castle Meadow, Norwich.

Wow and Flutter, 8 Trinity Street, Hastings – brilliantly quirky alt.music shop that reflects the creative revival of Hastings.

The Midlands
Back to Mono, 18 Guildhall Street, Lincoln.
The Polar Bear, 10 York Rd, Birmingham – much-loved Brummie shop.
Robs Records, 18 Hurts Yard, Nottingham – a bomb site of a used record shop with LPs stacked floor to ceiling.

The North
Astonishing Sounds, 3 Hall Street, Burnley.
Global Groove Records, 13 Bucknall New Road, Hanley, Stoke-on-Trent – leading dance music shop since 1992 that now also stocks many other vinyl treats.
Grey n Pink, 57 Brook Street, Chester – long-established used record shop with an emphasis on collectors' vinyl. Run by men with a passion for prog (the shop is named after a Caravan album).
Muse Music, 38 Market St, Hebden Bridge – Yorkshire shop known for its owner Sid's passion for all things prog/space rock.
Spin-It Records, Trinity Market, Kingston-upon-Hull – a much-loved oldies specialist store that boasts the widest vinyl collection in the north. Plus CDs, tapes, videos and memorabilia.
Tall Bird Records, Chesterfield – run by a very tall woman who provides Chesterfield with new music after Hudson's, the 105-year-old family-owned record shop, closed in 2012.
Vinyl Demand, 7 Charter Square, Sheffield, S1– small used record shop.

Wales
Diverse Music, 10 Charles Street, Newport – this south Wales record shop and record label has been trading since 1988.
Mudshark, 128 High Street, Bangor.
Retro Vibe Music, 8–10 High Street, Cardiff – lots of used CDs, LPs and 78s.
The Tangled Parrot, Upper Floor, 32 King Street, Carmarthen – highly regarded local hub comprising of record shop, veggie café and venue.
Terminal Records, Riverside Market, Haverfordwest – West Wales's finest record shop.

Scotland
Apollo Music, 48 Causeyside St, Paisley PA1 – long-established new and used record shop.
Avalanche Records, 63 Cockburn Street, Edinburgh – for all your Scottish music wants.
Coda Music, 12 Bank Street, On the Mound, Edinburgh – Scotland's foremost folk/acoustic music record shop. Open 363 days a year!

Northern Ireland
Belfast
The capital of Northern Ireland lost its most famous shop, Good Vibrations, in 2015 when Teri Hooley finally decided to call it a day. Yet Ireland's oldest record shop Premier Record Stores, 3-5 Smithfield Square, has existed in some form or other for almost a century and reflects traditional Irish musical tastes, while several new startups serve a city full of musicians and music lovers. Dragon Records, 58 Wellington Place, stocks new and used with a passion for psych sounds and is oft heralded as the finest contemporary record shop in Ireland. Sick Records, 78 North Street, is very fresh with a stock of all new LPs, 45s and CDs. Very hip and especially strong on indie, metal and free jazz. Several Belfast shops mix vintage clothes with vinyl – Young Savage, 22 Church Lane, is small but concise; Time Slip Records is very well curated with lots of classic rock; Octopus Garden, 11a Wellington Street is the best place for hardcore crate diggers, offering an upstairs where 78s, 45s and 33s all retail for £1 a pop.

The Rest Of The UK...
Bug Vinyl, Ladygate, Beverly – opened in January, 2017, this new vinyl only shop is bright and well curated.

Vinyl Tap Records, 42, John William Street, Huddersfield – long established new and used record shop with a strong international reputation.

Wanted Records, 415 Croydon Road, Beckenham, Bromley – vast used record store on the outskirts of London.

Wah Wah Records, 15 Brook street Wakefield – new record shop 2014 in West Yorkshire.

Mo' Fidelity Records, 126 Murray Street, Montrose, newest record shop in North East Scotland.

Music's Not Dead, 71 Devonshire Road, Bexhill-on-Sea.

Revolution Records, 16 Park Place, Walsall, West Midlands.

Clocktower Music, Unit 10a, St. Michael's Art & Vintage Quarter, St. Michaels Trading Estate, Bridport.

Ben's Collector's Records, 5 Tunsgate, Guildford – much loved used record and CD shop.

Revo Records, 26 Westgate, Halifax, Yorkshire – new and used records and CDs.

Sound Of Vinyl, 32 Church Road, Crystal Palace (Thursday - Sunday), vintage vinyl, clothing, furniture. Deep stock, high quality, not cheap. Nearby is Haynes Lane vintage market, operating Friday - Sunday with at least 2 indoor record stalls. Fine selection and prices.

Project Vinyl, Carberry Road, London – one of the few new dance music shops. Stocks new and used dance 12s and LPs.

Grammar School Records, High Street, Rye, East Sussex. Large stock of used LPs, 45s, 78s, CDs, 8-tracks (!) et al.

Tamla Coffee Bar, 35 Drummond Road, Skegness: this small, vinyl only soul shop is packed with great records and run by David Raistrick, a true aficionado.

Select Bibliography

Ackroyd, Peter (2000) *London: The Biography*, Chatto & Windus.

Anderson, Paul (2014) *Mods: The New Religion*, Omnibus.

Baker, Danny (2012) *Going to Sea in a Sieve*, Phoenix.

Barrow, Steve, Stuart, Baker and Hawks, Noel (2012) *Reggae 45 Soundsystem: The Label Art of Reggae Singles*, Soul Jazz Books.

Bradley, Lloyd (2013) *Sounds Like London*, Serpents Tail.

Branson, Richard (1998) *Losing My Virginity: The Autobiography*, Virgin Publishing.

Brewster, Bill and Broughton, Frank (2010) *The Record Players*, Ebury Publishing.

Broken, Michael (2003) *The British Folk Revival: 1944–2002*, Ashgate.

Chelsea Space (2013) *Dobell's Jazz Folk Blues*, Exhibition.

Cohen, Michael and Donaldson, Rachel Clare (2014) *Roots of the Revival*, University of Illinois Press.

Cosgrove, Stuart (2016) *Young Soul Rebels*, Polygon.

Davies, Hunter (1968) *The Beatles*, Ebury Press.

De Koningh, Michael and Cane-Honeysett, Laurence (2003) *Young, Gifted and Black: The Story of Trojan Records*, Sanctuary Publishing.

Desert Island Discs: Morrissey (4 December 2009), BBC Radio 4.

Doggett, Peter (2016) *Electric Shock*, Vintage.

Elborough, Travis (2008) *The Long-Player Goodbye: How vinyl changed the world*, Sceptre.

Elms, Robert (2006) *The Way We Wore*, Picador.

Epstein, Brian (1964) *A Cellarful of Noise*, Byron.

Firminger, John and Chapman, Gus M. (2009) *Shades of Violet: Remembering Sheffield's Vinyl Goddess Violet May*, You Books.

Gillett, Charlie (1970) *Sound of the City*, Da Capo.

Good Vibrations (2012) Directed by Lisa Barros D'Sa and Glenn Leyburn, Universal.

Hawks, Noel and Floyd, Jah (2012) *Reggae Going International 1967–1976: The Bunny 'Striker' Lee Story*, Jamaican Recordings.

Heylin, Clinton (2002) *Can You Feel the Silence? Van Morrison – A New Biography*, Penquin.

Hickey, Dave (1997) *Air Guitar*, Arts Issues Press.

Horn, Adrian (2010) *Juke Box Britain*, Manchester University Press.

Hornby, Nick (1995) *High Fidelity*, Victor Gollanz Ltd.

Hynde, Chrissie (2015), *Reckless*, Ebury Press.

James, Francis (1998) *The E.M.G. Story*, Old Bakehouse Publications.

Johns, Adrian (2011) *Death of a Pirate*, Norton.

Johnson, Alan (2013) *This Boy*

Jones, Mark (2013) *The B&C Discography: 1968 to 1975*, The Record Press.

Katz, David (2000) *People Funny Boy*, Cannongate.

Katz, David (2003) *Solid Foundation*, Jawbone.

King, Richard (2012) *How Soon Is Now?*, Faber & Faber.

King, Richard (2015) *Original Rockers*, Faber & Faber.

Lewisohn, Mark (2013) *The Beatles Tune In*, Little, Brown.

MacInnes, Colin (1959) *Absolute Beginners*, Penguin.

Martland, Peter (1997) *Since Records Began: EMI – The First 100 Years*, B.T. Batsford Ltd.

Martland, Peter (2013) *Recording History: The British Record Industry, 1888-1931*, Scarecrow Press.

McGee, Alan (2013) *Creation Stories*, Pan Books.

Miles, Barry (2010) *London Calling*, Atlantic Books.

Morrissey, Steven, *Autobiography* (2013), Penquin Classics.

Nott, James J. (2002) *Music for the People*, Oxford University Press.

Peel, John (2005) *Margrave of the Marshes*, Corgi Books.

Peel, John (2008) *The Olivetti Chronicles*, Transworld Books.

Polhemus, Ted (2010) *Street Style*, PYMCA.

Richardson, Clive (2015) *Soul Citizen*, Clive R Books.

Robb, John (2009) *The North Will Rise Again*, Aurum.

Sante, Luc (2016) *The Other Paris*, Faber & Faber.

Savage, Jon (1991) *England's Dreaming*, Faber & Faber.

Taylor, Neil (2010) *Rough Trade: Document & Eyewitness*, Orion Books.

Time Out (2008) *London Calling*, Time Out Guides Ltd.

Ventura, Michael (1985) *Shadow Dancing in the USA*, Tarcher.

Vernon, Paul 'Sailor' (2008) *Last Swill and Testament*, Music Mentor Books.

Vickers, Miranda and Pettifer, James (2007) *The Albanian Question: Reshaping the Balkans*, I.B. Tauris.

Williams, David (2009) *The First Time We Met the Blues*, Music Mentor Books.

Williams, John (1997) *Faithless*, Serpent's Tail.

Wilmer, Val (1989) *Mama Said There'd Be Days Like This*, The Women's Press.

Blogs and websites

The essential site for all lovers of record shops is the British Record Shop Archive.
www.britishrecordshoparchive.org

'After You've Gone' is a brilliant blog about ephemera from the recent past. Its post on Levy's Records links Yiddish canters to Woolworths' Embassy label to, ahem, The Clash.
colinville.blogspot.co.uk/2013/06/the-home-of-music.html

Images of HMV's Oxford Street flagship shop in the 1960s. Such chic modernism!
www.voicesofeastanglia.com/2011/06/inside-the-oxford-street-hmv-store-in-the-sixties.html

This blog about West Hampstead's record shops is extremely informative.
westhampsteadlife.com/2012/10/04/music-and-record-shops-in-kilburn-and-west-hampstead/5094

Richard Williams' excellent blog, 'The Blue Moment', covers many things of interest in music. Here he reflects on visiting Transat Imports in Soho.
thebluemoment.com/tag/transat-imports/

Marvellous Manchester record shop blog.
www.manchesterbeat.com/shops/records/index.php

The Vinyl Factory has the best record shop blogs going: This one's on Notting Hill's record shops from the mid-1970s onwards.
www.thevinylfactory.com/vinyl-factory-releases/record-shop-culture-notting-hill/

While this one celebrates London's unsung record shops.
www.thevinylfactory.com/vinyl-factory-releases/diggers-delight-londons-8-best-secret-record-shops/

DJ Dave Hucker's excellent history – at least from the mid-1960s – of record shops in north Kensington to Ladbroke Grove.
northkensingtonhistories.wordpress.com/2015/01/10/record-shops-around-portobello/

Excellent jazz blog by Geordie saxophone player Lance Liddle. Contains many anecdotes about his time spent working at Windows, the great Newcastle record and instrument shop.
http://lance-bebopspokenhere.blogspot.co.uk/#uds-search-results

Engaging feature on Hawkeye Records – last reggae shop standing in Harlesden. The shop's run by Locksley Gichie, a founder member of pioneering Brit reggae band The Cimarrons.
roserouse.wordpress.com/tag/record-shop/

Birmingham's reggae history – including its shops – gets detailed here.
http://www.birminghamconservationtrust.org/2014/07/06/handsworth-reggae/

Stamford Hill history blog celebrating Rita & Benny's.
www.uncarved.org/blog/2011/08/the-secret-ska-history-of-stamford-hill/

Paul Bradshaw's evocative memories of buying reggae records in mid-1970s
Gloucester and London.
ancienttofuture.com/2011/10/21/the-art-of-buying-reggae-music-a-back-in-the-day-journey-from-dalston-junction-to-tottenham-high-road/

Chelsea Drug Store's *Clockwork Orange* cameo intensely analysed.
www.johncoulthart.com/feuilleton/2006/04/13/alex-in-the-chelsea-drug-store/

Old Dansettes are loved and restored here.
www.dansettes.co.uk/index.htm

Excellent blog on old reggae and Caribbean music by Big Mikey Dread.
bigmikeydread.wordpress.com/category/jamaican-and-caribbean-music/page/2/

In-depth interview with John Abbey, founder of *Blues & Soul* magazine and the
Contempo record label and shop.
www.soulmusic.info/index.asp?s=1&T=38&ART=&A=

Why Record Store Day is bad for independent record shops: an articulate
argument from the owner of Taunton's Black Cat Records.
thequietus.com/articles/19946-record-store-day-2016-shops-bad-reissues-bleugh

Why the vinyl revival is proving detrimental to independent labels and shops by
the owner of Sonic Cathedral.
www.theguardian.com/music/musicblog/2016/dec/09/vinyl-record-sales-up-but-indie-labels-dont-see-benefit

Several Welsh and Scottish record shops are celebrated here.
www.wow247.co.uk/2014/11/25/13-cool-record-shops-you-have-to-visit/

The UK's smallest record shops – true cottage industries! Earworm Records
(York), The Record Shop (Cheltenham), Marrs Plectrum (Peterborough) and Vod
Music (Flintshire). Note that People Music in Guildford has since closed.
thevinylfactory.com/news/the-uks-five-smallest-records-shops-revealed/

Ray Smith and his jazz record shop are lovingly celebrated here. https://cargocollective.com/raysjazz/The-Jazz-Shop

Acknowledgements

If I'd had the slightest inkling when first undertaking *Going for a Song* of the vast amount of metaphorical grappling around in a dark room it would involve, I would never, ever have begun such a task. To research this book largely involved scrabbling around for info, as very little of note has been published on UK record shops. I interviewed, chatted with and called upon well over 100 people. Sometimes a conversation in a pub led to a memory being dusted off about a certain record shop; other times an email or phone number was passed my way with the advice that the recipient had tales to tell. They often did. Along the way, I press-ganged people at record stalls and gigs, in shops and markets, hunting for traces of what once was. Time and time again they were willing to help, and almost all of them replied when it came to clarifying details and illuminating darkness. Their willingness to do so has enabled this book to be written when for most of the shops covered here, all that's left of them is old record bags, advertisements, 78 sleeves and the very occasional photo (even the successful Beggars Banquet shops have left little trace). For this I'm extremely grateful – the positives in *Going for a Song* are all theirs, the faults all mine.

The seed of this book was planted by my pal Leon Parker: as shops such as Virgin, Selectadisc and Beanos crashed, he spun tales of a golden age where Dobell's and Collet's attracted everyone from raggedy anarchists through jazz loving MPs to the most celebrated musicians alive. Leon and I met in a Camberwell bookshop when I was reading from my book on Gypsy music (*Princes amongst Men*) and we've been friends ever since. Leon knows more about British record shops than anyone else alive and his website (www.britishrecordshoparchive.org) is home to a vast amount of images and information. It was Chris Carr who introduced me to Chris Marksberry at his Flood Gallery in Greenwich, and then I had a publisher. Chris Marksberry immediately 'got' *Going for a Song* and has been as helpful and understanding as a writer could want. Contract signed, I immediately turned to two friends – Ben Ayres at Rough Trade and Neil Scaplehorn at Ace Records – and both went out of their way to ensure I had access to record shop men who are today major players in the music industry. Gracias amigos! Tony Rounce has worked in more record shops than possibly anyone else ever and retains a near photographic memory of all the shops he has set foot in. Noel Hawks not only spoke eloquently of his time in the reggae shops but connected me with his contemporaries. Peter Burton, Nick Morgan, John Jack and Les Ong were fonts of knowledge on the pre-Second World War shops. Mike Gavin told remarkable stories of his father, Ray's Jazz and Soho – a book on the West End jazz shops could be written purely from Mike's recollections. As could a book by Chris Wellard on his New Cross shop. Jon Newey's wry recollections on the shops that shaped him demonstrate why he is editor of *Jazzwise*. Graham Griffiths and I go back years, but it wasn't until we sat in a Peckham greasy spoon that I learned how deep his engagement with London shops was. Iain Scott was grace personified as he answered my endless questions on northern mods, Indian record shops and such. Robert Urbanus is someone I came to admire when Stern's enlivened Warren Street, and this admiration has only increased over the years. DJ John Armstrong knows Latin music like no one else. David Katz is among the foremost reggae DJs and historians as well as a true friend. I met Steve Bronstein via Cigdem Aslan, the fabulous Hackney-based Alevi vocalist, and he shared with me secrets of the record men that I never would have found elsewhere. Jeff Dexter remains the source for all things mod. Gary Jeff and Petra Paignton shared real insight into R&TE. Paul Vernon's knowledge of blues and the shops that once sold black American music is only matched by his generosity. Everyone at Ace Records went out of their way to help (even linking me to Eukatech!) – Ace is the world's foremost reissue record label and has been making sure marvellous music gets heard by many ever since Ted Carroll first set up his Golborne Road stall. In deepest Suffolk, Andy Gray and Pete Stennett were gracious in detailing their time in the trade. Simon Robinson guided me through Sheffield's record shop history. Tim Everson chauffeured me across Norfolk, Suffolk and the North West with characteristic grace and kindness. Adrienne Connors was once my editor at *Culture* and her prescient touch is evident throughout. John Williams remains a font of stern Welsh wisdom. My brilliant friends Nick Nasev, Marc Engel and Ben Mandelson all alerted me to shops I was ignorant of. Chris Lane and Steve Barrow spoke forcefully of when reggae was king. Graham Robertson delivered on Pete Burns (RIP). Dave Clark connected me to UB40. Robert Elms and his knowledgeable listeners on BBC London helped out several times. Special thanks to Stewart Lee for stepping up.

I have no blood family in the UK but I do have an extended family of friends here who never let me down. Thanks then to Lesley Chan, Conrad Heine, Adam Blake and Errol Linton, Big Joe Louis, Dave Peabody, Alex and Ariane, Florence Joelle, Andy Jones, Andy Morgan, Martin Morales (@Ceviche!), Carina Westling, She'Koyokh (the world's finest klezmer–Balkan band), Gareth Evans, George Amponsah, Ian Bailey, Horace Panter, Donal Gallagher, all at *Songlines* magazine, the staff at Brixton's Ritzy cinema (Laura, Roger and the gang), Joe Cushley, Keith and Sarah Clark, Mark Edmonson, Max Reinhardt and Rita Ray, Rick Marshall, Sam Ford and Trudi Green, Steve Bunyon, Taib Akri, Quintina Valero, Eleanor Salter, Margaret and Roland Cartwright, Louise Stevens, Phil Minns and Tim Bennett, Steve at Wilsons Cycles SE15. Respect to 6 Music and The World Service for keeping the airwaves fresh. To friends who live in far-off lands – from Auckland to Addis Ababa – y'all hold a place in my heart. Kudos to all who work in record shops: in the UK, in New Zealand (Marbecks, Record Exchange, and Real Groovy being the three that shaped me), in the USA and further afield – your efforts are appreciated. And blessings to the musicians who made (and make) the music that keeps me returning to the oracles. My mum and dad who first took me to Marbecks to buy a Monkees EP when I was eight – I owe them for that. And plenty more. Finally, to Dr Sophie – for the good times.

A grant from the Society of Authors allowed this book to be completed: thank you, SOA.

Garth Cartwright
London SE15, UK.

Leon Parker has supplied some 50 images for this book.
He has many more at the British Record Shop Archive.
britishrecordshoparchive.org

Soho Record Centre shenanigans: Alex Strickland and Peter Sellers, 1969.
Courtesy of Nigel Strickland.

Garth Cartwright is a New Zealand born, London based, oft' travelling author, journalist, critic and DJ/music promoter. He has written for many publications including The Sunday Times, The Guardian, The New European, The FT, Songlines, Record Collector, fRoots and Jazzwise. He is the author of several books including Princes Amongst Men: Journeys With Gypsy Musicians, More Miles Than Money: Journeys Through American Music and Miles Davis: The Complete Illustrated History.

Photo: Quintina Valero